PIANO • VOCAL • GUITAR

Anthology of BROADWAY SONGS

gold EDITION

ISBN 978-1-4234-8964-1

7777 W. BLUEMOUND RD. P.O. BOX 13819 MILWAUKEE, WI 53213

Visit Hal Leonard Online at
www.halleonard.com

ALL I ASK OF YOU

from THE PHANTOM OF THE OPERA

Music by ANDREW LLOYD WEBBER
Lyrics by CHARLES HART
Additional Lyrics by RICHARD STILGOE

D♭maj7
G♭6/D♭
C♭
A♭/C
3fr
here, with you, be - side you, to guard you and to guide you.
D♭
B♭m7
E♭m7
6fr
A♭
4fr
D♭/F
B♭m7
CHRISTINE:
Say you love me ev - ery wak - ing mo - ment, turn my head with talk of
E♭m7
E♭m7/A♭
D♭
B♭m7
E♭m7
A♭
sum - mer - time. Say you need me with you now and al - ways;
D♭/F
G♭
D♭/A♭
E♭m/A♭
A♭6
E♭m7/A♭
prom - ise me that all you say is true, that's all I ask of
rit.

RAOUL:
D♭
D♭maj7
G♭6/D♭
Let me be your shel-ter, let me be your light; you're safe, no one will find you your
you.
a tempo
mf
C♭
A♭/C
D♭
CHRISTINE:
fears are far be-hind you. All I want is free-dom, a world with no more night; and
D♭maj7
G♭6/D♭
C♭
A♭/C
D♭
B♭m7
RAOUL:
you, al-ways be-side me, to hold me and to hide me. Then say you'll share with me one
E♭m7
A♭
D♭/F
B♭m7
E♭m7
G/A♭
A♭
A♭6
A♭7
love, one life-time; let me lead you from your sol-i-tude.

D♭ B♭m7 E♭m7 A♭ D♭/F G♭

Say you need me with you, here be - side you, an - y - where you go, let me go

D♭/A♭ E♭m7/A♭ A♭6 E♭m7/A♭ D♭ B♭m7

CHRISTINE:

too. Chris - tine, that's all I ask of you.

Say you'll share with me one

rit. *molto rit.* *a tempo* *f*

E♭m7 A♭ D♭/F B♭m7 E♭m7 A♭ A♭7

love, one life - time; say the word and I will fol - low you.

D♭ B♭m7 E♭m7 A♭ D♭/F G♭

TOGETHER:

Share each day with me, each night, each morn - ing.

CHRISTINE: *8vb*

Say you love me!

RAOUL:

You know I

rit.

D♭/A♭
E♭m7/A♭
A♭6
E♭m7/A♭
D♭
B♭m7
RAOUL & CHRISTINE:
do. Love me, that's all I ask of you.
molto rit.
a tempo
E♭m7
A♭
D♭/F
B♭m7
E♭m7
G/A♭
A♭
A♭6
A♭9
D♭
B♭m7
E♭m7
A♭
D♭/F
G♭
CHRISTINE & RAOUL:
An - y - where you go, let me go
f
ff largo
D♭/A♭
E♭m7/A♭
A♭6
E♭m7/A♭
D♭
RAOUL & CHRISTINE:
too; love me, that's all I ask of you.
mp
molto rit.

AS IF WE NEVER SAID GOODBYE
from SUNSET BOULEVARD

Music by ANDREW LLOYD WEBBER
Lyrics by DON BLACK and CHRISTOPHER HAMPTON,
with contributions by AMY POWERS

Fm7
but I'm not in an-y hur-ry, and I
D♭ A♭/C B♭7 E♭maj7
need a mo-ment. The whis-pered con-ver-sa-tions
Fm/E♭
in o-ver-crowd-ed hall-ways, the
E♭ E♭maj7 D♭maj7
at-mos-phere as thrill-ing here as al-ways.

A♭/C
3fr
Feel the early morning madness, feel the
Fm7
magic in the making. Why, ev-'ry-thing's as if we
E♭maj7/B♭
3fr
A♭/B♭
4fr
E♭
3fr
never said goodbye. I've
mf
E♭maj7
3fr
spent so many mornings, just trying to resist you.
Fm/E♭

E♭
3fr
E♭maj7
3fr
I'm trem - bling now, you can't know how I've
D♭maj7
A♭/C
3fr
missed you, missed the fair - y tale ad - ven - tures
Fm7
in this ev - er - spin - ning play - ground. We were
D♭
A♭/C
3fr
B♭7
E♭maj7
3fr
young to - geth - er. I'm com - ing out of make - up,
f

A♭/E♭
the light's al - read - y burn - ing, not
E♭
E♭maj7
D♭maj7
long un - til the cam - eras will start turn - ing,
A♭/C
and the ear - ly morn - ing mad - ness, and the
Fm
E♭maj7/B♭
mag - ic in the mak - ing, yes, ev - 'ry - thing's as if we

Fm7/B♭
E♭
3fr
never said good - bye.
molto accel.
Gm7
Cm7
3fr
Gm7
I don't want to be a - lone, that's all in the
Cm7
3fr
B♭
Cm
3fr
past. This world's wait - ed long e - nough,
Gm
3fr
Cm
3fr
B♭7
E♭maj7
3fr
I've come home at last, and this time will be big - ger,
f assai

Ab/Eb
and bright - er than we knew it.
So
Eb
Ebmaj7
Dbmaj7
watch me fly, we all know I can do it.
Ab/C
Could I stop my hand from shak - ing?
Has there
Fm7
Db
Ab/C
ev - er been a mo - ment with so much to

B♭7
E♭maj7
3fr
live for? The whis-pered con-ver-sa-tions in
p
Fm/E♭
E♭
3fr
o-ver-crowd-ed hall-ways, so much to say, not
E♭maj7
3fr
D♭maj7
just to-day, but al-ways. We'll have
A♭/C
3fr
Fm
ear-ly morn-ing mad-ness, we'll have mag-ic in the mak-ing,
f

E♭maj7/B♭
3fr
A♭6/B♭
yes, ev - 'ry - thing's as if we nev - er said good -
Cm
3fr
Cm/A
4fr
E♭maj7/B♭
3fr
bye, yes, ev - 'ry - thing's as if we
A♭6/B♭
B♭7
E♭
3fr
D♭/E♭
A♭
4fr
B♭sus
nev - er said good - bye. We taught the
mp
E♭
3fr
B♭
A♭/E♭
E♭
3fr
world new ways to dream.
f

ALL OF YOU

from SILK STOCKINGS

Words and Music by
COLE PORTER

A♭/B♭
B♭7
G7♯5
G7
C7♭9/D♭
C7
cer - tain love - ly lass, and it's
Fm7
B♭7
B♭dim7
B♭7
not a pass - ing fan - cy or a fan - cy pass.
A♭/E♭
E♭
I love the looks of you, the
A♭m6
A♭/E♭
E♭
lure of you. I'd love to make a

A♭m6
4fr
E♭/G
3fr
G♭dim7
4fr
tour of you, the eyes, the arms, the
B♭9/F
B♭7
E♭/G
3fr
B♭m7/F
C7/E
mouth of you, the east, west, north and the
Fm
B♭7
A♭/E♭
south of you. I'd love to gain com -
E♭
3fr
A♭m6
4fr
A♭/E♭
plete con - trol of you and han - dle

E♭
3fr
C7
e - ven the heart and soul of you. So
A♭
4fr
Adim7
G7♯5
G7
love at least a small per - cent of me, do,
B♭m6/D♭
2fr
C7
Fm
C7/G
Fm/A♭
B♭7
for I love all of
1
E♭
3fr
B♭dim7
B♭7
you. I love the
2
E♭
3fr
you.

ALMOST LIKE BEING IN LOVE

from BRIGADOON

Lyrics by ALAN JAY LERNER
Music by FREDERICK LOEWE

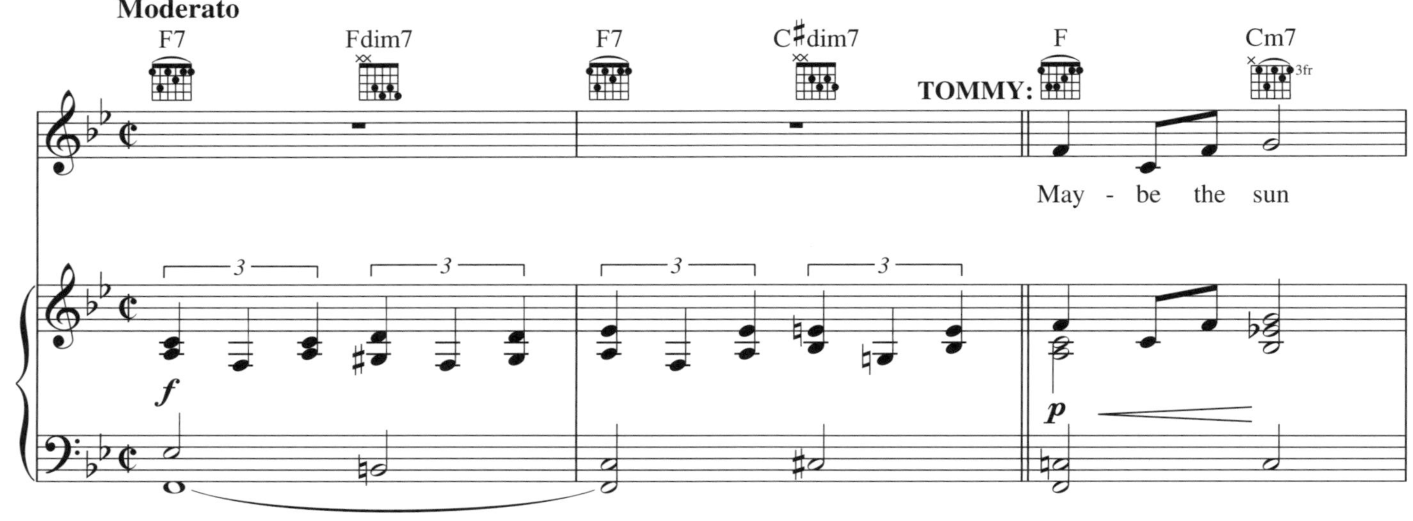

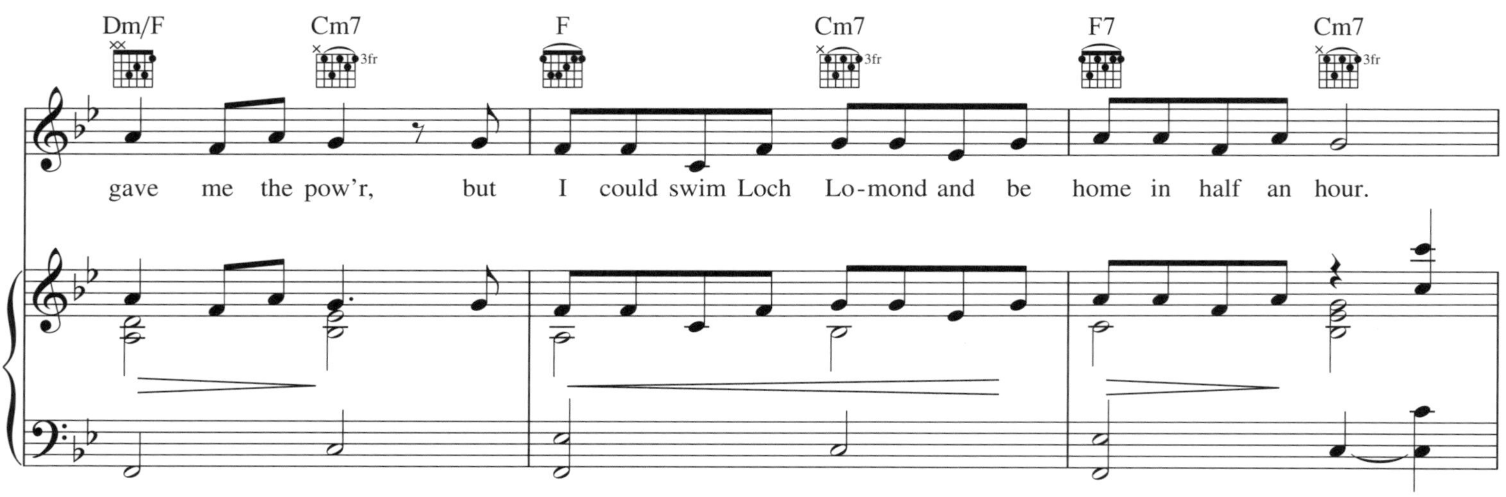

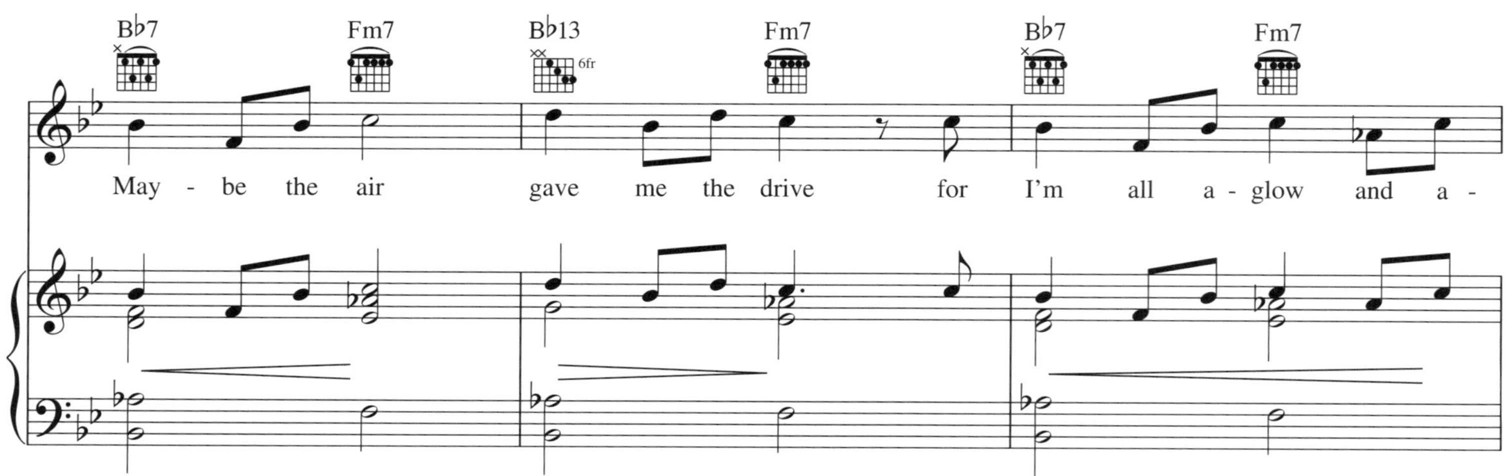

B♭7
E♭
Cm7
F7
live. What a day this has been! What a
L.H.
mf
F/B♭
F+
B♭6
Cm7
rare mood I'm in! Why, it's al - most like
Cm7/F
A/F
B♭
B♭6
B♭7♯5
be - ing in love. There's a
E♭
Cm7
F7
F/B♭
F+
smile on my face for the whole hu - man

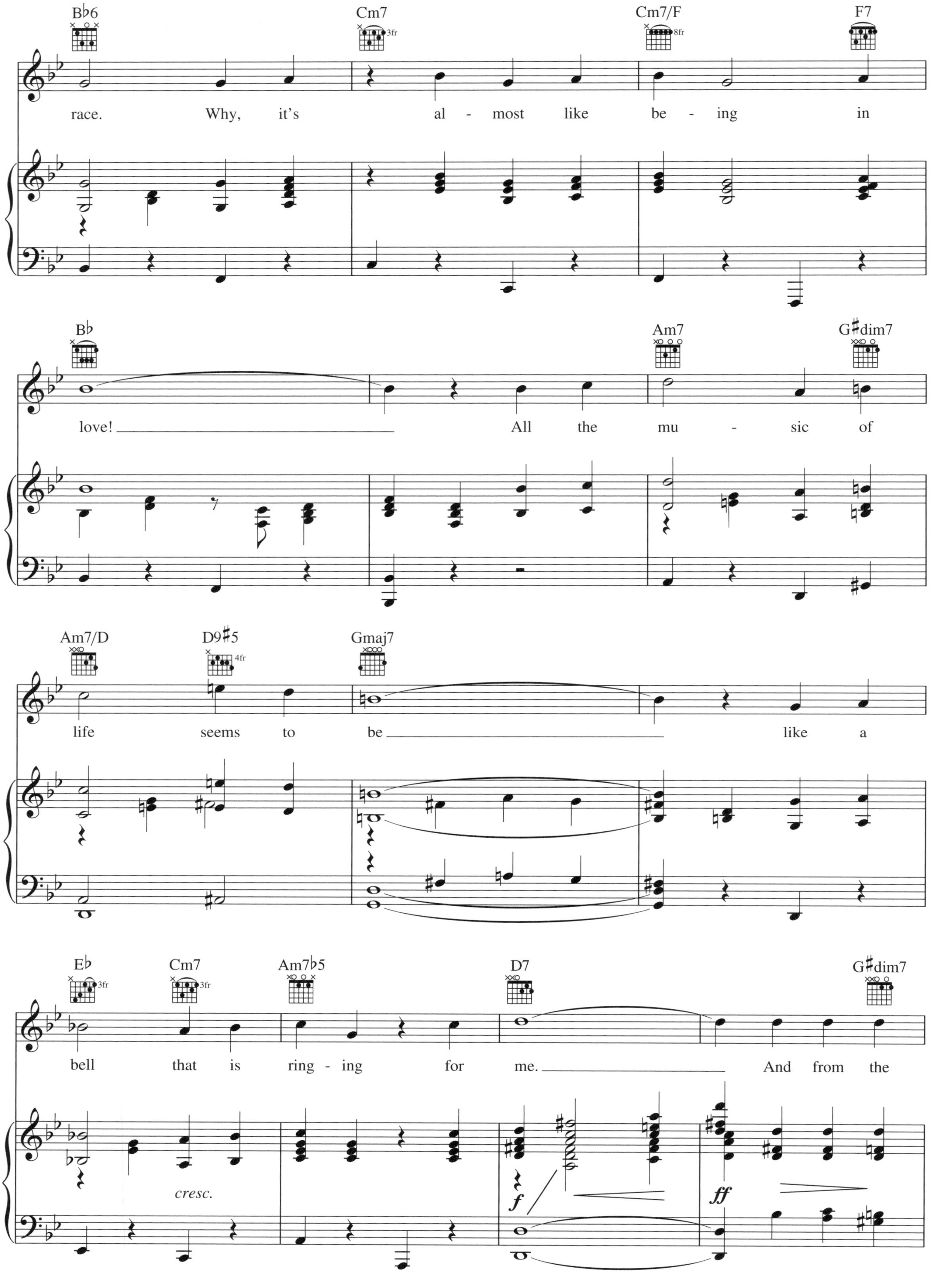
B♭6
Cm7
3fr
Cm7/F
8fr
F7
race. Why, it's al - most like be - ing in
B♭
Am7
G♯dim7
love! All the mu - sic of
Am7/D
D9♯5
4fr
Gmaj7
life seems to be like a
E♭
3fr
Cm7
3fr
Am7♭5
D7
G♯dim7
bell that is ring - ing for me. And from the
cresc.
f
ff

E♭
3fr
Cm7
3fr
F7
F/B♭
F+
way that I feel when that bell starts to
B♭6
Cm7
3fr
E♭/D♭
B♭/F
peal, I would swear I was fall - ing, I could swear I was
C9
G♭7
B♭/F
Em7♭5
F13
F7
fall - ing. It's al - most like be - ing in
1
B♭
Fm7
Fm6
Fm7
B♭7
2
B♭
love. What a love.
f
ff
8va

ALWAYS TRUE TO YOU IN MY FASHION

from KISS ME, KATE

Words and Music by
COLE PORTER

F♯7 F♯7♭5 B7♯5 B7 Em C♯dim7 Dm7 G7 G+
3fr
had more cash in the bank. _
C Dm7 G7 C G7
Each time we try ro - man - tic flights,
C G7 C G7
he begs for my ex - clu - sive rights.
C Am G7 C Am6 B7
My re - ac - tion is to give in, but the ris - in' cost of liv - in' fills my

Em
Em7
A7
C/D
G7
heart with fear, so I al - ways say to him, "Lis - ten, dear, If a
C
Fmaj7
C
cus - tom tai - lored vet asks me out for some - thing wet,
hi - o, Mis - ter Thorne calls me up from night 'til morn.
Fm(maj7)
C
C/E
E♭dim7
G7
when the vet be - gins to pet, I cry, 'Hoo - ray!'
Mis - ter Thorne once cor - nered corn and that ain't hay.
C/E
C+/E
F6
D♯dim7
But I'm al - ways true to you, dar - lin', in my
But I'm al - ways true to you, dar - lin', in my

C/E
Dm7♭5
C/G
fash - ion. Yes, I'm al - ways true to you,
fash - ion. Yes, I'm al - ways true to you,
D7
Fm/G
G7
C
F
C/E
E♭dim7
Dm7
G7
dar - lin', in my way. I've been
dar - lin', in my way. From Mil -
C
Fmaj7
C
asked to have a meal by a big ty - coon in steel.
wau - kee, Mis - ter Fritz of - ten dines me at the Ritz.
Fm(maj7)
C
C/E
E♭dim7
If the meal in - cludes a deal, ac - cept I may.
Mis - ter Fritz in - vent - ed Schlitz and Schlitz must pay!

G7
C/E
C+/E
F6
D♯dim7
But I'm al - ways true to you, dar - lin', in my
But I'm al - ways true to you, dar - lin', in my
C/E
Dm7♭5
C/G
D7
Fm/G
G7
fash - ion. Yes, I'm al - ways true to you, dar - lin', in my way.
fash - ion. Yes, I'm al - ways true to you, dar - lin', in my way.
C
F
C/E
Dm7
C
F
Fmaj7
F6
Fm
There's an oil man known as 'Tex' who is
Mis - ter Har - ris, plu - to - crat, wants to
C
Cmaj7
C6
C7
F
A7/E
keen to give me checks, and his checks, I fear, mean that
give my cheek a pat. If the Har - ris pat means a

D9
4fr
G
Gmaj7
G7
G6
A7
D7♯5
G7
'Tex' is here to stay! But I'm
Par - is hat, bé - bé! But I'm
C/E
C+/E
F6
D♯dim7
C/E
al - ways true to you, dar - lin', in my fash - ion.
al - ways true to you, dar - lin', in my fash - ion.
Dm7♭5
C/G
D7
Fm/G
G7
Yes, I'm al - ways true to you, dar - lin', in my way."
Yes, I'm al - ways true to you, dar - lin', in my way."
1
C
F
C/E
E♭dim7
Dm7
G7
"From O -
2
C
F
C/E
Dm7
C

ANTHEM
from CHESS

Words and Music by BENNY ANDERSSON,
TIM RICE and BJÖRN ULVAEUS

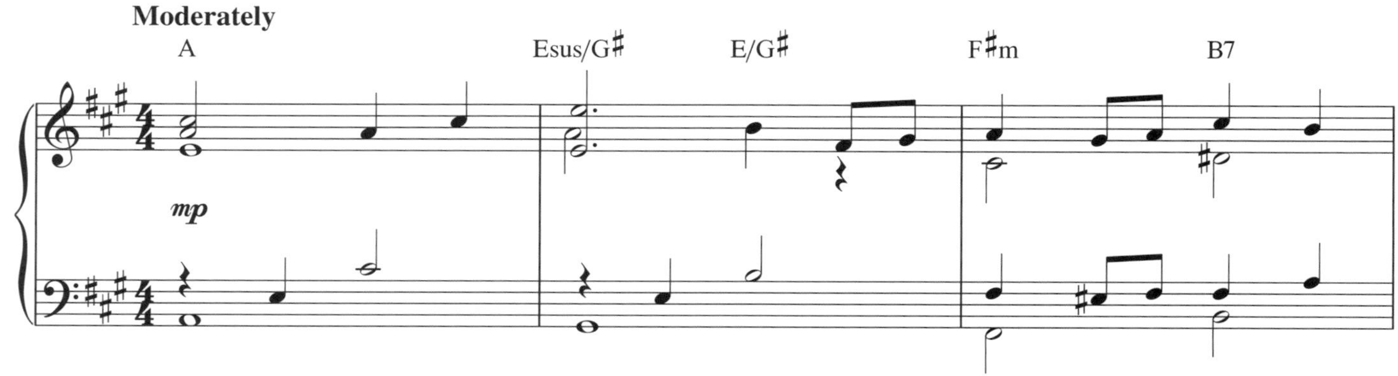

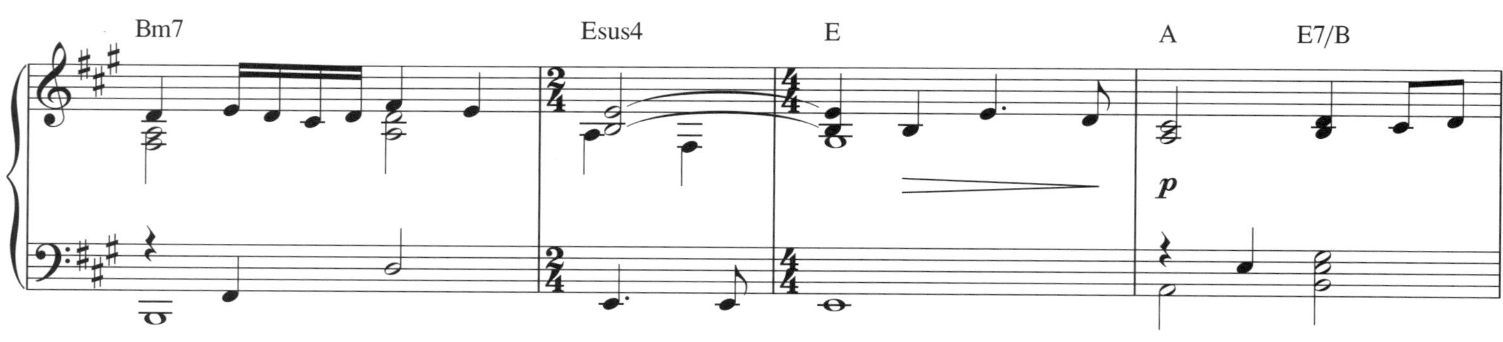

A E7/B A/C♯ A E/G♯ F♯m A/E
No man, no mad - ness, though their sad pow - er may pre -
mp
D♯m7♭5 E F♯7/E Bm/D F♯/C Bm F♯m/A
vail, can pos - sess, con - quer my coun - try's heart; they
D/E E7 A E7/B
rise to fail. She is e -
A/C♯ D/F♯ Dm/F A/E
ter - nal. Long be - fore na - tions' lines were drawn, when no

F♯m B B/D♯ E B/D♯ E A/C♯
flags flew, when no ar - mies stood, my
cresc.
Bsus B E F♯m
land was born. And you ask me why I
mf
mp
Amaj7/E D A/C♯
love her though wars, death, and de - spair.
D A/C♯ Asus2/B A/C♯ D Bm7
She is the con - stant, we who don't

Esus E F♯m Amaj7/E
care. And you won - der, will I leave her? But
Dmaj7 A D E E7
how? I cross o - ver
cresc.
mf
A E/G♯ A D Asus2/E E A
bor - ders but I'm still there now.
D A/C♯ E7sus E7
f

A
D6
E
A
D/F#
Esus
E
A
D
How can I
A/C#
E7sus
E7
C#7/G#
C#7b5/G
leave her? Where would I start?
D
E/D
A/C#
E/G#
A
D/F#
Let man's pet - ty na - tions tear them -

Asus2/E E7 F♯m F♯m/E D E
selves a - part. My land's on - ly
A E A D Asus2/E E Esus
bor - ders lie a - round my
A D/A E/A D/A A D/A
heart.
E/A D/A A
rit.

ANY PLACE I HANG MY HAT IS HOME

from ST. LOUIS WOMAN

Words by JOHNNY MERCER
Music by HAROLD ARLEN

F
N.C.
F
home!
Sweet - 'nin' wa-ter,
cher-ry wine, _
thank you kind-ly,
suits me fine. _
Bb F F+ Db Gm7b5 F Bb7
Kan - sas Cit-y, Car-o - line, _
that's my hon-ey-comb _ 'cause
F Gm Fdim Gm F Ab G Gb Fm
3fr 8fr 8fr 3fr 4fr
an-y place I hang my hat is home.
Birds roost-in' in the

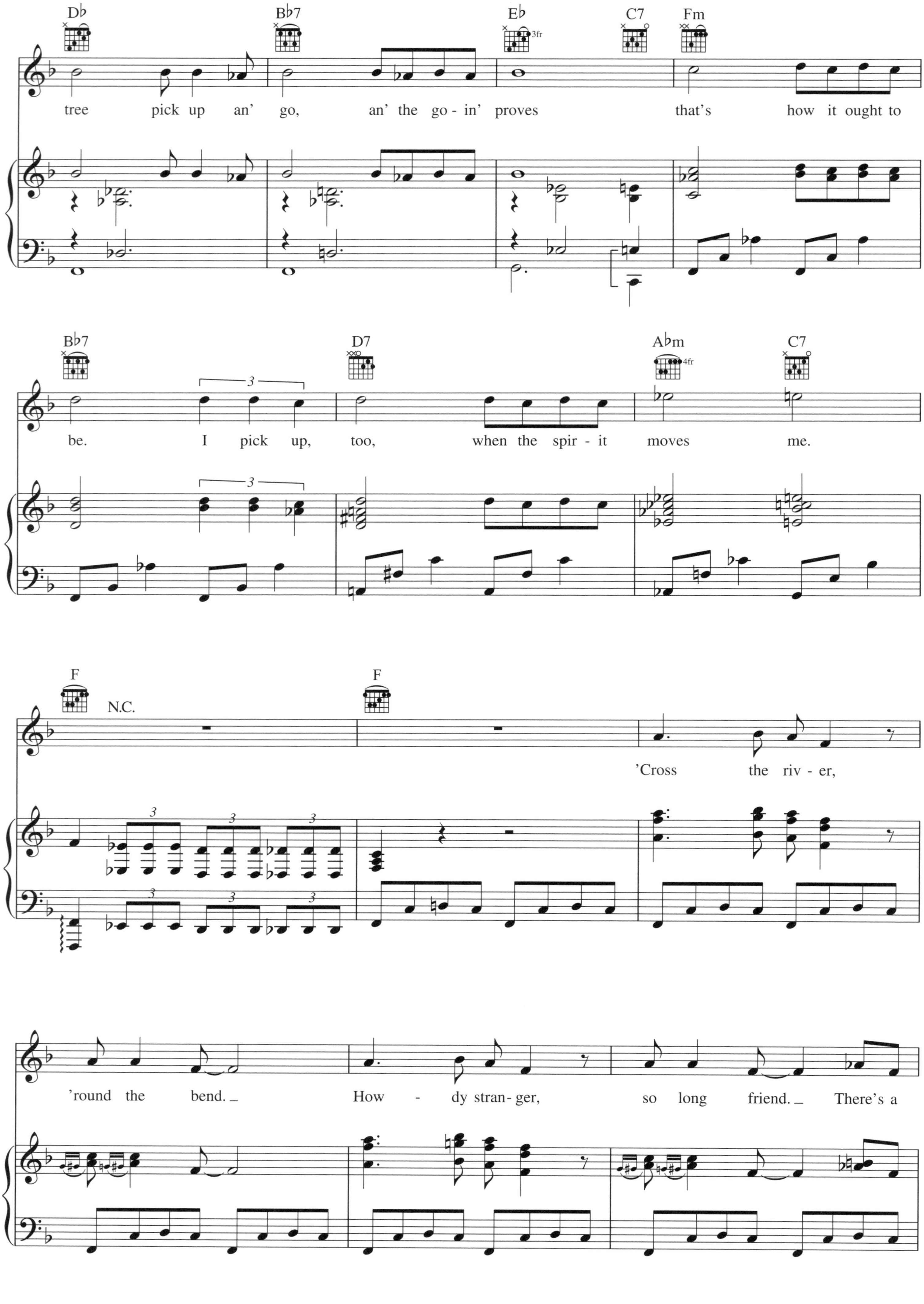
D♭
B♭7
E♭
3fr
C7
Fm
tree pick up an' go, an' the go-in' proves that's how it ought to
B♭7
D7
A♭m
4fr
C7
be. I pick up, too, when the spir-it moves me.
F
N.C.
F
'Cross the riv-er,
'round the bend. How-dy stran-ger, so long friend. There's a

G7♯5
C9
G7
Gm7
F
voice in the lone - some win' that keeps whis - per - in', "Roam!"
C7
B♭
E♭m
6fr
Fdim
8fr
F♯dim
9fr
I'm go - in' where a wel - come mat is, no mat - ter where that is, 'cause
Gm
3fr
an - y place I hang my hat is home.
1
N.C.
2
home!

BALI HA'I
from SOUTH PACIFIC

Lyrics by OSCAR HAMMERSTEIN II
Music by RICHARD RODGERS

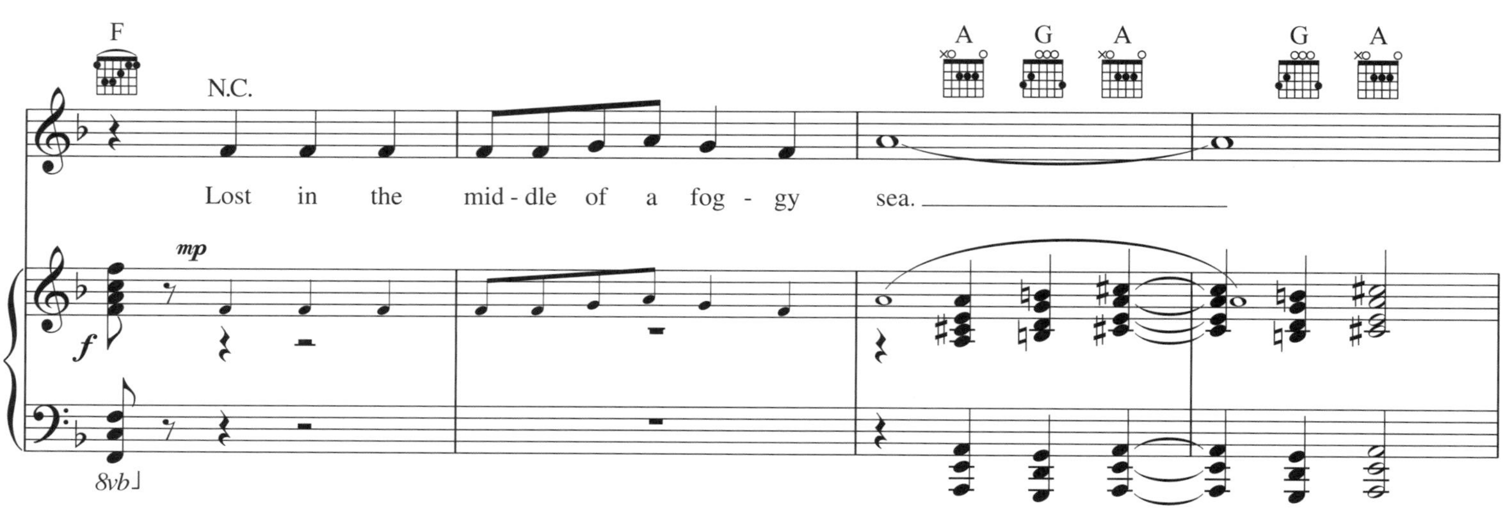

Gm7
C
C7
One where they know they would like to be. Ba - li
rit.
8vb
Refrain (slowly)
Fdim
8fr
F
Ha'i may call you an - y night, An - y day. In your
p-mf
E/F
D♭7/F
C7
heart you'll hear it call you: "Come a - way, Come a - way." Ba - li
Ha'i will whis - per On the wind of the sea: "Here am

E/F
D♭7/F
F
D♭7/F
C7
F
I, Your spe - cial is - land! Come to me, Come to me!" Your
B♭
B♭+
own spe - cial hopes, Your own spe - cial dreams
mf
3
3
Gm
3fr
B♭m/D♭
C7
Bloom on the hill - side And shine in the streams. If you
mp
Fdim
8fr
F
Fdim
8fr
F
try, You'll find me, Where the sky Meets the sea. "Here am

E/F
D♭7/F
F
D♭7/F
C7
I, Your spe - cial is - land! Come to me, Come to
F7
B♭
C9
me!" Ba - li Ha'i, Ba - li Ha'i, Ba - li
cresc.
1
F6
Edim7/F
8fr
Dm/F
Ha'i! Some day you'll see me,
mf
mp
Edim7/F
8fr
Dm/F
Gdim7/F
Float - ing in the sun - shine, My head stick - ing out From a low - fly - ing

F6
Gdim7/F
Dm/F
cloud.
You'll hear me call you,
Gdim7/F
Dm/F
G♭
A♭
B♭
A♭
B♭
Sing - ing through the sun - shine,
Sweet and clear as can
D♭
E♭
F
be.
"Come to me,
Here am I,
come to
mf
C7
me!"
Ba - li
2
F6
Ha'i!
cresc.
f
f

BEAUTY AND THE BEAST

from Walt Disney's BEAUTY AND THE BEAST: THE BROADWAY MUSICAL

Lyrics by HOWARD ASHMAN
Music by ALAN MENKEN

F(add9)
Am
Bare - ly e - ven friends, then some - bod - y
B♭(add9)
6fr
B♭/C
C7sus
C7
F(add9)
bends un - ex - pect - ed - ly. Just a lit - tle
C7sus
B♭/C
C7
F(add9)
F
Cm7
3fr
F7
change. Small, to say the least. Both a lit - tle
B♭(add9)
6fr
B♭maj7
Am7
Gm7
B♭/C
C7
scared, nei - ther one pre - pared, Beau - ty and the
rall.

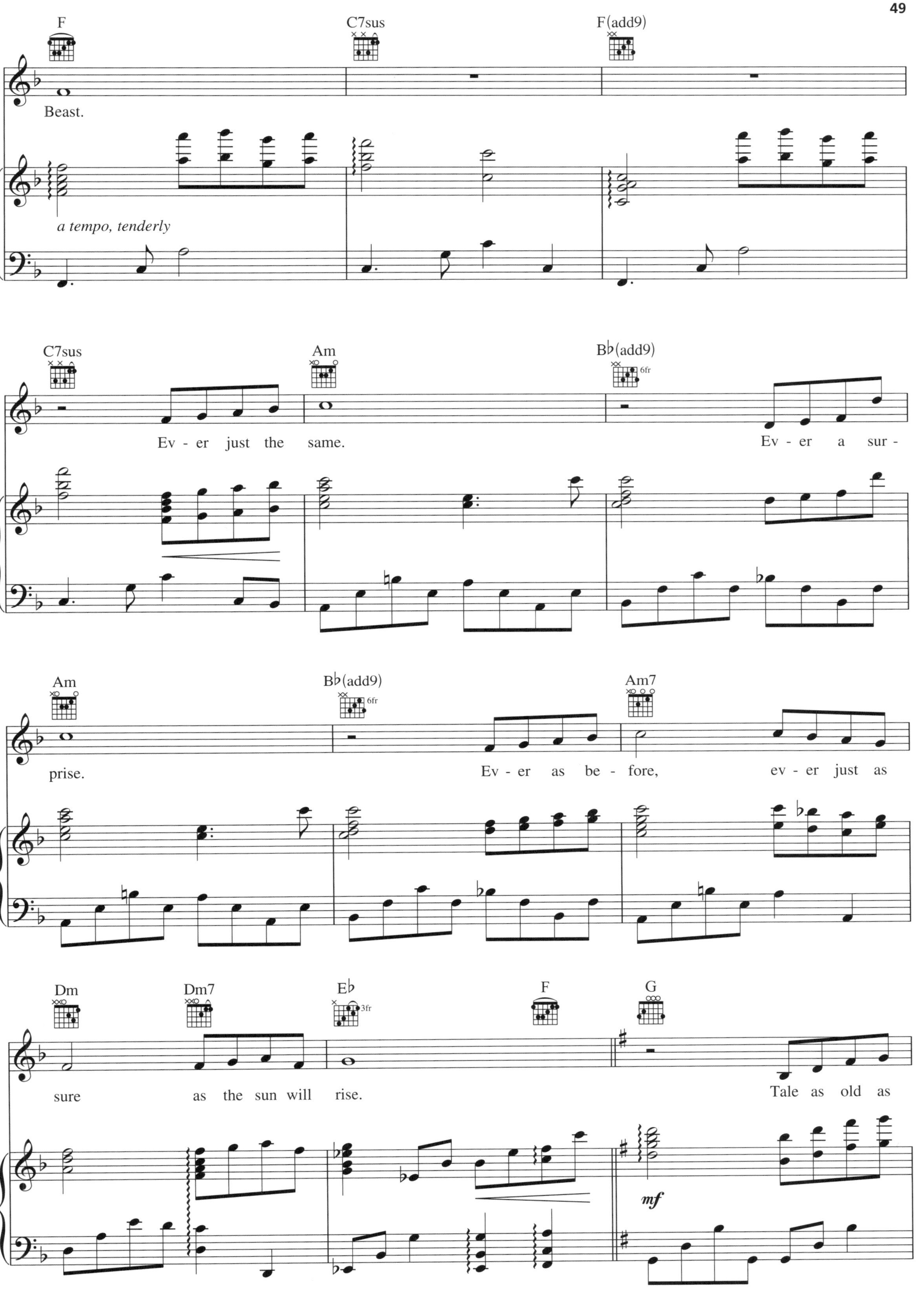
F
C7sus
F(add9)
Beast.
a tempo, tenderly
C7sus
Am
B♭(add9)
6fr
Ev - er just the same.
Ev - er a sur -
Am
B♭(add9)
6fr
Am7
prise.
Ev - er as be - fore,
ev - er just as
Dm
Dm7
E♭
3fr
F
G
sure
as the sun will rise.
Tale as old as
mf

D7sus
D7
G
D7sus
D7
time,
tune as old as song.
G
Bm
Bit - ter - sweet and strange,
find - ing you can
C
D7sus
D7
G(add9)
change,
learn - ing you were wrong.
Cer - tain as the
dim.
D7sus
D7
G(add9)
G
Dm7
G7
sun
ris - ing in the East,
tale as old as

C Cmaj7 Bm7 Am7 D7sus D7
time, song as old as rhyme, Beau - ty and the
G D/F♯ Em G/D C Cmaj7 Bm7
Beast. Tale as old as time, song as old as
mp
dim.
p
rall.
Am7 D7sus D7 G(add9) Gsus D D9
3fr
4fr
rhyme, Beau - ty and the Beast.
8va
a tempo
G(add9) Gsus
3fr
8va
molto rall.
8vb.

BILL
from SHOW BOAT

Music by JEROME KERN
Words by P.G. WODEHOUSE and OSCAR HAMMERSTEIN II

Dm Dm♯5 Gm6 Dm Gm6/D A7
3fr
al - ways used to fan - cy then, he'd be one of the God - like
is - n't tall and straight and slim, and he dress - es far worse than
Dm A7 Dm Dm/B F/C C9 C7 F/C
kind of men; with a gi - ant brain and a no - ble head, like the
Ted or Jim. And I can't ex - plain why he should be just the
C9 C7 F Gm7 F7 B♭
he - roes bold in the books I read. But a - long came Bill, who's
one, one man in the world for me. just my Bill, an
Cm7 F9 F+ B♭ B♭/D D♭dim F7sus F7 G/B
3fr
4fr
not the type at all. You'd meet him on the street and nev - er no - tice him. His
or - di - nar - y boy. He has - n't got a thing that I can brag a - bout. And

Cm F7 F7♯5 B♭6 B♭ B♭/A Gm C9
form and face, his man - ly grace are not the kind that you would
yet to be up - on his knee so com - fy and room - y feels
F7 Cm7 F7 B♭ Cm F9 F7♯5
find in a sta - tue. And I can't ex - plain, it's sure - ly not his brain that
nat - ur - al to me. And I can't ex - plain, it's sure - ly not his brain that
B♭7 E♭maj7 E♭6 C7
makes me thrill. I love him be - cause he's
makes me thrill. I love him be - cause he's,
rall.
B♭ B♭6 Cm7 F7 B♭ B♭
won der - ful, be - cause he's just old Bill. He's
I don't know, be - cause he's just my Bill.

CLOSE AS PAGES IN A BOOK

from UP IN CENTRAL PARK

Words by DOROTHY FIELDS
Music by SIGMUND ROMBERG

D7 G E♭7

fore I hear your laugh, my laugh breaks through;

Fm7 Fm6 E♭maj7 E♭7 A♭ F7

And when a tear starts to ap - pear, my eyes grow mist - y,

B♭7sus B♭7♯5 E♭ B♭m7 E♭7

too. Our dreams won't come tum - bling to the ground,

p

A♭ E♭7 A♭ A♭7 F7

we'll hold them fast. Dar - ling, as the

Cm7
F7
B♭
F7
B♭7
strong - est book is bound,
we're bound to last.
Gm
E♭
Gm
G7
G7♯5
G7
Cm
Your life is my life and while life beats a - way in my
A♭6
B7
E♭
B♭m6
C7
heart
we'll be close as pag - es in a book,
mp
Fm7
B♭9♯5
1
E♭
B♭dim
B♭7
2
E♭
nev - er to part.
part.
mf
f

BLUE SKIES

from BETSY
featured in BLUE SKIES

Words and Music by
IRVING BERLIN

C6/G G6 Gm6 A7 Bm F♯+
cloud - y day for me. Then good luck came a -
worst looks like the best. I should mind if they
F♯7 D7 G Gmaj7 G7
knock - ing at my door. Skies were gray, but they're
say it can't be true. I should smile; that's ex -
C6/G C7 G B7♯5 Em
not gray an - y - more.
act - ly what I do.
Blue skies
B+/D♯ B7/D♯ G/D C♯m7♭5 Cm6/E♭ G/D
smil - ing at me. Noth - ing but blue skies
3fr
4fr

C9
D+
G
Em
do I see.
Blue - birds
B+/D♯
B7/D♯
G/D
C♯m7♭5
4fr
Cm6/E♭
G/D
sing - ing a song;
noth - ing but blue - birds
C9
D+
G
all day long.
Nev - er saw the sun
Cm/G
3fr
G
Cm/G
3fr
G
Cm/G
3fr
G
shin - ing so bright.
Nev - er saw things go - ing so right.
No - tic - ing the days

Cm/G G Cm/G G D7 G B7♯5
hur - ry - ing by; when you're in love, my how they fly.
Em B+/D♯ B7/D♯ G/D C♯m7♭5 Cm6/E♭
Blue days, all of them gone. Noth - ing but
G/D C9 D+ G
blue skies from now on.
G
rit.

BRING HIM HOME

from LES MISÉRABLES

Music by CLAUDE-MICHEL SCHÖNBERG
Lyrics by HERBERT KRETZMER and ALAIN BOUBLIL

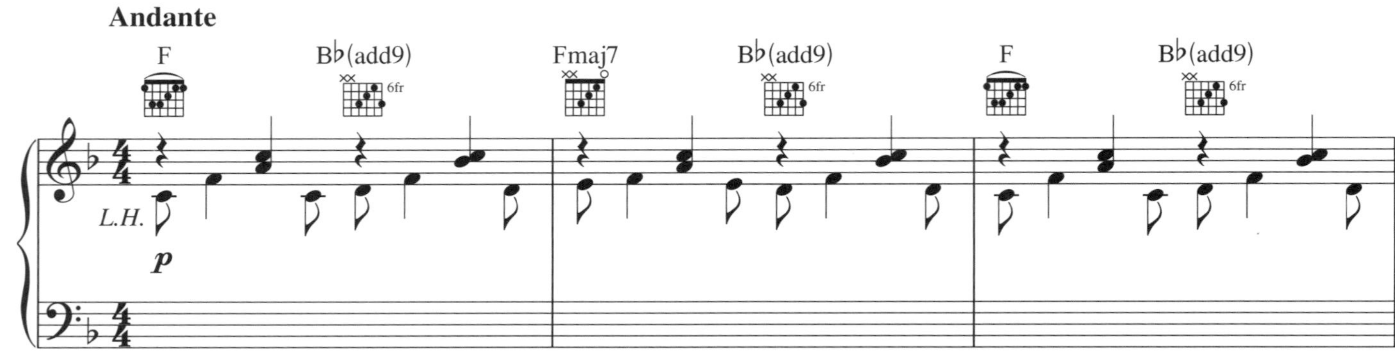

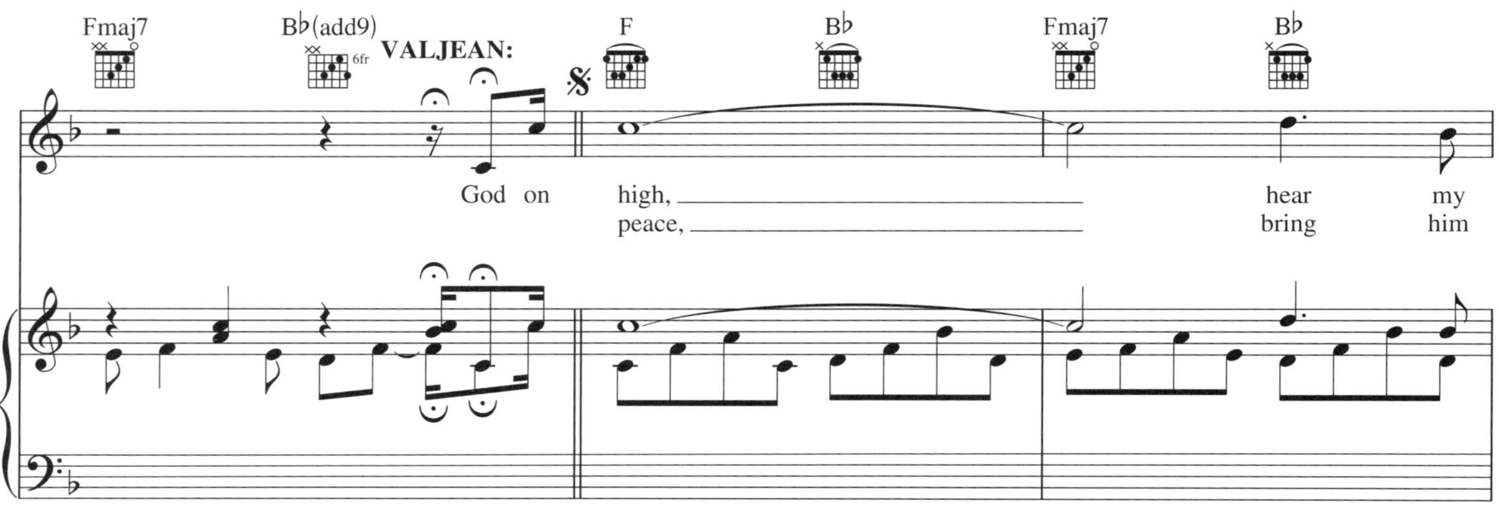

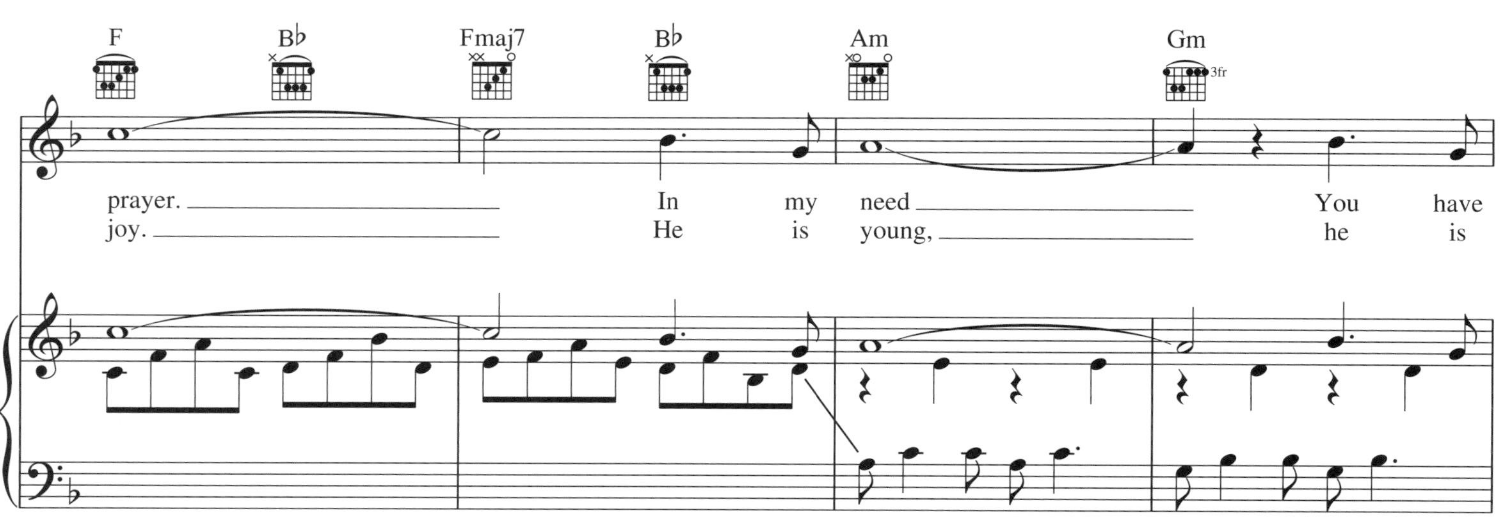

C
C7
F
Gm7/F
al - ways been there.
on - ly a boy.
He is young,
You can take,
Fmaj7
B♭/F
F
Gm7/F
Fmaj7
B♭/F
he's a - fraid.
You can give.
Let him
Let him
A
A7
Dm
rest,
be,
heav - en blessed.
let him live.
Dm/C
B♭
B♭/A
To Coda
Bring him home,
If I die,
bring him
let me
poco più mosso

Gm
C7
F
home, bring him home.
rall.
mf più mosso
Am
Gm
Dm
He's like the son I might have known if God had grant-ed me a
C
B♭
F/A
B♭
son. The sum-mers die one by one. How soon they fly on and
F/A
Gm
A
C
D.S. al Coda
on. And I am old and will be gone. Bring him
rit. e dim.
rall.
p

CODA
Gm
3fr
C7
F
Gm/F
Fmaj7
B♭/F
die, let him live. Bring him
rall.
p a tempo

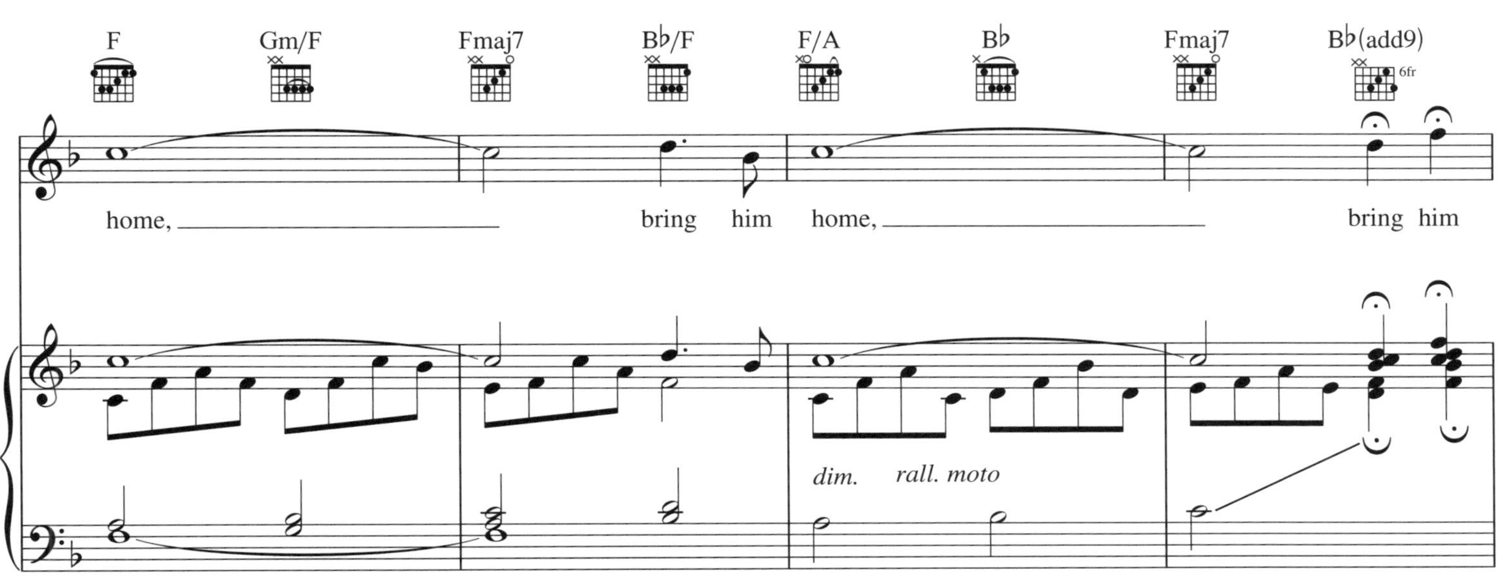
F
Gm/F
Fmaj7
B♭/F
F/A
B♭
Fmaj7
B♭(add9)
6fr
home, bring him home, bring him
dim.
rall. moto

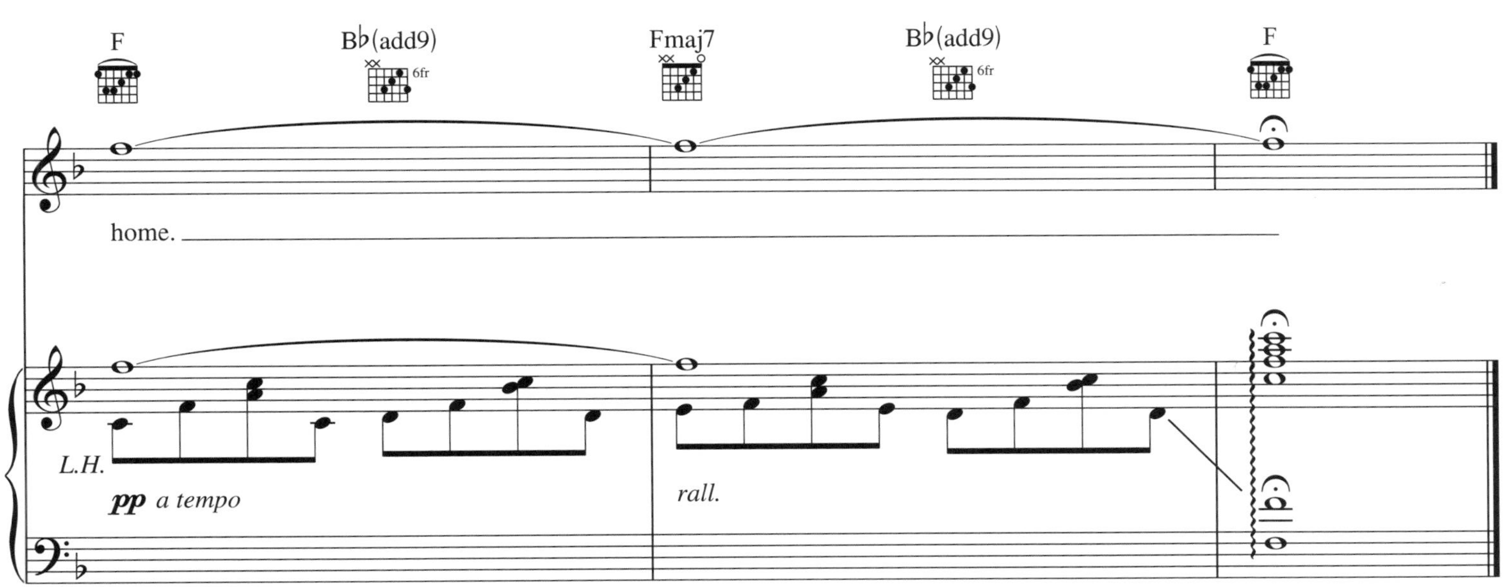
F
B♭(add9)
6fr
Fmaj7
B♭(add9)
6fr
F
home.
L.H.
pp a tempo
rall.

BROTHERHOOD OF MAN

from HOW TO SUCCEED IN BUSINESS WITHOUT REALLY TRYING

By FRANK LOESSER

C9
F
F♯dim
9fr
B7
all hu - man hearts and minds
in - to one
in that fra - ter - ni - ty,
the great big
1
C
F/C
C
D7
G7
Dm7
G7
broth - er - hood of man.
Your life - long
2
C
Am
Dm7
G7
C
G7
broth - er - hood of man?
C
G7
C7

C'EST MAGNIFIQUE

from CAN-CAN

Words and Music by
COLE PORTER

Gm
3fr
F
But be pa - tient and soon you will find, if you fol - low your
Bb
F7
3
heart, not your mind, love is wait - ing there a - gain,
poco rit.
Slow and easy
Gm
A7
D7
G
to take you up in the air a - gain.
G
When love comes in and takes you for a

E7
Am
Am6
spin, oo la la-la, c'est mag-ni-fi-que.
Am
E7
Am
Am7
When ev-'ry night your loved one holds you
Am
D9
4fr
D+
G6
Gmaj7
tight, oo la la-la, c'est mag-ni-fi-que.
G6
G
But when, one day, your loved one drifts a-

G9 9fr
G7
Cmaj7
C6
way, oo la la - la,
it is so tra - gi - que.
Am
C6
Cm6 3fr
G
C
But when, once more,
he
she
whis - pers "je t'a -
rit. poco a poco
G
A7
D13 4fr
1
G
dore" c'est mag - ni - fi - que.
a tempo
D7
2
G
D7
G
When
que.
rit.

CABARET
from the Musical CABARET

Words by FRED EBB
Music by JOHN KANDER

Adim7
Gm
3fr
C9
cab - a - ret, old chum,
Fm7
B♭9
1
E♭
3fr
Fm7
B♭9
come to the cab - a - ret.
2
E♭
3fr
A♭m
4fr
ret. Come taste the wine, come hear the
E♭
3fr
Cm
3fr
Cm(maj7)
8fr
Cm7
3fr
F9
band, come blow the horn, start cel - e - brat - ing,

B♭7
E♭(add9)
B♭9
B♭9♯5
right this way, your ta - ble's wait - ing.
No use per - mit - ting some
Start by ad - mit - ting from
E♭(add9)
B♭7♯5
E♭
E♭maj9
proph - et of doom to wipe ev - 'ry smile a -
cra - dle to tomb is - n't that long a
B♭m7
E♭7
A♭
Adim7
To Coda
way;
stay;
Life is a cab - a -
Gm7
C9
Fm7
A♭/B♭
E♭
ret, old chum, come to the cab - a - ret.

D.S. al Coda
CODA
Gm7
C9
Come taste the
ret, old chum,
A♭
Adim7
on - ly a cab - a -
Gm7
C9
Fm7
ret, old chum, so come to the
A♭/B♭
E♭
B♭9♯5
E♭
cab - a - ret.
sfz
8vb

A COCKEYED OPTIMIST

from SOUTH PACIFIC

Lyrics by OSCAR HAMMERSTEIN II
Music by RICHARD RODGERS

Dm7
G7
Dm7
get ev - 'ry cloud I've ev - er seen,
G7
C
Cdim7
So they call me a cock - eyed
Gmaj7
G6
Am7
op - ti - mist Im - ma - ture and in -
D7
G(add9)
G
cur - a - bly green. I have

G+
3fr
G6
3
heard peo - ple rant and rave and bel - low
3
Dm7
G7
That we're done and we might as well be
Dm7
G7
C
dead, But I'm on - ly a
Cdim7
Gmaj7
G6
cock - eyed op - ti - mist And I

Am7
D7
G6
can't get it in - to my head.
G
Bm
Bm♯5
2fr
I hear the hu - man race is
sempre p
C♯m7
4fr
F♯7
Bm
fall - ing on its face And has - n't ver - y
Bm7
C♯m7
4fr
F♯7
C♯m7
4fr
F♯+
far to go,
But
poco rall.
a tempo

B
Bmaj7
C♯m7
4fr
ev - 'ry whip - poor - will Is sell - ing me a
F♯7
D
A13
5fr
bill, And tell - ing me it just ain't
Am7/D
D7
C/D
D7
G
so. I could say life is
G+
3fr
G6
3
just a bowl of jel - lo And ap -

Dm7
G7
Dm7
pear more in - tel - li - gent and smart,
G7
C
Cdim
3fr
But I'm stuck like a dope With a
poco cresc.
G
A7
D7
thing called hope, And I can't get it
D7♯5
Bm7
G
Gmaj7
G7
out of my heart!
dim.

Cmaj9 C Cmaj7 C6 Am7/D D7

Not ___ this ___

p

Am/D D7 C G C(add9) G

heart! ___

mf

E♭7/G G

dim.

(p)

Ped.

COMEDY TONIGHT

from A FUNNY THING HAPPENED ON THE WAY TO THE FORUM

Words and Music by
STEPHEN SONDHEIM

G
C
F
D7
Some - thing for ev - 'ry - one, a com - e - dy to - night!
Some - thing for ev - 'ry - one, a com - e - dy to - night!
G
C
D
B
Noth - ing with kings, noth - ing with crowns.
Noth - ing of Gods, noth - ing of Fate.
F
G
Am
B
C
D11
5fr
Bring on the lov - ers, li - ars and clowns!
Weigh - ty af - fairs will just have to wait.
G
C
D
G
C
D
Old sit - u - a - tions, new com - pli - ca - tions,
Noth - ing that's for - mal, noth - ing that's nor - mal,

G
Am
G
B♭m7
Noth - ing por - ten - tous or po - lite;
No re - ci - ta - tions to re - cite!
Am7
1
D7
G
Trag - e - dy to - mor - row, com - e - dy to - night!
O - pen up the cur - tain,
Am
D
G
Am
D
2
com - e - dy
D7
G
Am
D
G
to - night!
ff
sfz

DANCE ONLY WITH ME

from SAY, DARLING

Words by BETTY COMDEN and ADOLPH GREEN
Music by JULE STYNE

C7 Gm6 3fr C9 F Dm
Love, love, love on - ly me
Gm 3fr C7 Eb7b5 D7 G7#5
all of our days from now on. Dance
f
C7#5 8fr Am7 D7b9 4fr G9 9fr C7b9
on - ly with me, till all our sweet mu - sic is
dim.
1 F 2 F
gone. gone.
rall.
mf

DANCING ON THE CEILING

from SIMPLE SIMON

Words by LORENZ HART
Music by RICHARD RODGERS

C7♭9
F
F/A
face I see. At night I creep in bed
A♭dim7
Gm7
F
and nev - er sleep in bed, but look a - bove in the air,
Fm
F
C7
C7♭9
and to my great - est joy, my boy is
F
Am
D7
there! It is my prince who walks

Gm
3fr
C7
F
in - to my dreams and talks.
He danc - es
A+
B♭6
G7
C
Em
o - ver - head on the ceil - ing near my bed,
Gm7
C7
F
B♭6
C7
in my sight, through the
F
A+
night. I try to hide in vain

B♭6 G7 C Em Gm7 C7
un - der - neath my coun - ter - pane; there's my
F B♭6 C7 F
love up a - bove!
C7 F6
I whis - per, "Go a - way, my lov - er; it's not fair."
C7 C7♭9
But I'm so grate - ful to dis - cov - er

F
Cdim7
C7
F
he's still there.
I love my
A+
B♭6
G7
C
Em
ceil - ing more since it is a danc - ing floor
Gm
3fr
C7
1
F
just for my love.
Gm7
C7
2
F
love.

DAY BY DAY

from the Musical GODSPELL

Music by STEPHEN SCHWARTZ
Lyrics by RICHARD OF CHICHESTER (1197-1253)

1
Dm
G
Cmaj7
fol - low Thee more
near - ly,
day by day.
2
Light Rock feeling
Cmaj7
Fmaj7
Gm/F
day by day.
Day by day,
Fmaj7
Gm7/F
B♭maj7
Am7
day by day,
oh, dear Lord, three
Gmaj7
2nd time, play these 4 measures 4 times
Em
things I pray:
to see Thee more

A
Em
A
clear - ly,
love Thee more
dear - ly,
Dm
G
1
Cmaj7
fol - low Thee more
near - ly,
day by day.
2
Cmaj7
Fmaj7
day by day.
Cmaj7
Fmaj7
Amaj7
Day by day, by
day by day by
day.

DO YOU HEAR THE PEOPLE SING?

from LES MISÉRABLES

Music by CLAUDE-MICHEL SCHÖNBERG
Lyrics by ALAIN BOUBLIL, JEAN-MARC NATEL
and HERBERT KRETZMER

Dm Gm C7 F E Am
COMBEFERRE:
life a-bout to start when to-mor - row comes. Will you join in our cru-sade? Who will be
give all you can give so that our
Em Dm Am
COURFEYRAC:
strong and stand with me? Be-yond the bar - ri-cade is there a world you long to see? Then
ban - ner may ad-vance? Some will fall and some will live. Will you stand up and take your chance? The
F Dm7 G C
CHORUS:
join in the fight that will give you the right to be free!
blood of the mar-tyrs will wa - ter the mead-ows of France!
Do you hear the peo - ple sing, sing-ing the
f

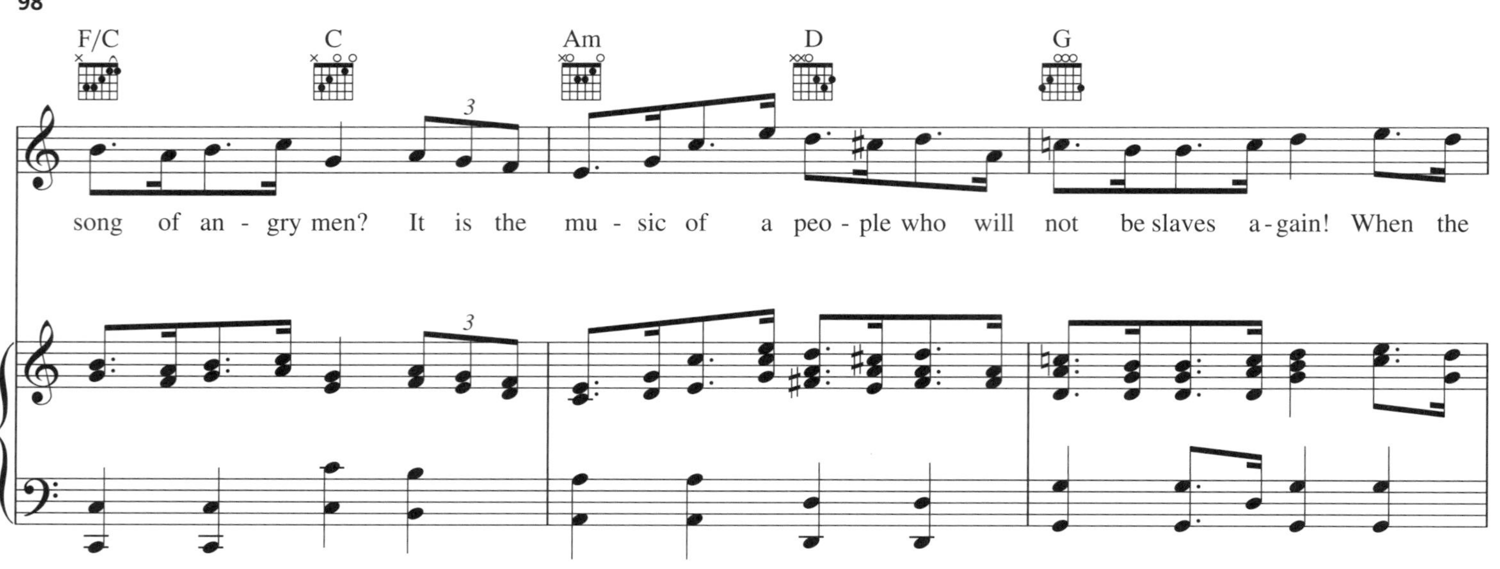
F/C
C
Am
D
G
song of an - gry men? It is the mu - sic of a peo - ple who will not be slaves a - gain! When the

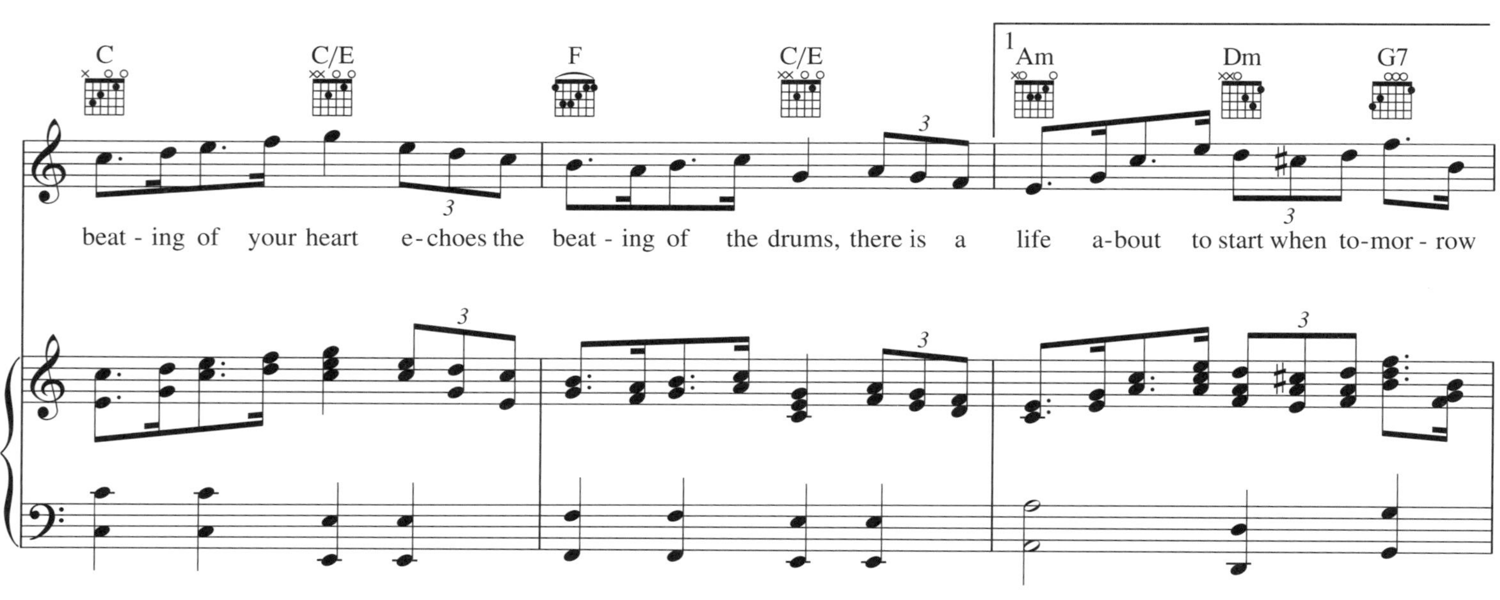
C
C/E
F
C/E
1 Am
Dm
G7
beat - ing of your heart e - choes the beat - ing of the drums, there is a life a - bout to start when to - mor - row

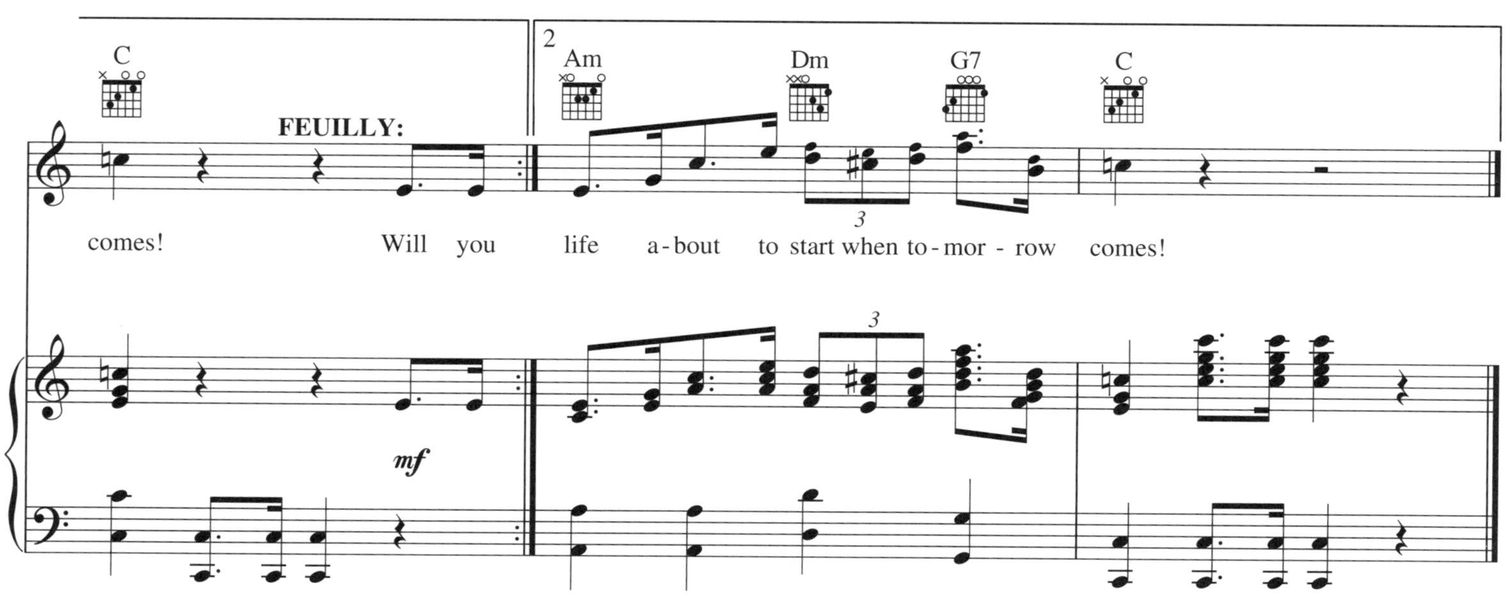
C
FEUILLY:
2 Am
Dm
G7
C
comes! Will you life a - bout to start when to - mor - row comes!
mf

EDELWEISS

from THE SOUND OF MUSIC

Lyrics by OSCAR HAMMERSTEIN II
Music by RICHARD RODGERS

B♭
F7/A
B♭/D
E♭/G
Small and white, Clean and bright,
B♭/F
F7
B♭
You look hap - py to meet me.
F7/A
F7
B♭
Blos - som of snow, may you bloom and grow,
mp
E♭
C/E
F
F7
Bloom and grow for - ev - er.

B♭ Fm6/A♭ E♭/G E♭m/G♭

E - del - weiss, E - del - weiss,

p

B♭/F F7 1 B♭

Bless my home - land for - ev - er.

2 B♭ *Optional final ending* B♭ Gm7

ev - er. ev - er.

mf

Ped. *

Cm7 E♭/F F9 B♭

p *rall.* *pp*

Ped. *

ELECTRICITY

from BILLY ELLIOT

Music by ELTON JOHN
Lyrics by LEE HALL

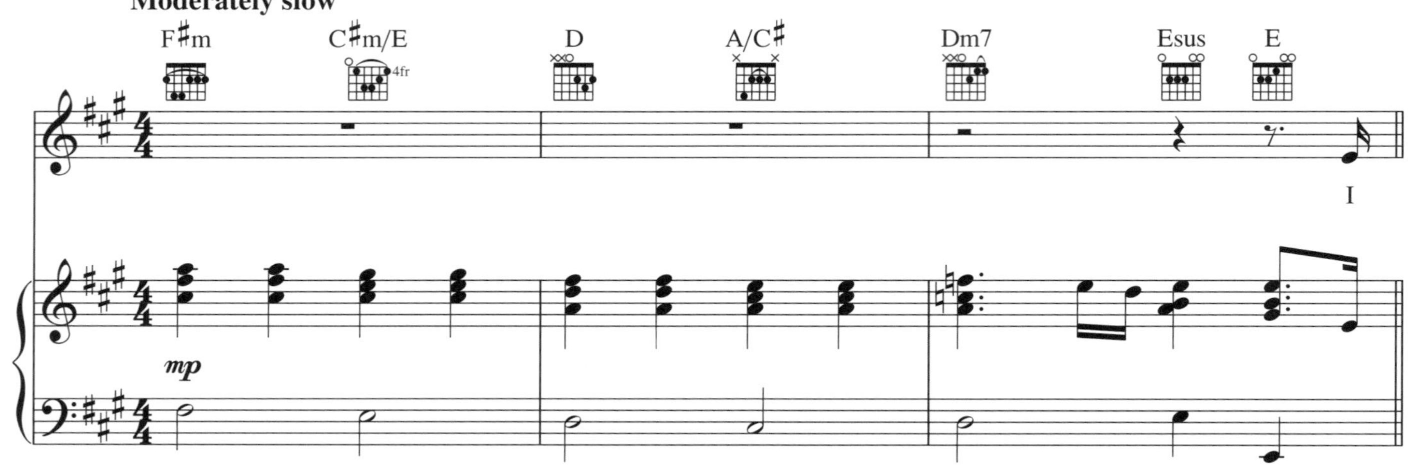

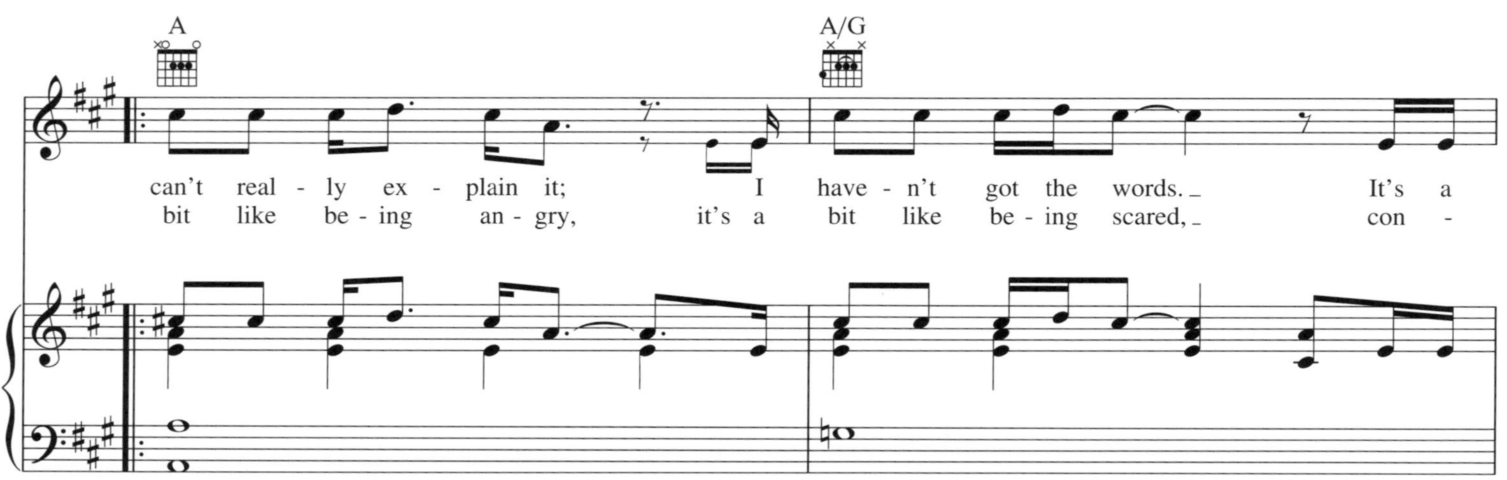

Bm7
F♯m
pose it's like for - get - ting, los - ing who you are, and at the
like when you've been cry - ing, and you're emp - ty, and you're full, but I
Dm7
Esus
E
same time some - thing makes you whole.
don't know what it is, it's hard to tell.
It's
Am
G6
F
C/E
like that there's mu - sic play - ing in your ear,
and I'm
but the
Am
G6
F
Esus
E
list - 'ning and I'm list - 'ning. And then I dis - ap - pear, and then I
mu - sic is im - pos - si - ble, im - pos - si - ble to hear. But then I

C
Am
feel a change like a fire deep in - side,
feel it move me, like a burn - ing deep in - side,
Dm7
C/E
D7/F♯
G
some - thing burst - ing me wide o - pen, im - pos - si - ble to hide. And
C
C/B♭
sud - den - ly I'm fly - ing, fly - ing like a bird, like e - lec -
F
Fm6
tric - i - ty. E - lec - tric - i - ty sparks in -

1
C/G
G7
C
side of me, and I'm free, I'm free.
It's a
2
C/G
side of me, and I'm
G7
F♯m
C♯m/E
4fr
free, I'm free,
D
A/C♯
Dm7
Esus
E
A
free, I'm free.
rit.

EVERYBODY'S GOT A HOME BUT ME

from PIPE DREAM

Lyrics by OSCAR HAMMERSTEIN II
Music by RICHARD RODGERS

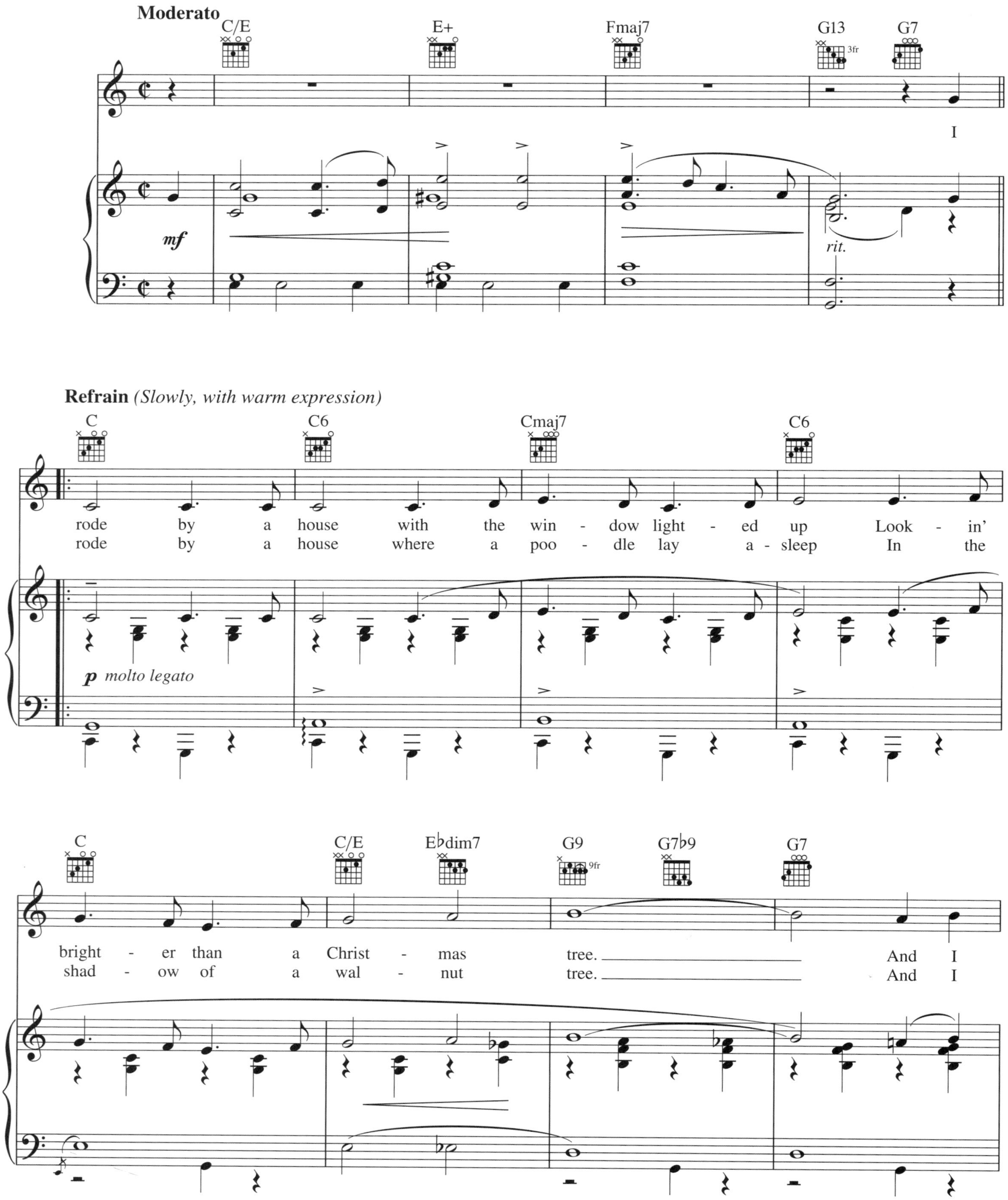

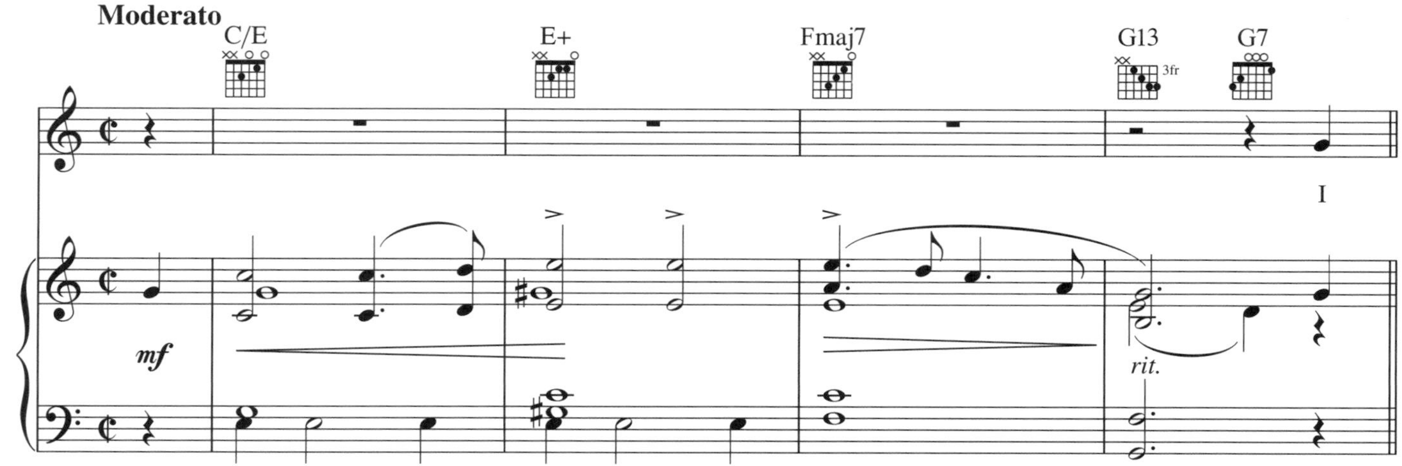

Moderato
C/E
E+
Fmaj7
G13
3fr
G7
I
mf
rit.
Refrain (Slowly, with warm expression)
C
C6
Cmaj7
C6
rode by a house with the win - dow light - ed up Look - in'
rode by a house where a poo - dle lay a - sleep In the
p molto legato
C
C/E
E♭dim7
G9
9fr
G7♭9
G7
bright - er than a Christ - mas tree. And I
shad - ow of a wal - nut tree. And I

C
C+
F6
D7
said to my - self as I rode by my - self, Ev - 'ry -
said to my - self as I rode by my - self, Ev - 'ry -
mf più espr.
cresc.
C
Dm7
G7
C(add9)
C
Cmaj7
C
bod - y's got a home but me. I
bod - y's got a home but me. I
C6
Cmaj7
C6
rode by a house where the moon was on the porch and a
rode by a house where a pi - geon had a roost on the
p
C
C/E
E♭dim7
G9
9fr
G7♭9
G7
girl was on her fel - ler's knee. And I
rig - gin' of a new T. V. And I

C
C+
F6
said to my - self as I rode by my -
said to my - self as I rode by my -
mf più espr.
cresc.
D7
C
Dm7
G7
self, Ev - 'ry - bod - y's got a home but
self, Ev - 'ry - bod - y's got a home but
C
A♭
4fr
me. I am free and I'm
me. I am free and I'm
mf
A♭6
3fr
C
hap - py to be free, To be
hap - py to be free, To be

Eb Eb6 Dm7(add4) Dm7 G7
3fr
free in the way I want to be. But
free in the way I want to be. But
C C6 Cmaj7
once in a while when the road is kind - a
once in a while when I'm talk - in' to my -
p
C6 C C/E Ebdim7
dark And the end is kind - a hard to
self And there's no one there to dis - a -
G9 G7b9 G7 C
9fr
see, I look up and I
gree, I look up and I
mf più espr.

C+
F6
D7
cry to a cloud go - in' by: "Won't there
cry to the big emp - ty sky: "Won't there
cresc.
C
Dm7
G7
Gm7(add4)
ev - er be a home for me, some -
ev - er be a home for me, some -
mf
C7
Fmaj7
F/E
Dm7
G7
where? Ev - 'ry - bod - y's got a home but
where? Ev - 'ry - bod - y's got a home but
1
C
G6
G7
me." I
f
2
C
C6
me."
f
Ped.
*

GUYS AND DOLLS

from GUYS AND DOLLS

By FRANK LOESSER

Dm7/C B+ B7 E7 B♭9♭5 A7
John wait - ing out in the rain Chanc - es
Doll with her dia - mond in hock Rest as -
3
Dm Dm7/C B♭7 A Fm6 G9
9fr
are he's in - sane as on - ly a John can be for a Jane.
sured that the rock has gone to re - stock some gen - tle - man Jock.
C G7♭9 Dm7/G G6 C G7♭9 Dm7 G
When you meet a gent pay - ing all kinds of rent
When you see a mouse hur - ry out of the house
C Cmaj7 C9 F(add2) G9 Cmaj7 G11 G9
For a flat that could flat - ten the Taj Ma -
And she runs twen - ty blocks for ci - gars and

C B+ Bb7 A7#5 Dm Dm7
hal Call it sad, call it
rye Call it dumb, call it
B+ B7 C Bb A7 A7#5
fun - ny, but it's bet - ter than e - ven mon - ey That the
clev - er, ah, but you can give odds for - ev - er That the
Dm C#+ Dm7/G G9/B Dm7 G7 C Db9b5
guy's on - ly do - ing it for some doll. On the
doll's on - ly do - ing it for some
1
9fr
G13 C Fdim C Bb9 Cmaj9
oth - er hand: When you guy.
2
3fr
8fr

THE GENTLEMAN IS A DOPE

from ALLEGRO

Lyrics by OSCAR HAMMERSTEIN II
Music by RICHARD RODGERS

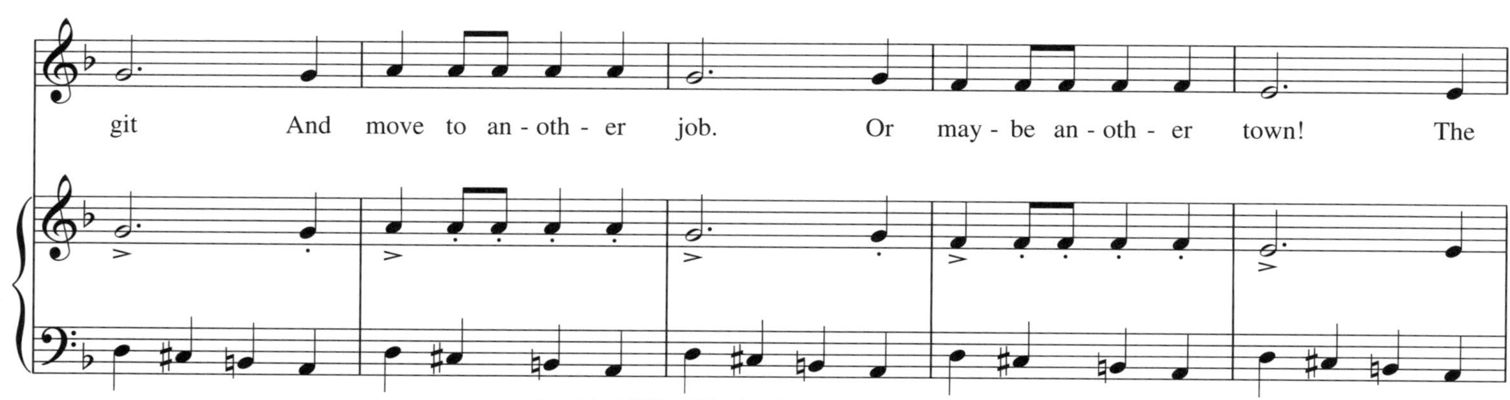

gen - tle - man burns me up! The gen - tle - man gets me down!
mf
R.H.
L.H.
Refrain
A7
Dm
The gen - tle - man is a dope a
p - mf leggiero
Dm6
B♭maj7
B7
man of man - y faults, A clum - sy Joe who would - n't know a
C7
F6
A7/E
Dm
Rhum - ba from a Waltz, The gen - tle - man is a dope and

G7
Bbmaj7
Bb7
not my cup of tea, (Why do I get in a dith - er? He
mf
Dm/A
E7
A7
Dm
Em7
A7
Dm
does - n't be - long to me!) The gen - tle - man is - n't bright,
mf
p
Dm6
Bbmaj7
he does - n't know the score A cake will come, he'll
B7
C7
F6
A7/E
Dm
take a crumb and nev - er ask for more! The gen - tle - man's eyes are blue

G7
Bbmaj7
but lit - tle do they see (Why am I beat - ing my
mf
Bb7
Dm/A
E7
A7
Dm
Dm/C
Dm/Bb
Dm/A
D7
brains out? He does - n't be - long to me!) He's
G
G/F#
G/E
G/D
C
C/B
C/A
C/G
3fr
some - bod - y els - e's prob - lem, She's
G
G/F#
G/E
G/D
C9
wel - come to the guy! She'll

F
F/E
F/D
F/C
B♭
B♭/A
B♭/G
B♭/F
nev - er un - der - stand him half as
E7
E7♯5
E7
E7♯5
E7
A7
A7♭9
A7
A7♭9
A7
Dm
well as I. The gen-tle-man is a dope
mf
p
Dm6
B♭maj7
he is - n't ver - y smart, He's just a lug you'd
B7
C7
F6
A7/E
Dm
like to hug and hold a - gainst your heart. The gen-tle-man does - n't know

G7
Bbmaj7
How hap - py he could be.
Look at me! Cry - ing my
mf
Bb7
Dm/A
E7
A7
Fmaj7
Bbmaj7
eyes out, As if he be - longed to me.
Em7(add4)
A7
D/F#
G
Ab7b5
A7
1 Dm
Em7(add4)
A7
He'll nev - er be - long to me!
The
f
mf
2 Dm6
Em7(add4)
A9
Dm
me!
f
sf
8vb

GOOD MORNING BALTIMORE

from Hairspray

Music by MARC SHAIMAN
Lyrics by MARC SHAIMAN and SCOTT WITTMAN

Bm
Gm/B♭
B♭7
D/A
rhy - thm of town starts call - ing me down. It's like a mes - sage from
rats on the streets all dance 'round my feet. They seem to say, "Tra - cy, it's
G♯m7♭5
E/G♯
D/A
A
D/A
high a - bove
up to you."
Oh, oh, oh, Pull - ing me out to the
So, oh, oh, Don't hold me back, 'cause to -
G
Em9
A
D/A
A7
Dsus
D
smiles and the streets that I love. Good morn - ing, Bal - ti - more!
day all my dreams will come true. Good morn - ing, Bal - ti - more!
G(add9)
G
Ev - 'ry day's like an o - pen door. Ev - ry night is a
There's the flash - er who lives next door. There's the bum on his

Dsus D
D/A Asus
fan - ta - sy. Ev - 'ry sound's like a sym - pho - ny.
bar - room stool. They wish me luck on my way to school.

A D/A A7 Dsus$^{2}_{4}$ D
D7/C
Good morn - ing, Bal - ti - more! And some day when I

G/B Gm/B♭ D/A
take to the floor, the world's gon - na wake up and see

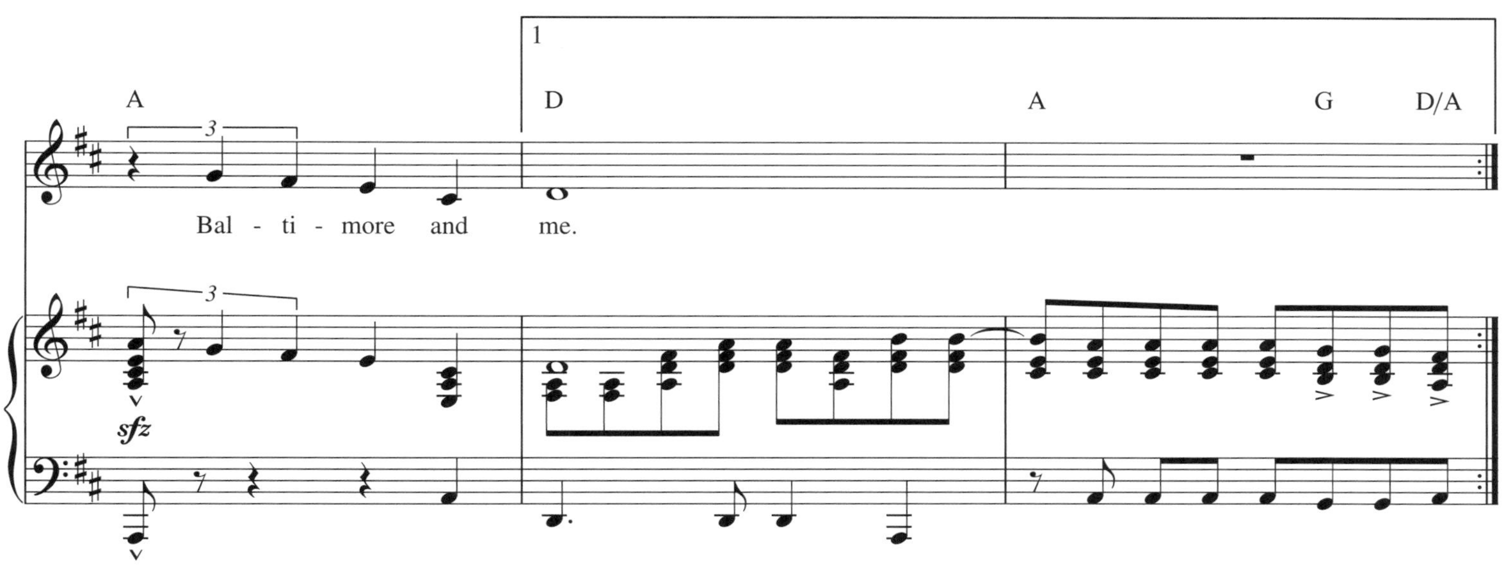
1
A
D
A
G
D/A
Bal - ti - more and me.
sfz

2
D
B♭
me.
I know ev - 'ry step. I
mp

F/A
Gm7
Gm/A
F/A
know ev - 'ry song. I know there's a place where I be - long. I

C
G/B
Am7
G/B
see all those par - ty lights shin - ing a - head. So some - one in - vite me be -
Asus
A
D
fore I drop dead!
So, oh, oh,
D/F♯
G
Bm/A
A
G
Give me a chance, 'cause when I start to dance I'm a mo - vie star.
D
D/F♯
G♯m7♭5
E/G♯
Oh, oh, oh, Some - thing in - side of me makes me move when

F♯7♭9/A♯
Bm
Gm/B♭
B♭7
I hear the groove. My ma tells me, "No," but my feet tell me, "Go."
D/A
G♯m7♭5
E/G♯
It's like a drum - mer in - side my heart.
D/A
A
D/A
G
Em7
Oh, oh, oh, Don't make me wait one more mo - ment for my life to
mf
D/A
A7sus
D/A
A7sus
B♭7sus
start.

B♭ E♭/B♭ B♭7 E♭sus2/4 E♭
I love you, Bal - ti - more! Ev - 'ry day's like an
ff
A♭2 A♭
o - pen door. Ev - 'ry night is a fan - ta - sy.
E♭sus E♭
Ev - 'ry sound's like a sym - pho - ny.
E♭/B♭ B♭sus B♭ E♭/B♭ B♭7
And I pro - mise,
E♭sus2/4 E♭ E♭7/D♭ A♭/C
Bal - ti - more, that some day when I take to the floor, the

A♭m/C♭
E♭/B♭
world's gon - na wake up and see,
Am7♭5
A♭/B♭
B♭
gon - na wake up and see
Bal - ti - more and
sfz
E♭ E♭sus E♭
B♭9
E♭ E♭sus E♭
me.
Bal - ti - more and me,
B♭
B♭ A♭(add9)
E♭
Bal - ti - more and me!
rit.

GOODNIGHT, MY SOMEONE

from Meredith Willson's THE MUSIC MAN

By MEREDITH WILLSON

G
C
G7
night. Sweet dreams be yours, dear, if dreams there
C
D♯dim
6fr
C
G7
be; sweet dreams to car - ry you close to me. I
C
C7
F
D7
D♯dim
6fr
C
wish they may and I wish they might. Now good - night, my
G
1
C
C♯dim
4fr
G7
2
C
F/C
Fm6/C
C
some - one, good - night. Good - night.

HAUNTED HEART

from INSIDE U.S.A.

Words by HOWARD DIETZ
Music by ARTHUR SCHWARTZ

Fm7
Edim7
E♭m6
Dm7♭5
Adim7
E♭6
ghost of you my lost ro - mance.
E♭maj7
3fr
E♭6
F♯dim7
Fm7
B♭7
B♭+
Lips that laugh, eyes that
E♭maj9
E♭6
Fm9
B♭7
E♭6
dance.
Haunt - ed heart
In the night,
B♭7♭9
E♭6
E♭dim7
B♭7
won't let me be,
though we're a - part,

E♭6
E♭maj7
3fr
B♭m7/E♭
6fr
E♭7
dreams re - peat a sweet but lone - ly song to me.
B♭m7
E♭7
A♭
4fr
E♭6
Fm7
F♯dim7
Dreams are dust, it's you who must be -
E♭
3fr
Adim7
long to me and thrill
A♭6
3fr
B♭7
E♭
3fr
E♭9
E♭7♯5
my haunt - ed heart. Be

To Coda
A♭maj7
A♭dim7
B♭7♭9
E♭
E♭6
still, my haunt - ed heart.
E♭dim7
Fm7
E♭
E♭6
E♭dim7
Fm7
E♭maj7
E♭
E♭dim7
B♭7
B♭7♯5
Gm
E♭maj9
E♭6
Time rolls on try - ing in vain to cure me,
A♭7
A♭9♭5
A♭9
Fm7
B♭7♯5
E♭
you are gone but you re - main to lure me.

Fm7
B♭dim7
Fm7
B♭7
Gm7
E♭dim7
You're there in the dark and I call, you're there but you're
Bdim7
Cm
A♭6
B♭7
E♭maj7
Fm
not there at all. Oh, what will I do without
3fr
8va
rall.
B9♯5
B9♭5
B♭13
D.S. al Coda
CODA
E♭
you, with - out you.
heart.
8va
molto rit.
E♭dim7
Fm7
E♭6
rall.
8vb

HE WAS TOO GOOD TO ME

from SIMPLE SIMON

Words by LORENZ HART
Music by RICHARD RODGERS

A♭
E♭6 Dm F/C
B♭ B♭/A♭
G7
Cm Edim E♭dim
gain, I was a good sport, Told him Good-bye, Eyes dim, But why com -
accel.
Slowly, with feeling
F7
B♭ B♭maj7
Am7♭5
E♭/F Dm/F Am7♭5 F7
plain? He was too good to me. How can I get a - long now?
rit.
p - mf
B♭ B♭maj7
Am7♭5
E♭/F Dm/F
Am7♭5 F7
B♭
So close he stood to me, Ev'-ry - thing seems all wrong now! He would have
B♭/A♭ Gm7 E♭m/G♭ B♭/F C7/E F7/E♭ B♭/D B♭m6/D♭ F/C C7/B♭
brought me the sun. Mak-ing me smile That was his

F/A Eb/F Bb/F F7 Bb Bbmaj7 Am7b5 Eb/F Dm/Eb
fun! When I was mean to him He'd nev - er say, "Go
Am7b5 F7 Bb Cm7/Bb Bb/F Am7b5 Eb/F Dm/F Am7b5 F7
'way now." I was a queen to him, Who's goin' to make me gay now?
Bb Bb/A Bb/Ab Gm7 Ebm/Gb Bb/F C7/E Ebm6 Bb/D Gm Cm7
It's on - ly nat - 'ral I'm blue - ooo, He was too good
F9 Bb Edim Ebmaj7 F7 Bb Ebmaj7 Bb
to be true. true.
rall.
a tempo
cresc.
dim.
Ped.

HEY, LOOK ME OVER

from WILDCAT

Music by CY COLEMAN
Lyrics by CAROLYN LEIGH

D7
Am7/E
Fm6
D7/F♯
G
B7
E7
don't pass the plate, folks, don't pass the cup; I
A7
D7
fig - ure when - ev - er you're down and out, the on - ly way is up. And I'll be
G
B7
F♯m7/C♯
Ddim7
B7/D♯
up like a rose - bud, high on the vine;
E7
Am
don't thumb your nose, bud, take a tip from mine. I'm a

Cmaj7
F9
G/B
E7
To Coda
lit - tle bit short of the el - bow room, but let me get me some.
And look
Hear me
Am7
D7
G
out, world, here I come.
Interlude (ad lib.)
No - bod - y in the world was ev - er with - out a pray'r;
F
how can you win the world, if no - bod - y knows you're there.

E
Kid, when you need the crowd, the tick - ets are hard to sell;

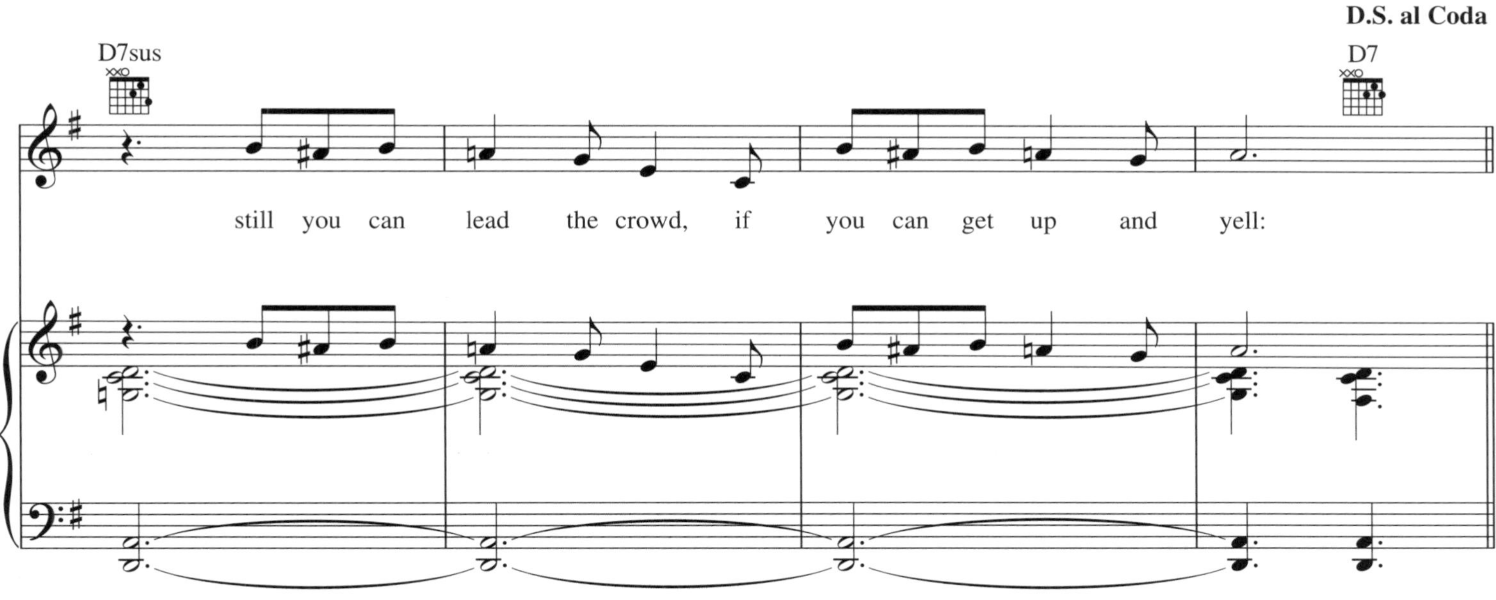
D.S. al Coda
D7sus
D7
still you can lead the crowd, if you can get up and yell:

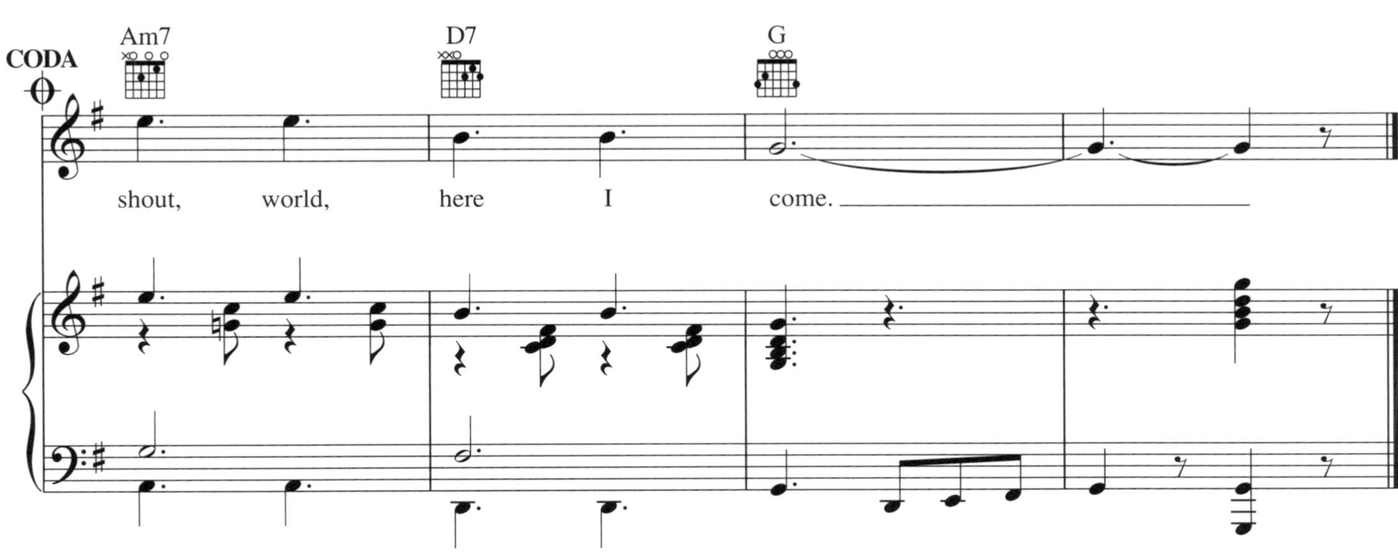
CODA
Am7
D7
G
shout, world, here I come.

HOW ARE THINGS IN GLOCCA MORRA

from FINIAN'S RAINBOW

Words by E.Y. "YIP" HARBURG
Music by BURTON LANE

C13 Gm7 C13 G♭dim Gm7 Edim F7 G7 D♭dim C7
2fr 2fr 3fr 4fr
breeze; it well may be it's fol - lowed me a - cross the
F B♭/F F C7♭9 F B♭/F F Gm7/C
seas. Then tell me, please: how are things in Gloc - ca
B♭/F Fmaj7 Gm7 Fmaj7 Gm7 C7 Gm7
Mor - ra? Is that lit - tle brook still leap - ing there?
C7 Gm7 C13 Gm7 C13
2fr 2fr
Does it still run down to Don - ny cove? Through Kil - ly - begs, Kil -

F
B♭
F/A
B♭
F/A
Gm7/C
B♭/F
Fmaj7
Gm7
ker - ry and Kil - dare?
How are things in Gloc - ca Mor - ra?
Fmaj7
Gm7
C7
Gm7
C7
Is that wil - low tree still weep - ing there?
Does that lad - die / las - sie with the
Gm7
C13
2fr
C7
twin - klin' eye come whis - tlin' / smil - in' by
and does he / she walk a - way, sad and
Gm7
C7
F
C7/F
F
A7
dream - y there not to see me there?
So I

B♭ C7 F A7 B♭ C7 F A7
ask each weep - in' wil - low and each brook a - long the way, and each
B♭ Gm7 C7 Fmaj7 D7♭9
lad that comes a - whis - tlin' too - ra - lay, "How are
lass a - sigh - in'
4fr
Gm Am Gm7/C C7
3fr
1 F
things in Gloc - ca Mor - ra this fine day?
Gm7/C
2 F
How are things in Gloc - ca day?"

I AM WHAT I AM

from LA CAGE AUX FOLLES

Music and Lyric by
JERRY HERMAN

G
Bm
So come take a look, give me the
Em
Am7
D7
hook or the o - va - tion. It's
G
B7
Em
Em/G
my world that I want to have a lit - tle pride in,
A7sus
A7
Am7♭5
my word and it's not a place I have to hide in.

Moderately
G
Bm
Life's not worth a damn till you can
mp
Em
Am7
D9sus
say, "Hey, world! I am what I
rit.
Moderately fast
G
E♭7sus
E♭7
am!"
cresc.
A♭
Cm
I am what I am. I don't want
mf

Fm
E♭7sus/B♭
6fr
E♭7
praise. I don't want pit - y.
A♭
4fr
Cm
3fr
I bang my own drum. Some think it's
Fm
B♭m
E♭7
noise. I think it's pret - ty. And
A♭
4fr
C
Fm
so what if I love each feath - er and each span - gle.

B♭m7
Slowly
E♭7♭9
Why not try to see things from a dif - f'rent an - gle.
Moderately fast
A♭
Cm7
Your life is a sham till you can
Fm
B♭m
E♭7
D♭/E♭
shout out loud, "I am what I
rit.
Fast
A♭
am!"
cresc.

E13
A
I am
C♯m
what I am, and what I
F♯m
F♯m(maj7)
F♯m7
Bm11
am needs no ex - cus - es.
E13
E7sus
E7
A
I deal my own
f
mf

C♯m
4fr
C♯m7
4fr
F♯m
deck, some - times the ace,
some - times the deuc - es.
G♯m7
4fr
E7
Amaj7
G♯m7♭5
C♯
It's one life and there's
F♯m
no re - turn and no de - pos - it.

B9
Moderately slow
N.C.
One life, so it's
rit.
Bm
A
G♯dim
F♯m7
Fm
Em
Dm
Bm7♭5
time to o - pen up your clos - et.
cresc.
rit.
f
B♭
F
B♭
Dm
A
Dm
Life's not worth a damn till you can
mf a tempo
Slowly, freely
Gm
Gm(maj7)
Gm7
Gm6
Cm7
shout, "Hey, world! I am what
rit.

Fast
Moderately
Eb/F
Bb
Gm7
Eb
3fr
Ebm
6fr
A
Bb
I
am!"
f
ff
rit.

I BELIEVE MY HEART
from THE WOMAN IN WHITE

Music by ANDREW LLOYD WEBBER
Lyrics by DAVID ZIPPEL

A
B
E
You smile and I feel as though
A
B
E
A
I've known you for years.
How do I know to
E/G♯
F♯
B
trust what I'm feel - ing?
E
B7/E
E
A
E
LAURA:
I be - lieve my heart.
What else can I

B
E/G♯
A
B9
E
do when ev - 'ry part of ev - 'ry thought
C♯m
B
E
B7/E
E
HARTRIGHT:
leads me straight to you? I be - lieve my heart.
A
E/G♯
B
E/G♯
A
There's no oth - er choice, for now when - ev - er
B9
E
C♯m
B
E
my heart speaks I can on - ly hear your voice.

A B E A B E
LAURA:
The life-time be - fore we met has fad - ed a - way.
A E/G♯ F♯ B
HARTRIGHT:
How did I live a mo - ment with - out you?
A B E A B
LAURA:
You don't have to speak at all, I know what you'd
E E7 A E/G♯
say.
HARTRIGHT:
And I know ev - 'ry se - cret a -

F♯
B
A/B
B
E
B
E
bout you.
I be - lieve my heart.
A
E
B
E/G♯
A
It be - lieves in you.
It's tell - ing me that
B9
E
C♯m
4fr
B7sus
2fr
B7
what I see is com - plete - ly true.
E
B
E
A
E
LAURA:
I be - lieve my heart.
How can it be

B
E/G♯
A
B9
E
wrong? It says that what I feel for you,
C♯m
B7sus
B7
E
I will feel my whole life long.
p cresc.
A
E7/A
A
D
A
BOTH:
I be - lieve my heart. It be - lieves in
f
E
A/C♯
D
E9
A
you. It's tell - ing me that what I see

F♯m
Bm7/E
E7
A
E7/A
is com - plete - ly true.
And with all my
A
D
A
E
soul I be - lieve my heart.
The
A/C♯
D
E9
A
F♯m
por - trait that it paints of you is a per - fect
Bm7/E
E7
A
Bm7/A
A
work of art.
ff

I GOT LOST IN HIS ARMS

from ANNIE GET YOUR GUN

Words and Music by
IRVING BERLIN

A7♯5
Dm(add9)
5fr
Dm
Dm7
It was dark in his arms And I lost my way.
D♭7
4fr
C7
Gm11
F♯dim
9fr
Fm7
From the dark came a voice And it seemed to say,
C6/E
Am/G
Dm7
Gdim7
Dm7/G
Fm6/G
"There you go… there you go."
G7
G7♯5
C(add9)
C
Cmaj7
C6
How I felt as I fell I just can't re - call;

A7♯5
Dm(add9)
Dm
Dm7
But his arms held me fast And it broke the fall,
D♭7
C7
Gm11
Fmaj7
Fm6
And I said to my heart As it fool - ish - ly kept
C/E
E♭dim7
Dm7
G7
A7♯5(♭9)
A7♭9
Dm7
jump - ing all a - round, "I got lost but
G7
F/G
G7sus(♭9)
C6
Em7
Dm7
G7
G7♯5
C
Fmaj7
C6/9
look what I found." I got
rall.
a tempo
R.H.

I'LL NEVER FALL IN LOVE AGAIN

from PROMISES, PROMISES

Lyric by HAL DAVID
Music by BURT BACHARACH

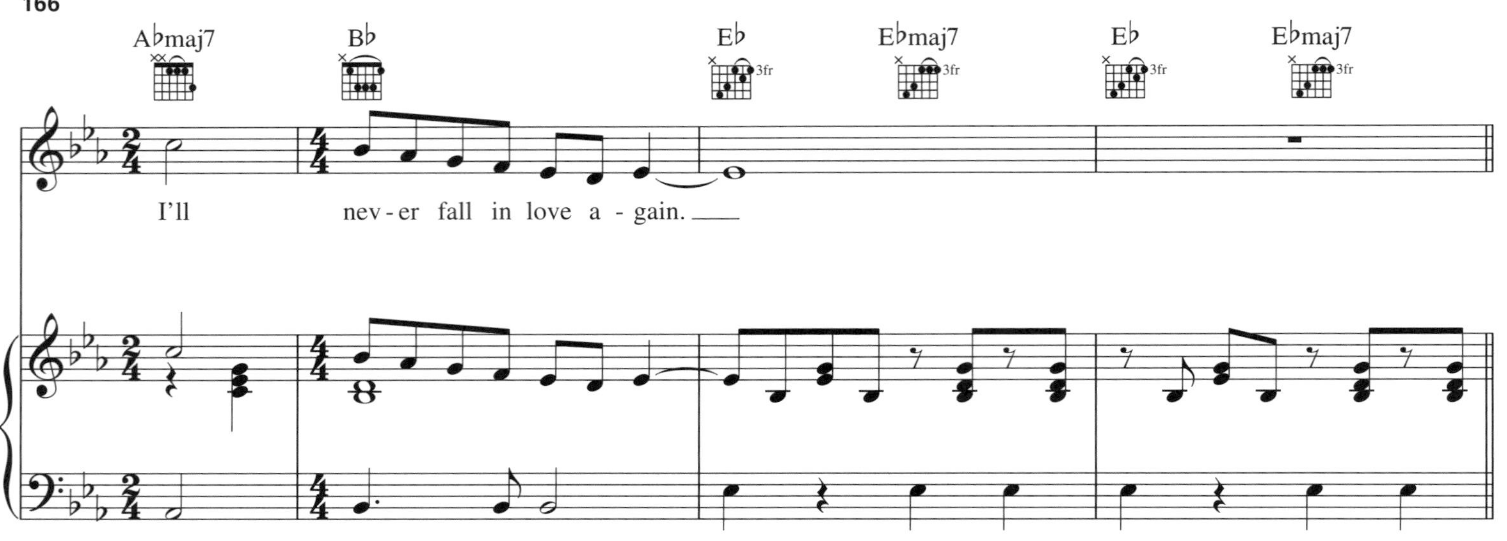
A♭maj7
B♭
E♭
E♭maj7
E♭
E♭maj7
3fr
I'll never-er fall in love a-gain.

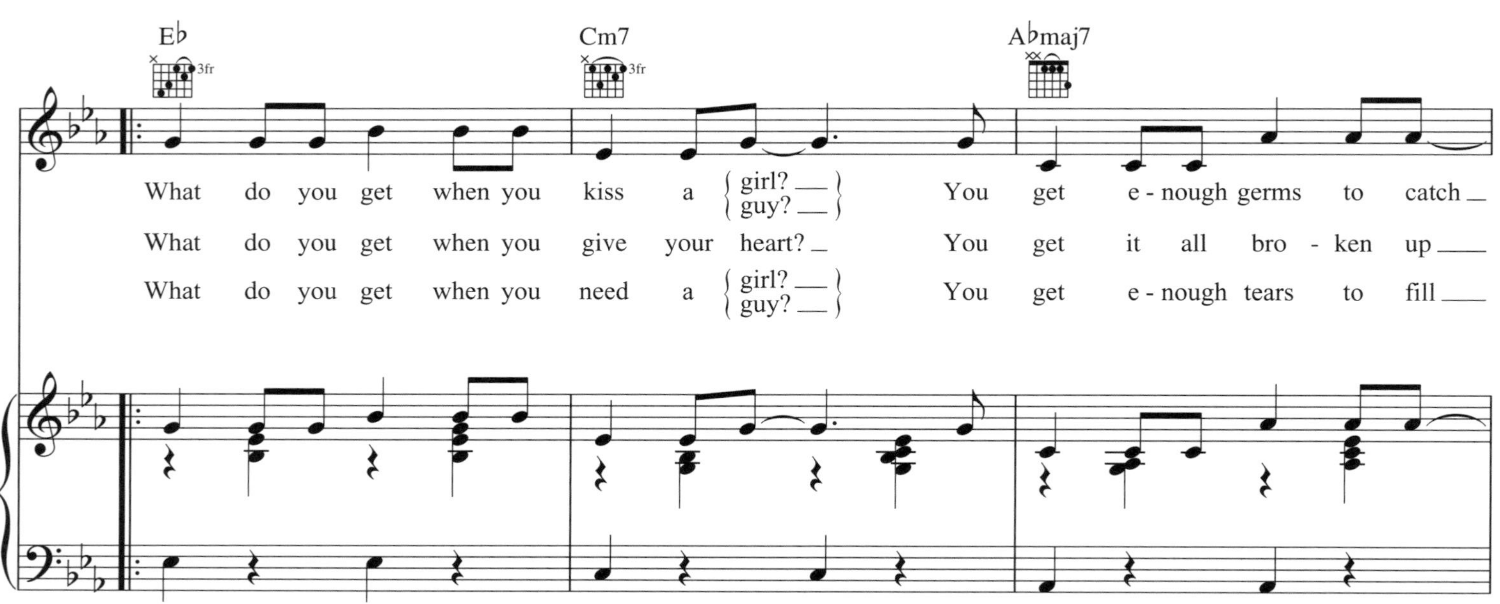
E♭
Cm7
A♭maj7
3fr
What do you get when you kiss a {girl? / guy?} You get e-nough germs to catch
What do you get when you give your heart? You get it all bro-ken up
What do you get when you need a {girl? / guy?} You get e-nough tears to fill

Gm7
Gm7/C
C7
pneu-mo-nia. Af-ter you do, {she'll / he'll} nev-er phone you.
and bat-tered. That's what you get, a heart that's shat-tered.
an o-cean. That's what you get for your de-vo-tion.

Fm7
B♭7
A♭7
E♭
I'll never fall in love a - gain.
A♭maj7
B♭
E♭
E♭maj7
I'll nev - er fall in love a - gain.
E♭
Fm7/B♭
E♭
Don't tell me what it's all a - bout, 'cause
Fm7/B♭
E♭
Gm
I've been there and I'm glad I'm out. Out of those chains, those

F7
B♭
chains that bind you, that is why I'm here to re-mind you.
E♭
Cm7
A♭maj7
What do you get when you fall in love? You on-ly get lies and pain
Gm7
Gm7/C
C7
Fm7
and sor-row. So, for at least un-til to-mor-row, I'll
B♭7
A♭7
E♭
1, 2
A♭maj7
nev-er fall in love a-gain. I'll

B♭
E♭
E♭maj7
E♭
E♭maj7
nev - er fall in love a - gain.
3
Fm7
B♭7
A♭7
I'll
nev - er fall in love a - gain.
E♭
A♭maj7
B♭
A♭/B♭
B♭7
I'll
nev - er fall in love a -
rit.
E♭
E♭maj7
E♭
E♭maj7
E♭
E♭maj7
E♭
gain.
a tempo

I KNOW HIM SO WELL

from CHESS

Words and Music by BENNY ANDERSSON,
TIM RICE and BJÖRN ULVAEUS

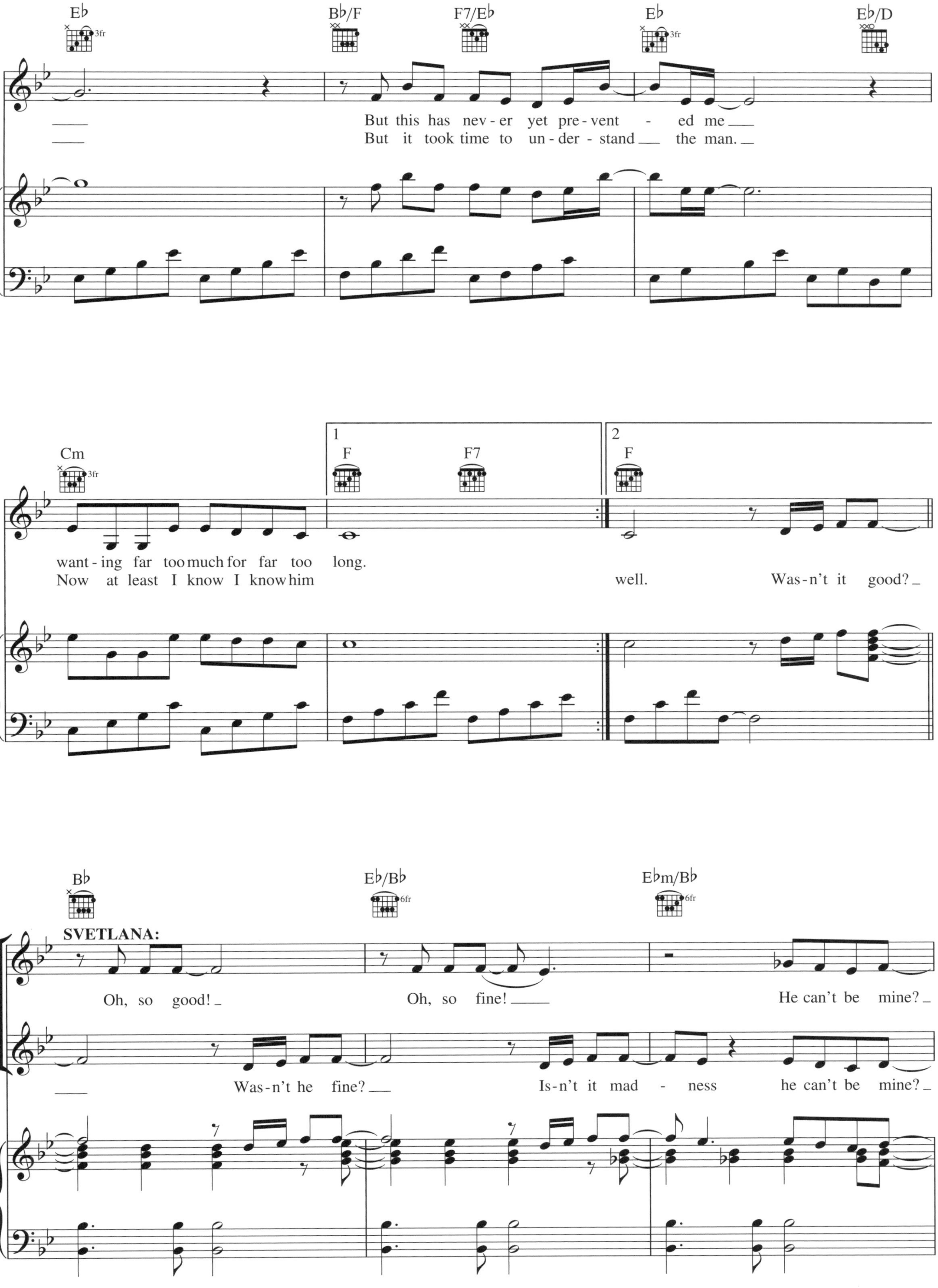

E♭ B♭/F F7/E♭ E♭ E♭/D

3fr 3fr

But this has nev - er yet pre - vent - ed me

But it took time to un - der - stand the man.

Cm F F7 F

3fr

1 2

want - ing far too much for far too long.

Now at least I know I know him well. Was - n't it good?

B♭
E♭m/G♭
B♭
F7/A
Gm
C7/E
But in the end he needs a lit-tle bit more than me, more se-
B♭/F
F/E♭
E♭
E♭/F
F
B♭
E♭m/B♭
E♭/F
F
He needs his fan-ta-sy and free-dom.
cu-ri-ty. I know him so well.
B♭
F7/C
B♭/D
B♭
B♭/A
Gm
Gm/F
No one in your life is with you con-stant-ly, no one is com-plete-ly on your
Look-ing back, I could have played it dif-f'rent-ly, learned a-bout the man be-fore I
(2nd time only)
Look-ing back, I could have played things some oth-er way.

E♭
B♭/F
F7/E♭
E♭
E♭/D
side. And though I move my world to be with him,
fell. But I was ev - er so much young - er then,
I was just a lit - tle care - less, may - be, I was so much young - er then,
Cm
1
F
F7
2
F
still the gap be - tween us is too wide.
now at least I know I know him well. Was - n't it good?
I know I know him well.
B♭
E♭/B♭
E♭m/B♭
Was - n't he fine? Is - n't it mad - ness he won't be mine?
Oh, so good! Oh, so fine! He won't be mine?
3fr
6fr

B♭
Em7♭5
Gm
3fr
Gm/F
Did-n't I know how it would go? If I knew from the start,
C
C/B♭
F/A
Gm7
F
B♭
Was-n't it good?
why am I fall - ing a - part?
E♭/B♭
6fr
E♭m/B♭
6fr
B♭
E♭m/G♭
3fr
Was-n't he fine?
He won't be mine?
Is-n't it mad - ness he won't be mine?
But

B♭
F7/A
Gm
C7/E
B♭/F
F/E♭
He needs his fan - ta - sy and
in the end he needs a lit-tle bit more than me, more se - cu - ri - ty.
E♭
E♭/F
F7
C7/E
E♭m6
B♭/D
C7
free - dom.
It took time to un - der - stand him.
I know him so well.
Cm7
E♭/F
F7
B♭
I know him so well.
I know him so well.
rall.

I LOVE PARIS

from CAN-CAN

Words and Music by
COLE PORTER

A7
D7
Fm6
cheers, or wheth - er soft be her tears, more and more
G7
C
C6
Cdim7
G7♭9
do I re - al - ize:
poco rit.
Slow Fox Trot
Cm
3fr
I love Par - is in the spring - time,
G7
I love Par - is in the fall,

I love Par - is in the win - ter when it driz - zles,
Fm
G7
Cm
3fr
I love Par - is in the sum - mer when it siz - zles.
7
C
I love Par - is ev - 'ry mo - ment,
C/E
E♭dim
G7/D
Dm7
G7
ev - 'ry mo - ment of the year.

F
C
I love Par - is; why, oh, why do I love Par - is?
1
G7
C
Cdim
G7
Be - cause my love is near.
3
2
G7
A7sus
A7
Dm7
Dm7/G
Be - cause my love, be - cause my love
G7sus
C
is near.

I SEE YOUR FACE BEFORE ME

from BETWEEN THE DEVIL

Words by HOWARD DIETZ
Music by ARTHUR SCHWARTZ

E♭
Cm6
D7
Gm
Gm7
could be tru - ly worth - y and true, yes, I met my i -
Gm6
D7
Gm
B♭m
C7
Fm7
B♭7
deal thing when I met you.
Slowly
E♭
E♭6
E♭
E♭6
E♭
E♭6
I see your face be - fore me crowd - ing my ev' - ry
Fm7
B♭7
Fm7
B♭7
Fm7
B♭7
dream, there is your face be - fore me,

Fm7
Eb
3fr
Bbdim
you are my on - ly theme.
It does - n't mat - ter
mp
Fm7
Bb7
Ebdim
6fr
Bb7
Ab
4fr
Eb
3fr
Cm
3fr
D7
where you are,
I can see how fair you are.
I close my eyes and
mf
p
Gm7
Bbm
C7
Fm7
Bb+
Eb
3fr
Eb6
there you are,
al - ways.
If you could share the
rit.
p a tempo
Eb
3fr
Eb6
Eb
3fr
Eb6
Fm7
Bb7
mag - ic,
if you could see me too,

Fm7
Bb7
Fm
Bb7
Fm7
Eb7
there would be noth - ing trag - ic in all my dreams of you.
cresc.
Ab
Ebdim
Eb
Ebdim
Bb7
Eb7
Would that my love could haunt you so; know - ing I
mf expressively
rit.
Ab
Abm
Eb
Eb7
Fm
Abm
Bb9
want you so, I can't e - rase your beau - ti - ful face be -
mf ten.
p calmato
molto rall.
Eb
1
Bb7
Eb
Bb7
2
D/A
Eb/Bb
B7b5
Bb7
Eb6
fore me.
mf a tempo
smoothly
mf
8vb

I WISH I WERE IN LOVE AGAIN

from BABES IN ARMS

Words by LORENZ HART
Music by RICHARD RODGERS

Am7
D7
G
Em7
A7
D7
sleep all night, Appetite and health restored.
G
C/E
A7
D7
G♯dim7
D7
You don't know how much I'm bored! The
G
Gdim7
G
sleepless nights, The daily fights, The quick toboggan when you
furtive sigh, The blackened eye, The words "I'll love you till the
p - mf
Gdim7
G
Gdim7
reach the heights; I miss the kisses and I miss the bites, I
day I die," The self-deception that believes the lie, I

D7 C♯dim7 D7 G Gdim7

wish I were in love a - gain! ___ The bro - ken dates, The end - less waits, The
wish I were in love a - gain! ___ When love con - geals It soon re - veals The

G Gdim7 G

love - ly lov - ing and the hate - ful hates, The con - ver - sa - tion with the
faint a - ro - ma of per - form - ing seals, The dou - ble - cross - ing of a

Gdim7 D7 G7

fly - ing plates, I wish I were in love a - gain!
pair of heels, I wish I were in love a - gain!

C Cm6 3fr G/B E7♭9 A7 D7 G G7

No ___ more pain, No ___ more strain,
No ___ more care, No ___ de - spair.

mf

C
Cm6
3fr
G/B
E7♭9
A7
Now I'm sane, but I would rath - er be
I'm all there now, But I'd rath - er be
D7
G
Gdim7
ga - ga! The pulled out fur of cat and cur, The
punch - drunk! Be - lieve me, sir, I much pre - fer The
p
G
Gdim7
G
fine mis - mat - ing of a him and her, I've learned my les - son, but I
clas - sic bat - tle of a him and her. I don't like qui - et and I
B7
Em
Am7
D7
1
G
Am7
D7
2
G
Am7
G
wish I were in love a - gain! The
wish I were in love a - gain!
mf

IN MY LIFE

from LES MISÉRABLES

Music by CLAUDE-MICHEL SCHÖNBERG
Lyrics by ALAIN BOUBLIL,
JEAN-MARC NATEL and HERBERT KRETZMER

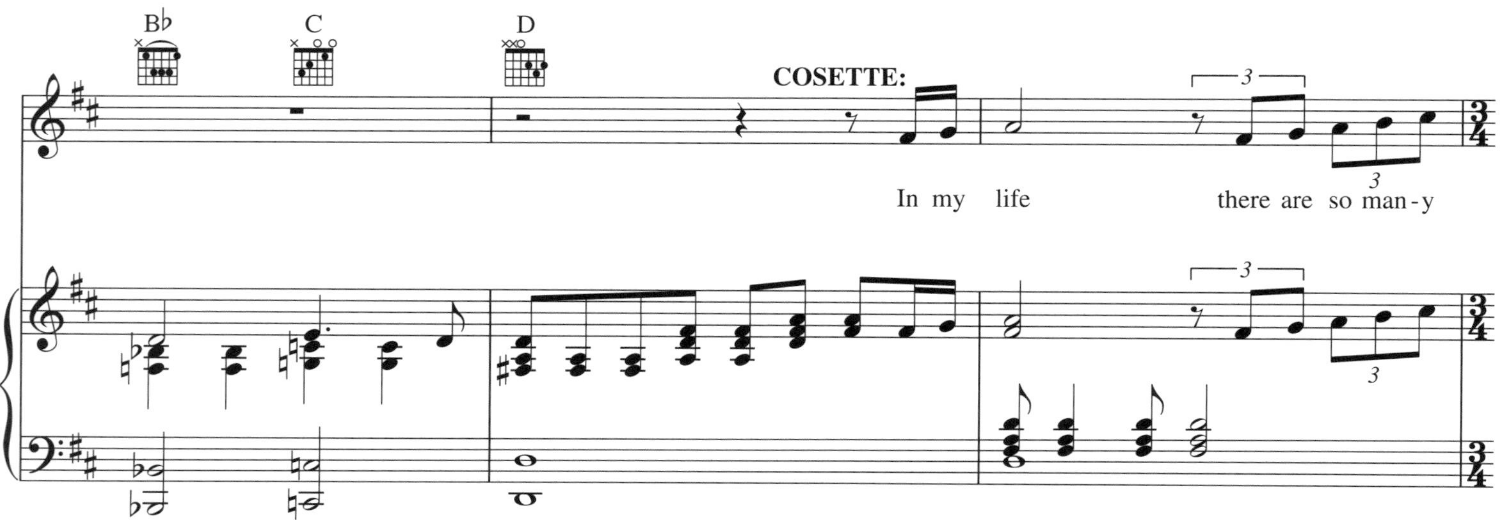

Em
Em/D
A/C♯
A7
life there are times when I catch in the si - lence the sigh of a far - a - way
D
D7
G
song. And it sings of a world that I long to see, out of
E
E7
A
A7
reach, just a whis - per a - way, wait - ing for me.
B♭/C
F
Does he know I'm a - live? Do I know if he's real?

B♭/C
D
Did he see what I saw? Does he feel what I feel? In my
D/C♯
Bm
D/A
life I'm no long - er a - lone. Now the love of my life is so
mf
E7
G
A7
D
D/C♯
Bm
near. Find me now. Find me here. In my
rall.
B♭
B♭/A
life I have all that I want. You are lov - ing and gen - tle and
a tempo

Gm
Cm
Cm7
good. But pa - pa, dear pa - pa, in your eyes I am
F
Bb
VALJEAN:
just like a child who is lost in a wood. No more
Bb/Ab
Eb
words. No more words, it's a time that is dead. There are
C
C7
F
COSETTE:
words that are bet - ter un - heard, bet - ter un - said. In my
rall.

D♭ D♭/C B♭m B♭m7 D♭/A♭
life I'm no long - er a child and I long for the truth that you
a tempo
Gm7♭5 G♭ A♭ D♭
VALJEAN:
know of the years, years a - go. You will
A♭m/C♭ E♭m7 A♭
learn. Truth is giv - en by God to us all in our time, in our
D♭ A♭m/C♭
turn.

E♭m7
6fr
A7
MARIUS:
In my
D
life she has burst like the
D/C♯
mu - sic of an - gels, the light of the
Bm
sun.
And my
Em
life
Em/D
seems to stop as if some-thing is
A
o - ver and
A7
some - thing has scarce - ly be -
D
gun.
E - po -
mf

D7
G
nine, you're the friend that has brought me here. Thanks to
E
E7
A
A7
you I am one with the gods and heav - en is near.
B♭/C
F
And I soar through a world that is new that is free.
f
più mosso
B♭/C
EPONINE:
D
Ev - 'ry word that he says is a dag - ger in me. In my

D/C♯
Bm
Bm/A
life there's been no one like him an - y - where. An - y - where where he
mf
E7
G
A
is, if he asked I'd be
D
C6
EPONINE & MARIUS:
his. In my life there is some - one who
G
A
D
MARIUS:
EPONINE:
touch - es my life, wait - ing near, wait - ing here.
rall.

IN MY OWN LITTLE CORNER

from CINDERELLA

Lyrics by OSCAR HAMMERSTEIN II
Music by RICHARD RODGERS

Refrain (with tender expression)
F
F6
F
C7
F
way.
In
my
own
lit - tle
cor - ner,
in
my
own
lit - tle
chair,
I
can
Eb
Eb6
Eb
3fr
C7
F
be
what - ev - er
I
want
to
be.
3
C7
F
On
the
wing
of
my
fan - cy
I
can

E♭
E♭6
E♭
C7
3fr
3fr
fly an - y - where And the world will
o - pen its arms to me.
F
I'm a
3
3
D
Em7
A7
F♯m
young Nor - we - gian prin - cess or a milk - maid,
legato
D
Bm
F♯7
I'm the great - est pri - ma don - na in Mi -

Bm
D+/G
Gm
3fr
D
Em7
A7
lan. I'm an heir - ess who has al - ways had her
D
A
silk made By her own flock of
E7
A
Gm7
C7
F
silk - worms in Ja - pan. I'm a girl men go
mp
E♭
3fr
E♭6
E♭
3fr
mad for, love's a game I can play with a

C7 F7

cool and con - fi - dent kind of air,

cresc.

B♭ B♭m/D♭

Just as long as I stay in my own lit - tle

mf

F/C B♭ F/C Gm/C C7

3fr

cor - ner, All a - lone in my own lit - tle

1 F Gm7 C7 | 2 F

chair. In my chair.

mf mf

JUST IN TIME
from BELLS ARE RINGING

Words by BETTY COMDEN and ADOLPH GREEN
Music by JULE STYNE

F13 Bb9 Fm Bb7

— the los - ing dice were tossed, — my bridg - es

Eb9 Ab

all were crossed, — no - where to go. —

D7 Gm D Gm D

— Now you're here, — and now I

Gm Bb/C Am/C Gm/C Bb/F

know just where I'm go - ing, no more doubt or fear, —

G7♯5(♭9) G7 G7♯5

I've found my way. For love came

C9 F7 B♭ F+

just in time. You found me just in time,

B♭ C7 Cm7 F7♭9

and changed my lonely life, that lovely

1 B♭ C9 F7

day.

2 B♭ B♭dim B♭ B♭dim B♭6

day.

IN THE STILL OF THE NIGHT

from ROSALIE

Words and Music by
COLE PORTER

Gm7
C7
At the moon in its flight, My thoughts all
F/A
Gm7(add4)
C7sus
C7
stray to you.
F
Fm6
In the still of the night,
F
Fm6
E
While the world is in slum - ber,

Am
Am/C
E7
Oh, the times with - out num - ber, Dar - ling, when I
Am(add9)
5fr
C7
say to you:
F
F/A
B♭
"Do you love me
C7sus
C7
C/B♭
F/A
As I love you?

F+/A
B♭
Are you my life - to - be,
C7sus
C7
C/B♭
Am7♭5
My dream come true?"
D7sus
D7
Am7/D
D7/F♯
Gm
3fr
Or will this dream of mine
Gm7♭5
B♭m/D♭
F/C
fade out of sight
Like the

Bdim7
C/B♭
moon
grow - ing
dim
on the
F/A
A♭dim7
rim
of the
hill
in the
Gm7
C
chill,
Still
of the
1
F
Fm6
night?

2
F
Fm6
night?
F
Fm6
F6
F

IT NEVER ENTERED MY MIND

from HIGHER AND HIGHER

Words by LORENZ HART
Music by RICHARD RODGERS

A7
D7
G7
walk in a daze now, I nev - er go to shows at night, But just to mat - in - ees now.
Csus
3fr
C
Cm6
3fr
C9
I see the show and home I go.
poco rit.
Refrain (slowly, with warm expression)
F
Am
Once I laughed when I heard you say - ing That I'd be play - ing
p - mf a tempo
sol - i - taire,
Un - eas - y in my eas - y chair.

Gm7 Gm E♭7 C7 F Am
It nev - er en - tered my mind. Once you told me
F Am F Am F Am
I was mis - tak - en That I'd a - wak - en with the sun
F Am F Am Gm7 F
And or - der or - ange juice for one. It nev - er en - tered my mind.
Am/C E+/B C7 F6 Gm7 B♭/C C7 Fmaj7 F6
You have what I lack my - self,
mf
p
mf
mp

Gm7
Bb/C
C7
F6
C7
F
Abdim7
C7
Bb/D
Am/C
And now I e - ven have to scratch my back my - self.
mf
marcato
Bb/D
Am/C
C7
F
Am
F
Am
F
Am
Once you warned me That if you scorned me, I'd sing the maid - en's
p
F
Am
F
Am
Am7b5
D7
Gm
3fr
C7
pray'r a - gain. And wish that you were there a - gain To get in - to my
Fmaj7
Bb6
C7
F6
1
G7
C7
2
hair a - gain. It nev - er en - tered my mind.
mf
p

IT ONLY TAKES A MOMENT
from HELLO, DOLLY!

Music and Lyric by
JERRY HERMAN

Cm Cm(maj7) Cm7 G9 Cm Cm(maj7)
3fr 8fr 3fr 9fr 3fr 8fr
heart knows in a mo - ment
Cm7 G9 Cm Cm(maj7)
3fr 9fr 3fr 8fr
you will nev - er be a -
Cm7 F9 B♭maj7 Gm7
3fr
lone a - gain.
I held her
Girl: He held me
Cm7 F7 B♭maj7 Gm7 Cm7 F7
3fr 3fr
for an in - stant, but
my
his

B♭maj7
B♭6
Gm
3fr
G7♭9
arms felt {sure / safe} and strong.
Cm7
3fr
Cm7♭5
It on - ly takes a
B♭
Gm
3fr
Cm7♭5
B♭
Gm
3fr
mo - ment to be loved a
To Coda
Cm7
3fr
F7
B♭
whole life long. I've heard it

Interlude
B♭maj7
B♭6
Cm7
3fr
said that love must grow,
F7
B♭maj7
B♭6
that to be sure, you must be
Cm7
3fr
F7
B♭maj7
slow. I saw you smile,
Gm7
and now I know I'll lis - ten to
3
3

Cm7♭5
F7♯5(♭9)
7fr
3
just my heart, that smile made me trust my heart.
D.S. al Coda
CODA
B♭
For it
long.
B♭maj7
B♭6
And that is all that love's a -
Cm7
3fr
F7
B♭maj7
bout, and we'll re - call

Gm7
C9
Cm7♭5
when time runs out that it
B♭
Gm
Cm7♭5
B♭
Gm
3fr
on - ly took a mo - ment
Cm7♭5
B♭maj7
Gm
Cm7
F7
to be loved a whole life
B♭
long.

IT'S DE-LOVELY

from RED, HOT AND BLUE!

Words and Music by
COLE PORTER

D7
Gm
E♭/G
I un - der - stand the rea - son why You're
Gm6
G
E♭/G
Edim
Gm
sen - ti - men - tal, 'cause so am I, It's de -
Gm
G♯dim
light - ful, it's de - li - cious, It's De -
F
G7
C7
F7
love - ly. You can tell at a glance
3fr

B♭
F7
F+
What a swell night this
B♭
B♭m6
6fr
is for ro - mance, You can hear dear Moth - er Na - ture mur - mur - ing
C7
F
low, "Let your - self go." So please be sweet, my
F+
F6
F
F+
Dm
F
chick - a - dee, And when I kiss you, just say to me, "It's de -

*Pronounced "delukes"

JUNE IS BUSTIN' OUT ALL OVER

from CAROUSEL

Lyrics by OSCAR HAMMERSTEIN II
Music by RICHARD RODGERS

Em
E
Em
E
B+/E♭
Bm/D
D♭7
4fr
Am/C
E/B
B7♯5
crowd of doubt - in' Thom - as - es Was pre - dict - in' that the Sum - mer'd nev - er
E
A/E
MEN:
come. But it's com - in' by gum, y' ken feel it come! Y' ken
mp
D
Am7/D
GIRLS:
feel it in your heart, y' ken see it in the ground. Y' ken hear it in the trees, Y' ken
D7
N.C.
ALL:
smell it in the breeze. Look a - round, look a - round, look a - round!
8va
f
sf

Refrain (brightly)
G G6 Gmaj7 G6 Gmaj9
June is bust - in' out all o - ver! All o - ver the
June is bust - in' out all o - ver! The sap - lin's are
June is bust - in' out all o - ver! The o - cean is
mf
G6 F♯dim7 Em Em/D♯
mead - ow and the hill! Buds 're bust - in' out - a
bust - in' out with sap! Love has found my broth - er,
full of Jacks and Jills. With her lit - tle tail a -
Em/D Em/C♯ C Em/B C/B♭ A7 D/F♯ Dm/F
bush - es And the romp - in' riv - er push - es Ev - 'ry lit - tle wheel that
jun - ior, And my sis - ter's e - ven lu - nier! And my ma is get - tin'
swish - in' Ev - 'ry la - dy fish is wish - in' That a male would come and

A7sus
A7
D
D7
G
G6
ALL:
wheels be - side a mill!
kit - ten - ish with pap!
grab her by the gills!
June is bust - in' out all
June is bust - in' out all
June is bust - in' out all
f
mf

Gmaj7
G6
Gmaj9
G6
NETTIE:
o - ver!
o - ver!
o - ver!
The feel - in' is get - tin' so in -
To la - dies the men are pay - in'
The sheep are - n't sleep - in' an - y -

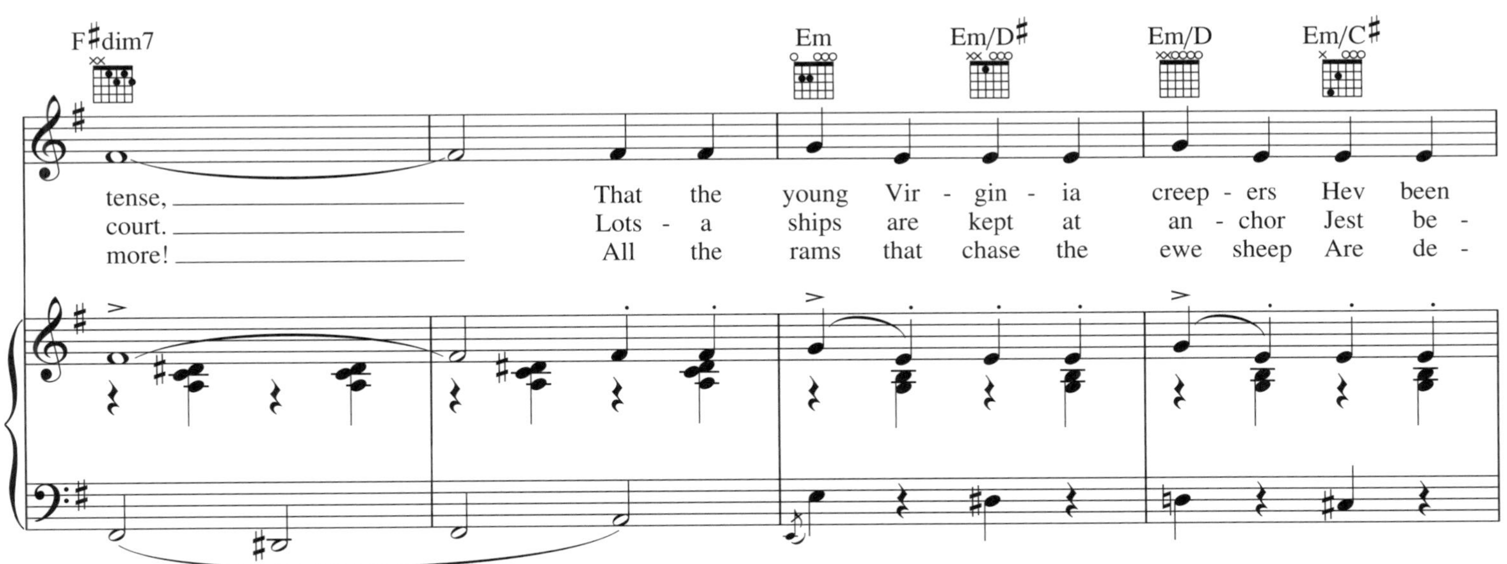
F♯dim7
Em
Em/D♯
Em/D
Em/C♯
tense,
court.
more!
That the young Vir - gin - ia creep - ers Hev been
Lots - a ships are kept at an - chor Jest be -
All the rams that chase the ewe sheep Are de -

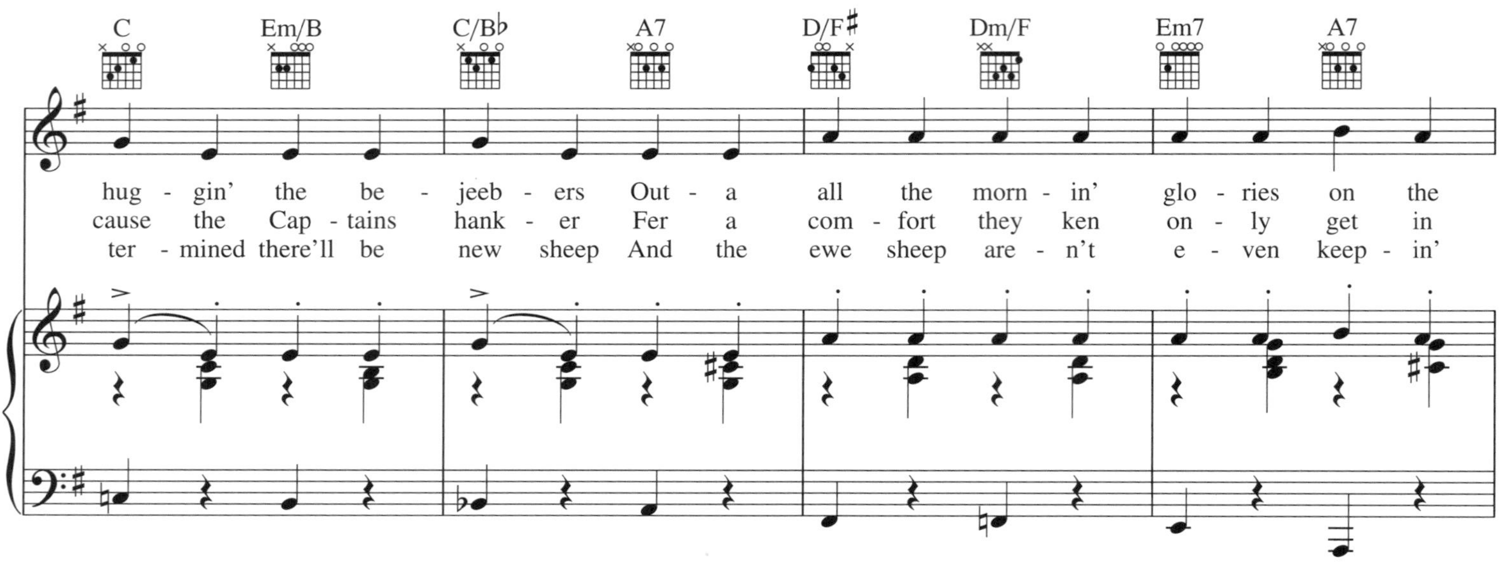
C
Em/B
C/B♭
A7
D/F♯
Dm/F
Em7
A7
hug - gin' the be - jeeb - ers Out - a all the morn - in' glo - ries on the
cause the Cap - tains hank - er Fer a com - fort they ken on - ly get in
ter - mined there'll be new sheep And the ewe sheep are - n't e - ven keep - in'

D
Cmaj9/D
5fr
D7
Gmaj9
G6
Gmaj9
MEN:
fence! Be - cause it's June! June, June,
port! Be - cause it's June! June, June,
score! On a - count - a it's June! June, June,
f

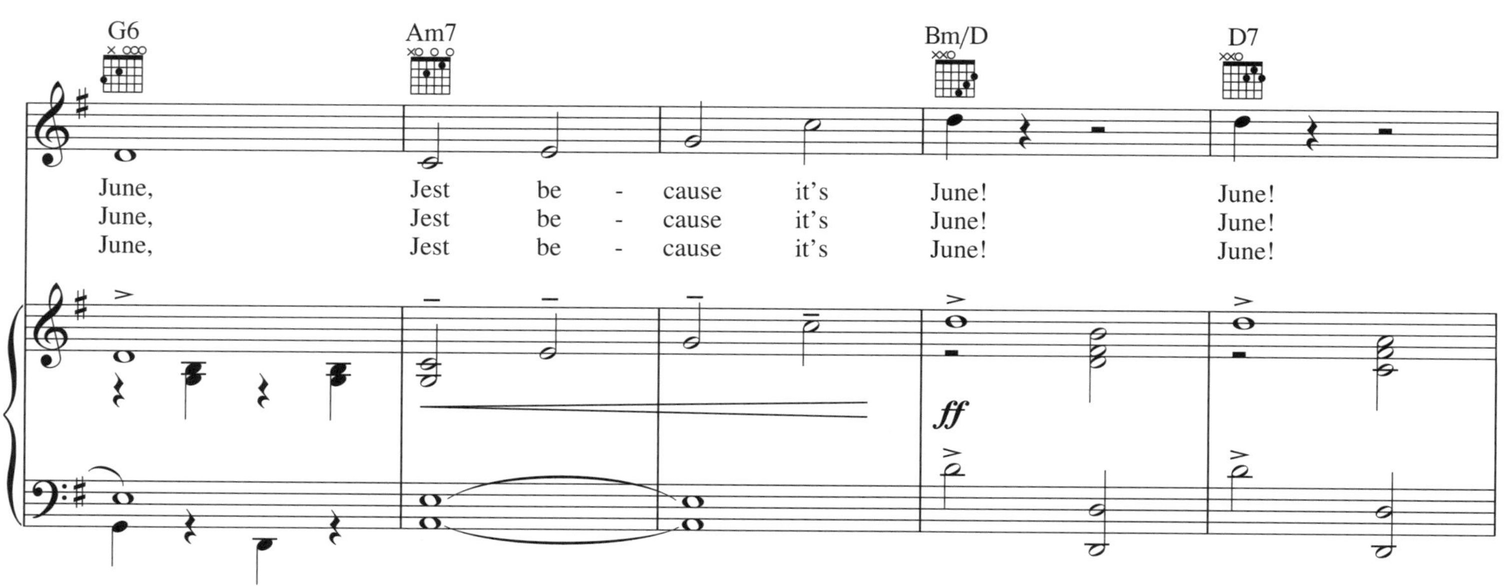
G6
Am7
Bm/D
D7
June, Jest be - cause it's June! June!
June, Jest be - cause it's June! June!
June, Jest be - cause it's June! June!
ff

1, 2
Gmaj9
G6
Gmaj9
G6
rit.
June!
June!
f
rit.
NETTIE:
Am7
E♭7
B6/E♭
D7
4fr
rit.
Fresh and a - live and gay and young, June is a love song sweet - ly sung.
June makes the bay look bright and new, Sails gleam - in' white on sun - lit blue.
rit.
3
Gmaj9
G6
Gmaj9
G6
June!
F6
A13
5fr
D
sf

LAMBETH WALK

from ME AND MY GIRL

By NOEL GAY, L. ARTHUR ROSE
and DOUGLAS FURBER

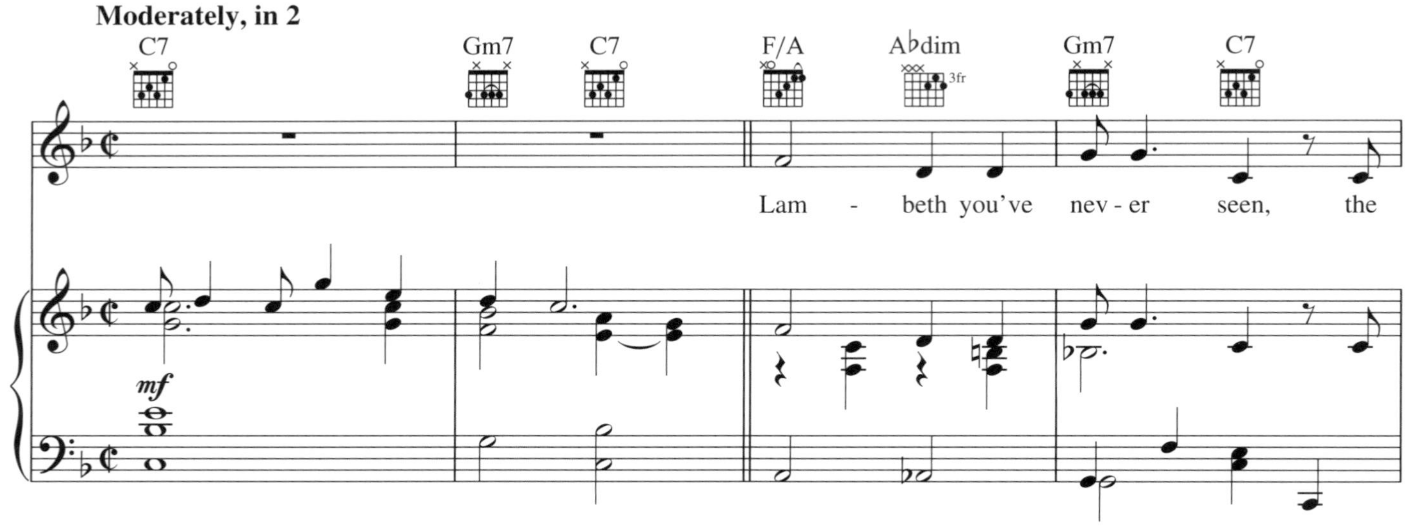

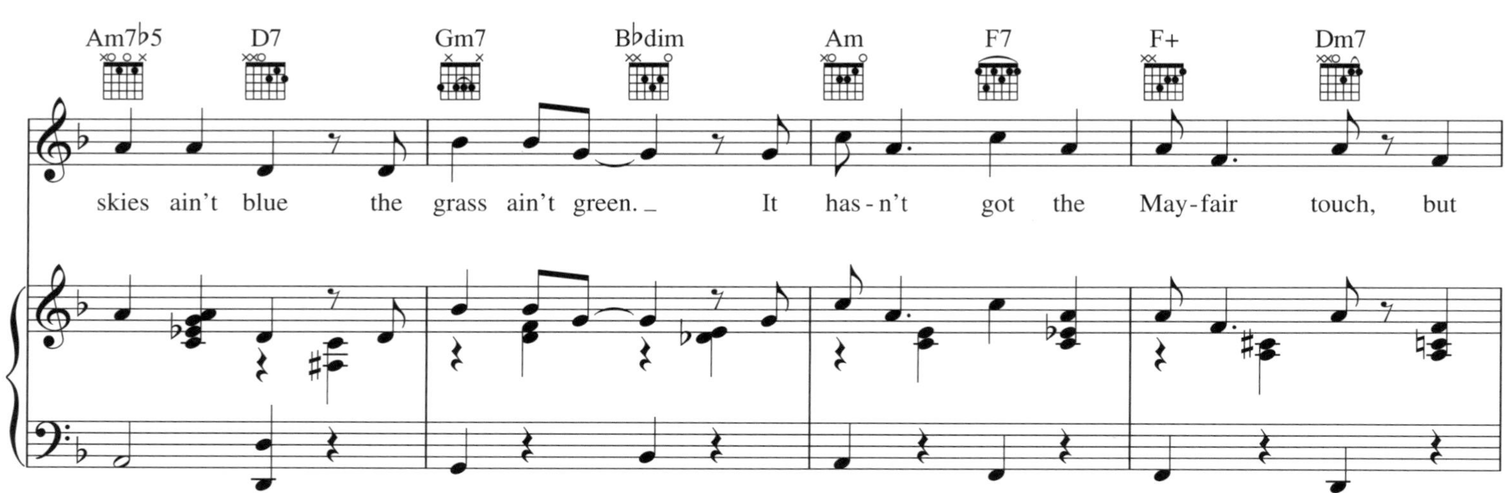

A6
Bm7♭5
E7
Am
F/A
not like you but a bit more gay, and when we have a
D7
G7♭9
C7
C7♯5
8fr
bit of fun oh, boy.
rit.
F
B♭/C
F
F
D7♯5
Any time you're Lambeth way, any evening
a tempo
Gm7
D7
Gm7
any day, you'll find us all

C7
F
B♭/C
C7
F
B♭/C
F
do - in' the Lam - beth walk.
Ev - 'ry lit - tle Lam - beth gal
D7♯5
Gm7
Dm7
Gm7
with her lit - tle Lam - beth pal,
you'll find 'em
C7
F
Dm7
G7
all
do - in' the Lam - beth walk.
Ev - 'ry-thing free and
C
G7
C
eas - y,
do as you darn well
pleas - ey,

Am F D7 C G7sus G7
why don't you make your way there, go there,
C7 C7♯5 F B♭/C F
8fr
stay there. Once you get down Lam - beth way,
D7 Gm7 D7 Gm7
ev - 'ry eve - ning, ev - 'ry day, you'll find your -
C7
1
F G9 C7♯5
9fr 8fr
2
F
self do - in' the Lam - beth walk. walk.

LET'S TAKE AN OLD-FASHIONED WALK

from the Stage Production MISS LIBERTY

Words and Music by
IRVING BERLIN

Gm7
C7
F6
out to some ro - man - tic spot.
say - ing, "The car - riage a - waits."
G7/F
C6/E
C♯dim7
Dm7
G7
But when you have - n't a sou,
But since you have - n't a sou,
C
Am7
D7
G7sus
G7
there's on - ly one thing to do.
and I have noth - ing to do,
C
Cmaj7
C6
Cmaj7
Let's take an old - fash - ioned walk.

C Cmaj7 Dm G7

I'm just burst - ing with talk. What a

C/E F6 C/G G7

tale could be told if we went for an old - fash - ioned

C6 F6 C6/E Dm7

walk.

C Cmaj7 C6 Cmaj7

Let's take a stroll through the park,

C
Cmaj7
Dm
G7
down a lane where it's dark, and a
C/E
F6
C/G
G7
heart that's con - trolled may re - lax on an old - fash - ioned
C6
F6
C6/E
B7♭9
walk.
Em
Em(maj7)
Em7
I know for a cou - ple who seem to be

A9
5fr
miles a - part,
G/D
Em7
Am7
D7
there's noth - ing like walk - ing and hav - ing a
G7
"heart to heart."
C
Cmaj7
C6
Cmaj7
I know a girl who de - clined.

C
Cmaj7
Dm
G7
Could - n't make up her mind.
She was
C/E
F6
C/G
G7
wrapped up and sold com - ing home from an old - fash - ioned
1
C6
F6
C6/E
Dm7
G7
walk.
2
C6
F6
Dm7
G7
C
walk.

LIFE IS JUST A BOWL OF CHERRIES

from GEORGE WHITE'S SCANDALS (1931 Edition)

Words and Music by LEW BROWN
and RAY HENDERSON

Bbm C7-9 Fm G7+5 G7 Cm
Where are we go - ing? It's time that we found out
F7 Cm7 F7 Abm6 C7 B7 Fm7 Bb9
We're not here to stay, We're on a short hol - i - day.
rall.
Eb Gm Eb6 Edim
Life Is Just A Bowl Of Cher - ries, Don't make it se - ri - ous, Life's too mys -
p-f
Bb7 Fm Bb9 Eb Bbm6 C7 Fm Bb9
te - ri - ous. You work, you save, you wor - ry so, But you can't take your dough when you

F9 Abm Bb7 Eb Gm Eb6
go, go, go, So keep re - peat - ing it's the Ber - ries The
Bbm6 C7 Fm Adim Gm C7
strong - est oak must fall. The sweet things in life, To you were just loaned, So
Fm Bb9 F9 Bb9 Eb Gm Bbm
how can you lose what you've nev - er owned. Life Is Just A Bowl Of
C7 F7 Fm7 Bb7 Eb Adim Fm Bb7 Eb
Cher - ries, So live and laugh at it all. all.
sfz

MAD ABOUT THE BOY

from WORDS AND MUSIC

Words and Music by
NOEL COWARD

C B7 G+ C F♯dim G7
3fr 9fr
spell. I bask'd in his at - trac - tion for a
down. I should have been ex - empt, for my par -
3
C F♯dim G7 C A7 D7 G7 E7
9fr
cou - ple of hours or so, his man - ners were a frac - tion too met - i - cu - lous. If he was
ti - cu - lar kind of fate has taught me such con - tempt for ev - 'ry phase of love, and now I've
Am C F♯dim G7 E C♯dim D7
9fr 4fr
real or not I could - n't tell, but like a sil - ly fool I
been and spent my last half - crown to weep a - bout a paint - ed
G7 C♯dim G C♯dim Dm7♭5 G7
4fr 4fr
fell. Mad a - bout the boy, I know it's stu - pid to be
clown. Mad a - bout the boy, it's pret - ty fun - ny, but I'm

Dm7♭5
G7
Cm
3fr
Mad a-bout the boy, I'm so a-shamed of it, but must ad-mit the
mad a-bout the boy. He has a gay ap-peal that makes me feel there's
F♯dim
9fr
G7
C
Fm
C
Dm7♭5
sleep-less nights I've had a-bout the boy.
may-be some-thing sad a-bout the boy.
G7
Dm7♭5
On the sil-ver screen he melts my fool-ish heart in ev-'ry sin-gle scene,
Walk-ing down the street, his eyes look out at me from peo-ple that I meet;
G7
Cm
3fr
D
al-though I'm quite a-ware that here and there are trac-es of the
I can't be-lieve it's true, but when I'm blue, in some strange way I'm

G G7 Cm D7 G7♭9 Cm D7
cad a - bout the boy. Lord knows I'm not a
glad a - bout the boy. I'm hard - ly sen - ti -
Gm Gm7♭5 C7 Fm
fool girl, I real - ly should - n't care;
ment - al, love is - n't so sub - lime,
G7 Cm D7♭9
Lord knows I'm not a school girl, in the flur - ry of her first af -
I have to pay my rent - al and I can't af - ford to waste much
G7 G+ Dm7♭5 G7
fair. Will it ev - er cloy? This odd di - ver - si - ty of
time. If I could em - ploy a lit - tle mag - ic that would

Dm7♭5
G7
Cm
mis - er - y and joy; I'm feel - ing quite in - sane and young a - gain, and
fi - nal - ly de - stroy this dream that pains me and en - chains me, but I
D7♭9
G7
1
Cm
D7
Dm7♭5
C
all be - cause I'm mad a - bout the boy.
can't be - cause I'm
Am
C
F
Am
G7
F/G
G7
It
2
Cm
Fm
C
mad a - bout the boy.

LOST IN THE STARS

from the Musical Production LOST IN THE STARS

Words by MAXWELL ANDERSON
Music by KURT WEILL

G
Edim7
D7
G
E7
Lord God hunt - ed through the wide night air for the lit - tle dark star on the
Am
Cm
3fr
G/B
C6
G/D
wind down _ there, and He stat - ed and prom - ised He'd take spe - cial care so it
Gm6
3fr
Cm6
3fr
D7
G
Cm7
3fr
E♭7
would - n't get lost a - gain. Now a man don't mind if the
B♭
Gm7
E♭m/G♭
3fr
Gm
3fr
stars grow dim and the clouds blow o - ver and dark - en him, so

Cm7
E♭7
B♭
Gm
E♭m/G♭
F7♯5
long as the Lord God's watch - ing o - ver them, keep - ing track how it all goes
E7
E♭7
D7
G
Edim7
D7
on. But I've been walk - ing through the night and the day till my
cresc.
mf
G
E7
Am
Cm6
G/B
eyes get wea - ry and my head turns gray, and some - times it seems may - be
Cm6
G/B
Cm6
God's gone a - way, for - get - ting the prom - ise that we heard Him say.
3fr

D
C/D
G
Em7
E♭7
And we're lost out here in the stars,
lit - tle stars, big stars,
G/D
C♯dim7
D
C/D
G
blow - ing through the night,
and we're lost out here in the stars,
Em7
E♭7
G/D
Am/C
Bdim7
B♭dim7
lit - tle stars, big stars,
blow - ing through the night,
D
G
E♭7
G6
and we're lost out here in the stars.

MAKIN' WHOOPEE!

from WHOOPEE!

Lyrics by GUS KAHN
Music by WALTER DONALDSON

E7 A A7
Wed-dings make a lot of peo-ple sad. But if you're not the groom, they're not so
D7 G D7
bad. An-oth-er bride, an-oth-er June, an-oth-er
year or may-be less, what's this I
G G7 C Am Am7♭5 G/D
sun - ny hon-ey-moon. An-oth-er sea - son, an-oth-er
hear? Well, can't you guess? She feels ne-glect - ed, and he's sus-
E♭ E♭7 D7 G Am7/E♭ D7
3fr
rea - son for mak-in' whoop-ee! A lot of
pect - ed of mak-in' whoop-ee! She sits a-

G D7 G G7
shoes, a lot of rice, the groom is nerv - ous, he an - swers
lone 'most ev - 'ry night, he does - n't 'phone her, he does - n't
C Am Am7♭5 G E♭ 3fr E♭7 D7
twice. It's real - ly kill - ing that he's so will - ing to make
write. He says he's "bus - y," but she says "is he?" He's mak - in'
G A♭dim7 Am
whoop - ee! Pic - ture a lit - tle love - nest,
whoop - ee! He does - n't make much mon - ey,
Cm 3fr G A♭dim7
down where the ros - es cling. Pic - ture the same sweet
on - ly five thou - sand per. Some judge who thinks he's

Am
Cm
3fr
G
love - nest, think what a year can bring. He's wash - ing
fun - ny, says "you'll pay six to her." He says, "Now
D7
G
G7
dish - es and ba - by clothes, he's so am - bi - tious, he e - ven
judge, sup - pose I fail?" The judge says, "Budge right in - to
C
Am
Am7♭5
G/D
E♭
3fr
E♭7
D7
sews. But don't for - get, folks, that's what you get, folks, for mak - in'
jail. You'd bet - ter keep her, I think it's cheap - er than mak - in'
1
G
G/F
F/E♭
E/D
E♭/D♭
D/C
2
G
D+
G
whoop - ee! An - oth - er whoop - ee!"

MAYBE THIS TIME

from the Musical CABARET

Words by FRED EBB
Music by JOHN KANDER

G7
C9
F
Fm
last. Not a los - er anymore, like the
C Gm7/B♭
A9
5fr
D7
G9
9fr
C
last time and the time be - fore.
Ev - 'ry - bod - y
C+
C6
C9
loves a win - ner, so no - bod - y loved me.
F
F+
F6
F♯dim7
La - dy Peace - ful. La - dy Hap - py. That's what I long to be.

G7
Am
D9
4fr
All the odds are in my fa - vor. Some - thing's bound to be - gin.
C/G
C+/G#
Dm9
3fr
Dm9/G
3fr
It's got to hap - pen, hap - pen some - time. May - be this time I'll
C
A♭7
4fr
D♭
D♭+
win. Ev - 'ry - bod - y loves a win - ner,
D♭6
D♭7
4fr
G♭
G♭+
so no - bod - y loved me. La - dy Peace - ful. La - dy Hap - py.

G♭6
Gdim7
A♭7
4fr
That's what I long to be.
All the odds are
B♭m
E♭9
in my fa - vor.
Some-thing's bound to be - gin.
D♭/A♭
4fr
D♭+/A♭
B♭m
D♭6/A♭
It's got to hap-pen,
hap-pen some - time.
May-be this time.
E♭m9
4fr
A♭13
4fr
D♭
A/C♯
D♭6
May - be this time I'll win.
rit.

MR. WONDERFUL

from the Musical MR. WONDERFUL

Words and Music by JERRY BOCK,
LARRY HOLOFCENER and GEORGE DAVID WEISS

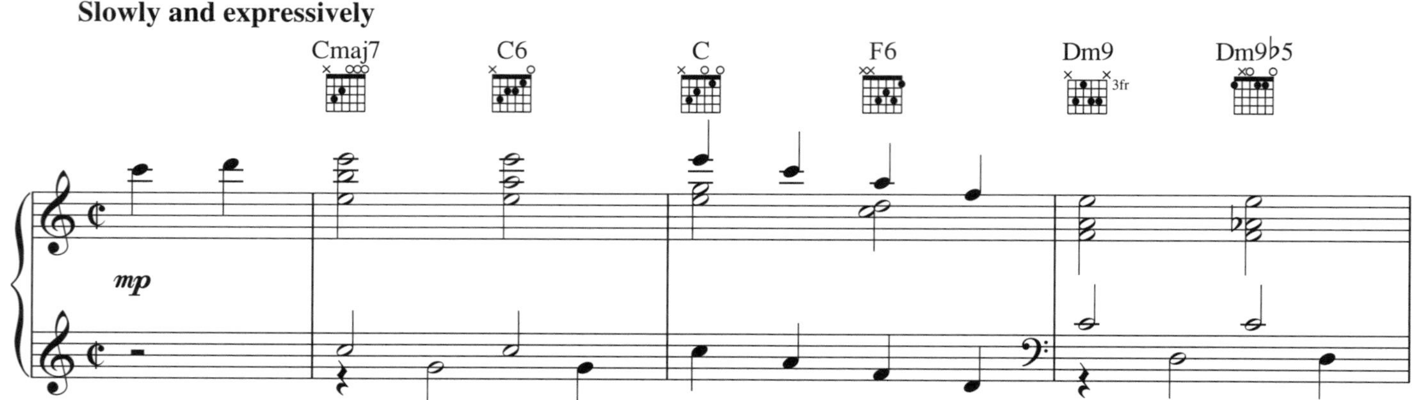

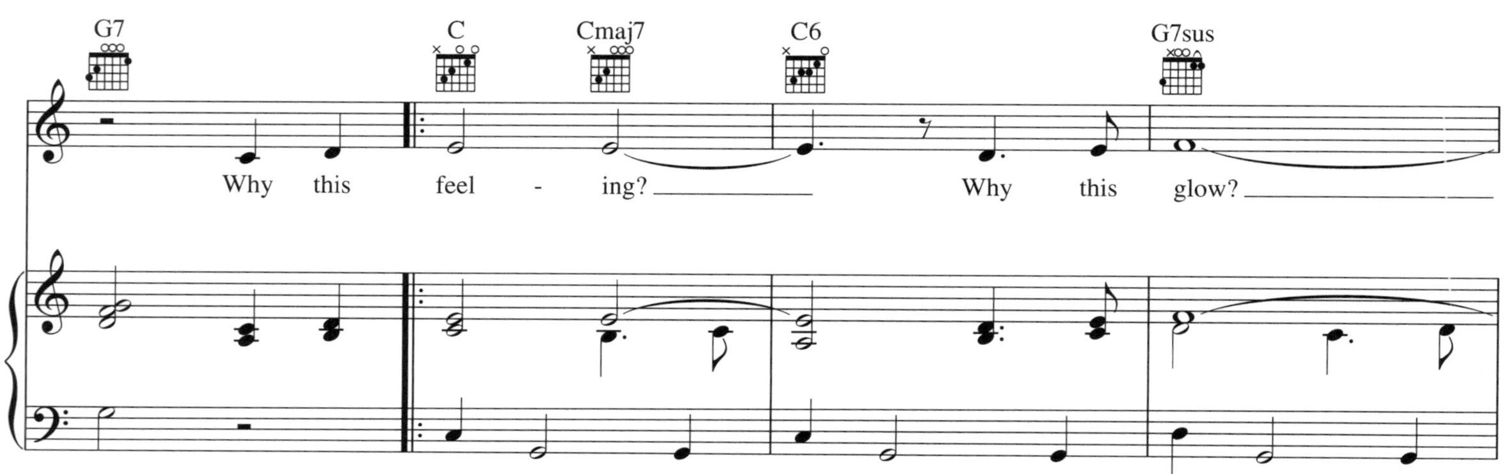

Dm/F
E7
Am
Am/G
F♯dim7
C/G
Gm6/B♭
It's a strange and ten - der mag - ic you do.
A7
Dm7
D9
4fr
Dm/G
B♭7/G
Mis - ter Won - der - ful, that's you!
G7
C
Cmaj7
C6
G7sus
Why this trem - bling when you speak?
G7
C
D7
G7
Why this joy when you touch my cheek?

Dm/F E7 Am Am/G F♯dim7 C/G Gm6/B♭
I must tell you what my heart knows is true:
A7 Dm7 G7 C F6
Mis - ter Won - der - ful, that's you!
C Gm7 C7 Fmaj7
And why this long - ing to know your charms,
F6 Am7 D7 G7
to spend for - ev - er here in your arms!

C
Cmaj7
C6
G7sus
Oh! there's much more I could say,
G7
C
D7
G7
but the words keep slip - ping a - way;
Dm/F
E7
Am
Am/G
F♯dim7
C/G
Gm6/B♭
and I'm left with on - ly one point of view:
A7
Dm7
G7
C
Dm7
Mis - ter Won - der - ful, that's you!
8va

Em7 E♭m7 G7sus G7 Cmaj9 C6 Em7 B♭7
One more thing, then I'm
(8va)
A7 Dm7 F♯dim7
through; Mis - ter Won - der - ful, Mis - ter
(8va)
C6 A7 Dm9 F6 F♯7 G7
Won - der - ful, Mis - ter Won - der - ful, I love
1 C F♯dim7/G Dm7/G G7
you! Why this
2 C Fm/C C C6
you!
rall.

OH, WHAT A BEAUTIFUL MORNIN'

from OKLAHOMA!

Lyrics by OSCAR HAMMERSTEIN II
Music by RICHARD RODGERS

A♭m/C♭
E♭/B♭
B♭7/A♭
E♭/G
The corn is as high as an el - e - phant's
They don't turn their heads as they see me ride
The breeze is so bus - y it don't miss a
A♭
E♭
eye, an' it looks like it's climb - in' clear
by, but a lit - tle brown mav' - rick is
tree, and a ol' weep - in' wil - ler is
mf
B♭dim
B♭7
E♭
up to the sky.
wink - in' her eye.
laugh - in' at me!
Oh, what a beau - ti - ful
mp
A♭sus
A♭
E♭
morn - in'.
Oh, what a beau - ti - ful

B♭7
E♭
day.
I got a beau - ti - ful
A♭
Adim
E♭
B♭7
feel - in'.
Ev - 'ry - thing's go - in' my
1, 2
E♭
B♭7
3
E♭
Fm7/B♭
B♭7
way.
All the
All the
way.
p
riten.
E♭
B♭7
E♭
Oh, what a beau - ti - ful day!

MORE I CANNOT WISH YOU

from GUYS AND DOLLS

By FRANK LOESSER

Am F Em Dm/F G C Dm/G
own true love, this day. Man - sions I can
C Dm/G C Dm/G C C7 F G G9
9fr
wish you, sev - en foot - men all in red, and call - ing cards up - on a sil - ver
C Dm7/G C Dm/G C Dm/G C Dm/G
tray. But more I can - not wish you than to wish you find your
E+ Am F Em Am Am/G
love, your own true love, this day.

D7/F♯ G D7
Stand - ing there gaz - ing at you, full of the bloom of
G C G D7/F♯ G A7♭9
youth. Stand - ing there gaz - ing at you, with the
Dm Gm Dm G C Dm/G C Dm/G
sheep's eye and the lick - er - ish tooth. Mu - sic I can wish you, mer - ry
C Dm/G C C7 F G G9 C Dm7/G
mu - sic while you're young, and wis - dom when your hair has turned to gray. But

C Dm/G C Dm/G C Dm/G E+ Am F
more I can - not wish you than to wish you find your love, your own true
Em Am Am/G Dm Gm
3fr
love, this day, with the sheep's eye and the
Dm G C Am Em Dm/G C Am
lick - er - ish tooth and the strong arms to car - ry you a - way.
Em Dm/G C Am Em Dm/G C
rall.

THE MOST BEAUTIFUL GIRL IN THE WORLD

from JUMBO

Words by LORENZ HART
Music by RICHARD RODGERS

Moderate Waltz tempo

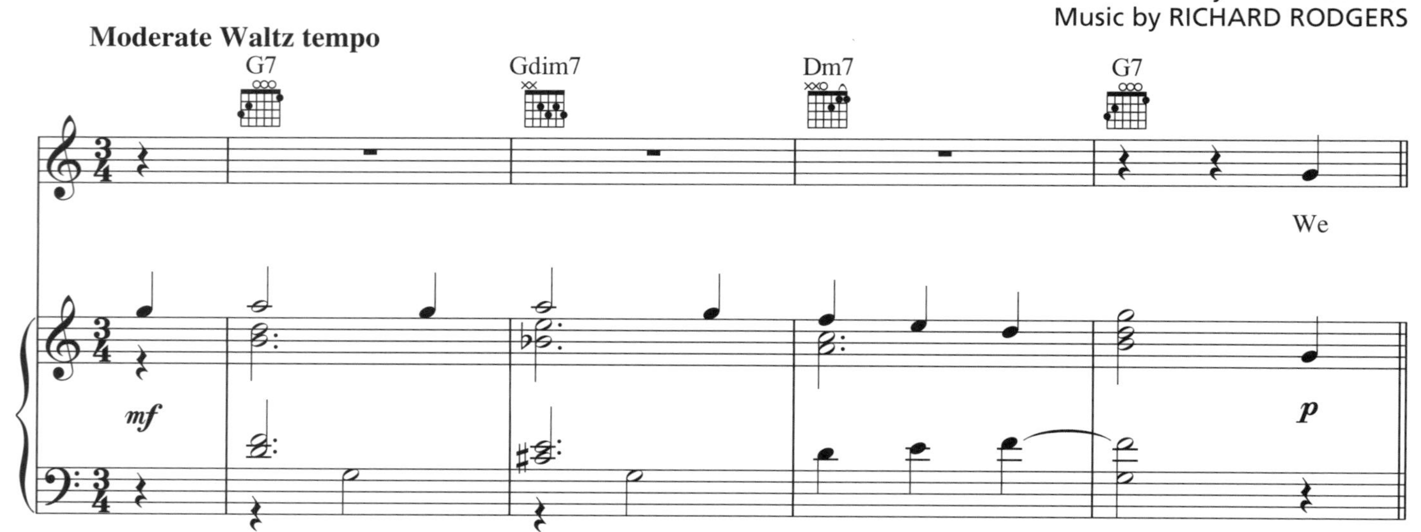

Dm7 G7 G+ 3fr C Dm7 G7
used to laugh and sing to - geth - er be - fore we learned how to
C G7 C/E
talk. With no
mf
p
E/F F G7 B/C C Am7 D7
rea - son for the sea - son spring would end as it would
Dm7 G7 C/E
start. Now the
mf
p

E/F F G7 B/C C Am7 D7

sea - son has a rea - son, And there's spring - time in my

cresc.

G B♭m6/D♭

heart.

f

C C7

The most

p

Fmaj7 Fdim7 Fmaj7 Fdim7/C

beau - ti - ful girl in the world Picks my ties out, eats my

Fmaj7
Fdim7/C
C7sus/G
3fr
C7
can - dy, Drinks my bran - dy, The most beau - ti - ful girl in the
F/A
Am/C
Gm7
C7
Fmaj7
world. The most beau - ti - ful star in the
mf
Fdim7
Fmaj7
Fdim7/C
Fmaj7
Fdim7/C
world is - n't Gar - bo, is - n't Diet - rich, But the
C7sus/G
3fr
C7
Cm/E♭
3fr
sweet trick who can make me be - lieve it's a beau - ti - ful
cresc.

Cm
Am7♭5
D7
Dm
G9
C7
world.
So - cial not a bit,
mf
Dm
G9
C7
Am7
Nat - 'ral kind of wit,
She'd shine
D7
G7sus/D
G7
Gm7
C
Gm
an - y - where
And she has - n't got plat - i - num hair.
C7
Fmaj7
Fdim7
Fmaj7
The most beau - ti - ful house in the world
has a mort - gage,
p

Fdim7/C Fmaj7 Fdim7/C C7sus/G C7
what do I care, it's good - bye care when my
Cm/E♭ Cm Am7♭5 D7
slip - pers are next to the ones that be - long To the
cresc.
Dm7 G7 Gm7 B♭7
1
F B♭
one and on - ly beau - ti - ful girl in the world!
f
F C7
2
F B♭ F
The most world!
mf

MY FAVORITE THINGS

from THE SOUND OF MUSIC

Lyrics by OSCAR HAMMERSTEIN II
Music by RICHARD RODGERS

Em
Cream - col - ored po - nies and crisp ap - ple
mf
mp
Cmaj7
stru - dels, Door - bells and sleigh - bells and schnitz - el with noo - dles,
Am7
D7
G/B
C/E
G/D
Wild geese that fly with the moon on their wings, These are a
C
F♯m7♭5
4fr
B7
E
few of my fa - vor - ite things.
f

A
Girls in white dress - es with blue sat - in sash - es, Snow - flakes that
mf
Am7
D7
stay on my nose and eye - lash - es, Sil - ver white win - ters that
G/B
C/E
G/D
C
F♯m7♭5
4fr
B7♭9
melt in - to springs, These are a few of my fa - vor - ite things.
Em
F♯m7♭5
4fr
B7
When the dog bites, When the bee stings,
mf

Em
C
When I'm feel - ing sad, I
A7/C♯
A7
sim - ply re - mem - ber my fa - vor - ite things and
G/D C/D G/D C/D G
D7♭9
4fr
D7
G
then I don't feel so bad.
cresc.
f
C
G/D
D7
G
sf

OLD DEUTERONOMY

from CATS

Music by ANDREW LLOYD WEBBER
Text by T.S. ELIOT

Fm
G
Old Deu - ter - on - o - my's lived a long time; he's a cat who has lived man - y
Old Deu - ter - on - o - my's bur - ied nine wives and more I am tempt - ed to
Dm
Am
Bm
C
D
lives in suc - ces - sion. He was fa - mous in pro - verb and fa - mous in rhyme a
say, nine - ty nine. And his nu - mer - ous prog - e - ny pros - pers and thrives, the
B♭
D
1 G
2 G
long while be - fore Queen Vic - to - ria's ac - ces - sion.
vil - lage is proud of him in his de - cline. At the
F♯/G
F/G
F♯/G
G
sight of that plac - id and bland phys - i - og - no - my, when he sits in the sun on the

F♯/G F/G E♭ D♭ B♭ D7
3fr
vic - ar - age wall; The Old - est In - hab - i - tant croaks: Well, of
G Fm G
all things, can it be real - ly? No! Yes! Ho! Hi! Oh my
all things, can it be real - ly? No! Yes! Ho! Hi! Oh my
Dm Am Bm C G/D
eye! My mind may be wan - der - ing but I con - fess, I be -
eye! My legs may be tot - ter - y, I must go slow and be
B♭ D7
1 G
2 G
lieve it is Old Deu - ter - on - o - my. Well, of
care - ful of Old Deu - ter - on - o - my.
rall.

ON MY OWN
from LES MISÉRABLES

Music by CLAUDE-MICHEL SCHÖNBERG
Lyrics by ALAIN BOUBLIL, JEAN-MARC NATEL,
HERBERT KRETZMER, JOHN CAIRD
and TREVOR NUNN

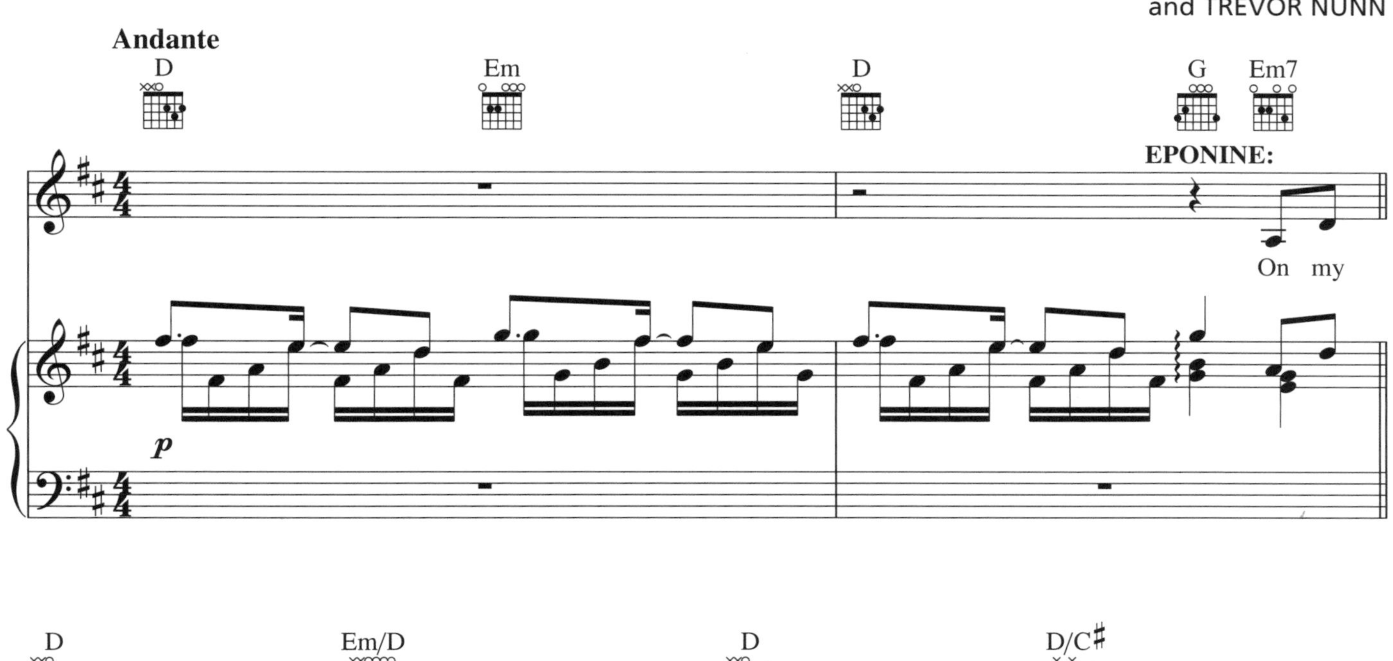

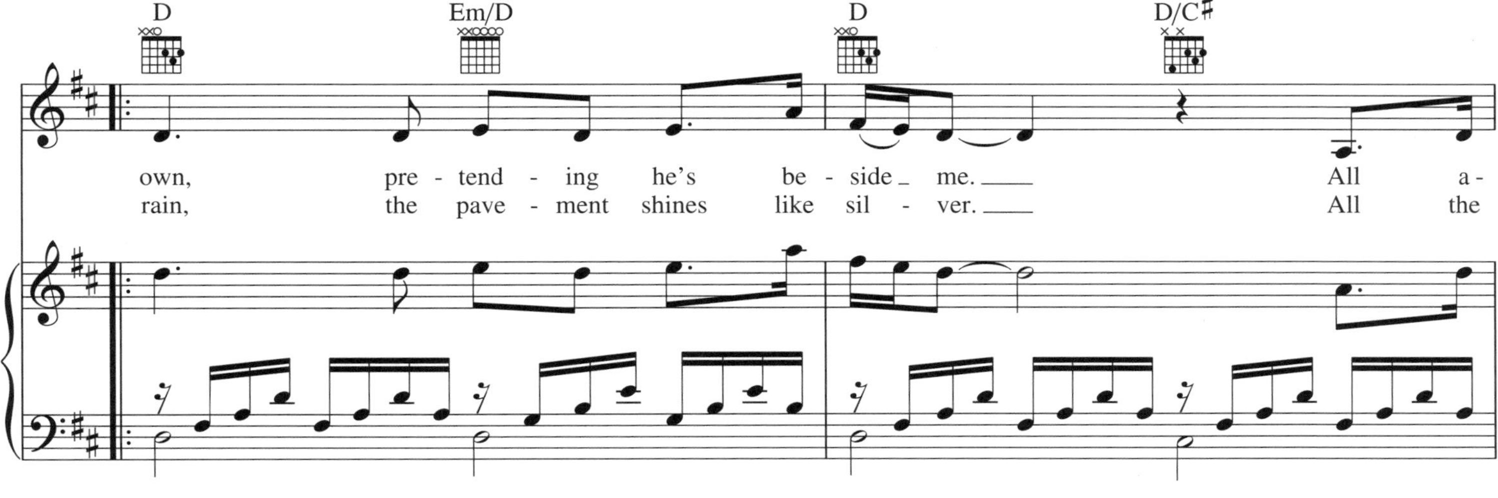

G
F♯7
Bm
him I feel his arms a - round me. And
dark - ness the trees are full of star - light. And
Em
Em/D
1
A
when I lose my way I close my eyes and he has found me. In the
all I see is him and me for - ev - er and for -
2
A
B♭
E♭m/B♭
6fr
ev - er. And I know it's on - ly in my
mf
più mosso
B♭
B♭/A
Gm
3fr
Gm/F
mind that I'm talk - ing to my - self and not to

E♭
3fr
Em
him. And al - though I know that he is
B
B7
Am7
C7
blind, Still I say there's a way for us. I
F
Gm/F
F
F/E
love him, but when the night is o - ver, he is
Dm
G7
C
C/B
gone, the riv - er's just a riv - er. With -

B♭
A
Dm
out him the world a - round me chang - es. The
Gm
3fr
Gm/F
C
trees are bare and ev - 'ry - where the streets are full of stran - gers. I
F
Gm/F
F
F/E
love him but ev - 'ry day I'm learn - ing all my
f
Dm
G7
C
C/B
life I've on - ly been pre - tend - ing. With -

B♭
A
Dm
out me his world will go on turn - ing. The
Gm
3fr
C
world is full of hap - pi - ness that I have nev - er known. I
p
F(add9)
F7/E♭
love him, I love him, I
Dm7
B♭m/D♭
F
love him, but on - ly on my own.
rall.

ON THE STREET WHERE YOU LIVE

from MY FAIR LADY

Words by ALAN JAY LERNER
Music by FREDERICK LOEWE

E♭m
B♭maj7
B♭6
sev - 'ral sto - ries high,
Know - ing
C7
F9
F7♯5
B♭6
I'm on the street where you live.
Cm7
F7♭9
B♭6
F7
Are there li - lac trees in the
B♭6
F7
B♭maj7
heart of town?
Can you hear a lark in

C♯dim7
C7
F7
Cm7
3fr
F7
Fdim7
an - y oth - er part of town?
Does en -
Cm7
3fr
E♭m
6fr
B♭maj7
B♭6
chant - ment pour
out of ev - 'ry door?
C7
F9
No, it's just on the street where you
B♭
D7
Am
Cdim
live.
And oh,
the tow - er - ing
mf

Eb6
Ebm
6fr
feel - ing, Just to know
Ebm/Gb
3fr
Gdim7
Bb
Gb7
Bb/F
3
somehow you are near! The o -
Em7b5
Em7/A
A7
D
A/C#
3
- ver - pow - er - ing feel - ing That an - y sec - ond you may
Am/C
Bb/C
C7
F7
Eb/F
F7
sud - den - ly ap - pear! Peo - ple
p

B♭6 F7 B♭6 F7

stop and stare, they don't both - er me; For there's

B♭6 C♯dim7 C7 F7 Cm7 F7 Fdim7

no - where else on earth that I would rath - er be. Let the

Cm7 Cm7♭5 D+ B♭/F

time go by, I won't care if I can be

mf

C9 F9 B♭ G♭6 B♭

here on the street where you live.

mf

THE OTHER SIDE OF THE TRACKS

from LITTLE ME

Music by CY COLEMAN
Lyrics by CAROLYN LEIGH

Dm7/G
G7
Cmaj9
C6
Em7/A
A9
5fr
put my shad - ows be - hind me, give my in - hi - bi - tions the
Dmaj7
D7
Dm7/G
G7
Cmaj7
Bm7
axe, and to - mor - row morn - ing you'll find me on the
Am7
D9
4fr
G6
D9
4fr
Gmaj9
Am7
Bm7
oth - er side of the tracks. On the oth - er side of that line,
Am7/D
Gmaj9
G6
Bm7
E9
where the life is fan - cy and free, gon - na

Amaj7 Bm7 Amaj9 Bm7 Amaj7 A6/9 C♯m7/F♯
9fr
sit and fan on my fat di-van while the but-ler but-tles the
F♯9 F♯m7/B B7 Emaj7 E7
3fr
tea! But for now I'm fac-in' the fenc-es, and I
Em7/A A7 Dmaj7 D7 Dm7/G G7
can't af-ford to re-lax when the whole ca-boo-dle com-
Cmaj7 Bm7 Am7 D9 G6 Gmaj9
4fr
menc-es on the oth-er side of the tracks. So I'm

C♯m7 F♯7 C♯m7 F♯7 Bmaj9 B6 Bmaj9
4fr 4fr
off and run-nin' o - ver the rail. I'm goin' gun-nin' af -
B6 Dm7 G7 Dm7 G7
- ter the quail! Off and run-nin', send me the mail, to the
Cmaj7 F13 Em7 A13
5fr
great big world on the oth-er side, the great big world on the far-ther side, the
Am7 G6/B
1
Cmaj7 C/D Gmaj9 Am7/D Gmaj9 Am7/D
great big world on the oth-er side of the tracks! On the

2
Cmaj7
C/D
B7sus
2fr
B7
Bm7/E
E9
G7/D
oth - er side of the tracks.
To the
Cmaj7
F13
Bm7
F7
great big world that - 'll o - pen wide,
E9
G7/D
Cmaj7(add6)
G6/B
Am7
C/D
to the great big world on the oth - er side of the
D7sus/G
D7
Gmaj9
Em7/D
D7sus/G
D7
G
tracks!

ONCE UPON A TIME

from the Broadway Musical ALL AMERICAN

Lyric by LEE ADAMS
Music by CHARLES STROUSE

Cm7
E♭/G
F7
Gm
E♭maj7
F7sus
F7
But that was once up - on a time,
The world was beau - ti - ful to see
ver - y long a -
ver - y long a -
B♭
B♭maj7
Cm7
F7sus
F7
B♭
B♭maj7
go.
go.
Once up - on a hill
On a night like this
B♭6
B♭maj7/F
Gm
we sat be - neath a wil - low tree,
we saw the ris - ing of the moon.
E♭
B♭
B♭maj7
E♭
B♭/D
E♭
count - ing all the stars
All the sil - ver stars
and wait - ing for the dawn.
like neck - lac - es were strung.

Cm7 Eb/G F7 Gm Ebmaj7 F7sus F7

— But that was once up - on a time. — Now the tree is

— We spoke of such im - por - tant things. — We were ver - y

Bb Bbmaj7 Bb6 Bbmaj7

A little faster

Cm7 F7 Bbmaj7 Bb6

gone. How the breeze

young. O - pen hearts,

Cm7 F7 Bbmaj7 Bb6 Am7 D7 Gm C7sus C7 F7sus F7

ruf - fled through her hair, how we al - ways laughed as though to - mor - row was - n't there.

noth - ing to con - ceal. Ev - 'ry lit - tle thought was so ex - cit - ing to re - veal.

F7/Eb Bb/D F7/Eb Bb/D Gm7 C7 F7

We were young and did - n't have a care. Where did it go?

All our dreams we knew would soon be real. Where did they go?

poco rit.

Tempo I
B♭
B♭maj7
B♭6
B♭maj7/F
Gm
3fr
Once up-on a time the world was sweet-er than we knew.
E♭
B♭
B♭maj7
B♭7
Ev-'ry-thing was ours, how hap-py we were
E♭
Cm7
E♭/G
F7
Gm
E♭maj7
Cm9
F7
Opt.
then. But some-how once up-on a time nev-er comes a-
B♭
B♭maj7
1
Cm7
F7sus
F7
2
E♭/B♭
6fr
gain.
8va
rit.

OUR LANGUAGE OF LOVE

from IRMA LA DOUCE

Music by MARGUERITE MONNOT
Original French Words by ALEXANDRE BREFFORT
English Words by JULIAN MORE,
DAVID HENEKER and MONTY NORMAN

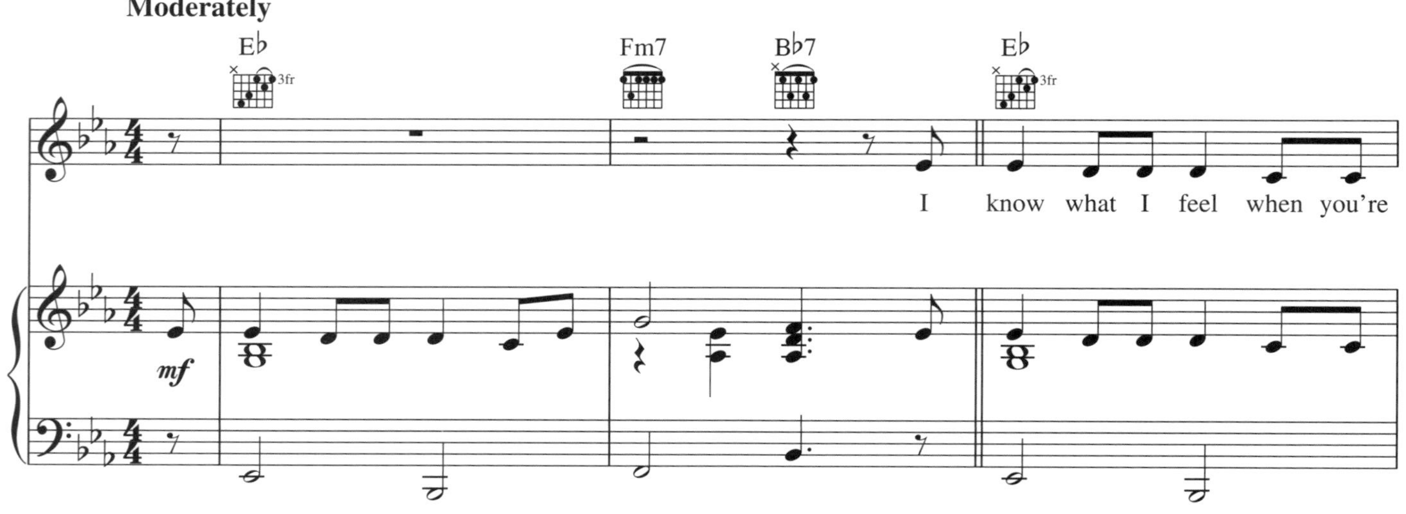

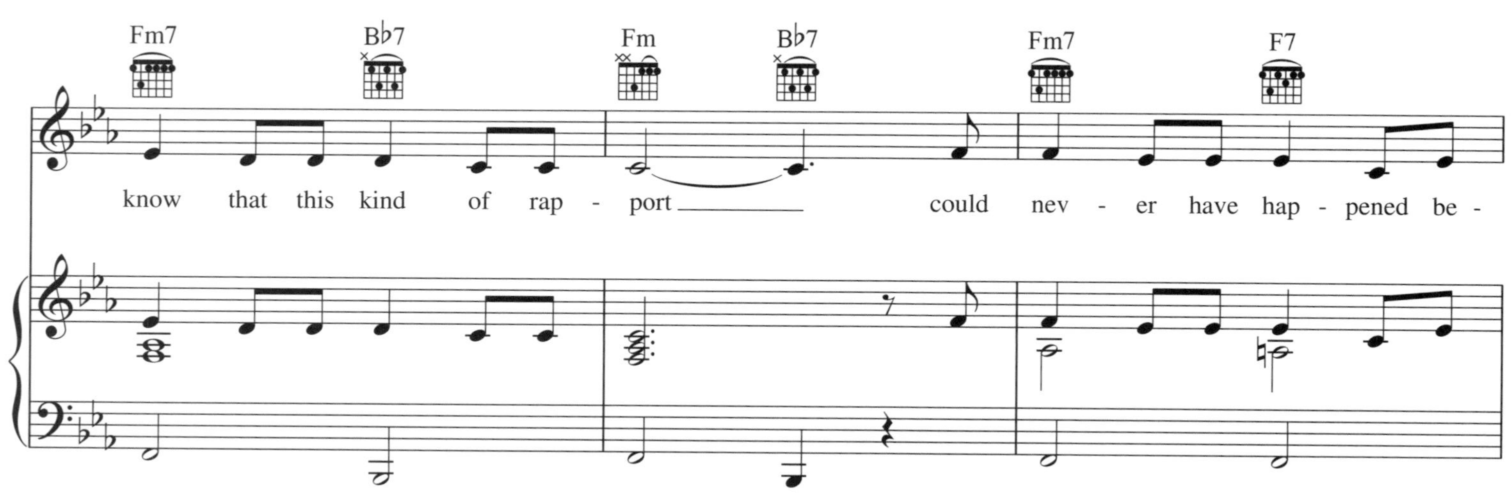

B♭7
E♭
3fr
E♭6
fore. No need to speak, no need to sing when just a
E♭maj7
3fr
E♭6
F7
glance means ev - 'ry - thing. Not a word need be spo - ken
B♭7
B♭7♭9
E♭
3fr
in our lan - guage of love. I'll touch your
E♭6
E♭maj7
3fr
cheek, you'll hold my hand, and on - ly we will un - der -

E♭6
F7
B♭7
B♭7♭9
stand that the si - lence is bro - ken by our lan - guage of
E♭
3fr
A♭
4fr
love. It's clear to you, it's clear to
A♭6
3fr
A♭maj7
A♭6
3fr
me this pre - cious mo - ment had to be, oth - er mo - ments out -
Gm
3fr
C7♭9
Fm
class - ing. Guard - ian an - gels are pass -

B♭7
E♭
3fr
ing. No words will do, no lips can
E♭6
E♭maj7
say the ten - der mean - ing we con -
E♭6
F7
B♭7
B♭7♭9
vey, "I love you" is un - spo - ken in our lan - guage of
E♭
1
2
love. No need to

THE PHANTOM OF THE OPERA

from THE PHANTOM OF THE OPERA

Music by ANDREW LLOYD WEBBER
Lyrics by CHARLES HART
Additional Lyrics by RICHARD STILGOE and MIKE BATT

Gsus
3fr
Gm
3fr
C
Dm
that voice which calls to me and speaks my name.
B♭maj7
Gm/B♭
C
Dm
And do I dream a - gain? for now I find
the phan - tom of the op - er - a is
B♭dim
Dm
D♭m
4fr
Cm
3fr
B
there in - side my mind.

B♭
A♭
B♭
D♭dim
Gm
PHANTOM: Sing once a -
mf
Csus
Cm
F
Gm
gain with me our strange du - et; my pow - er
o - ver you grows strong - er yet.
(8va basso)
And though you
E♭maj7
Cm/E♭
F
Gm
turn from me to glance be - hind, the

Cdim
3fr
F♯dim
9fr
phan - tom of the op - er - a is there in - side your
Gm
3fr
(loco)
F♯m
Fm
E
E♭
3fr
D
D7
mind.
Em
Asus
Am
D/F♯
CHRISTINE: Those who have seen your face draw back in
Em/B
Asus
Am
D/F♯
fear. I am the mask you wear,
PHANTOM: it's me they

Em/B
Cmaj7
Am/C
D
hear. PHANTOM & CHRISTINE: Your spi - rit and my voice in one com -
My spi - rit and your voice in one com -
Em
bined; the phan - tom of the op - er - a is
bined; the phan - tom of the op - er - a is
Cdim
3fr
Em
VOICES:
He's there, the phan - tom of the
there in - side my mind.
there in - side your mind.
C
Em
op - era. Be - ware the phan - tom of the

C
Fm
E♭
Fm
op - era.
PHANTOM: In all your
mp
D♭
E♭
Fm
fan - ta - sies, you al - ways knew that man and
D♭
E♭
Fm
mys - ter - y
CHRISTINE:
were both in you.
PHANTOM & CHRISTINE:
And in this
And in this
D♭maj7
B♭m/D♭
E♭
Fm
lab - y - rinth where night is blind, the
lab - y - rinth where night is blind, the
mf

Fm
Db dim
4fr
phan - tom of the op - er - a is there in - side my
phan - tom of the op - er - a is there in - side your
Fm
Db
mind.
mind.
PHANTOM:
(Spoken:) Sing, my angel of music!
CHRISTINE: He's
Fm
Db
there the phan - tom of the op - era.
Fm
Db
Ah!
PHANTOM: Sing, my angel, sing!

Gm
3fr
E♭
3fr
1
CHRISTINE:
Ah!
PHANTOM: (1st time only) Sing for me!
2
Am
F
CHRISTINE:
Ah!
PHANTOM: Sing, my
Am
F
CHRISTINE:
Ah!
Ah!
angel of music!
Am
Ah!
Ah!

SABBATH PRAYER

from the Musical FIDDLER ON THE ROOF

Words by SHELDON HARNICK
Music by JERRY BOCK

Am
D
Am7
D
Am
D
May you be de - serv - ing of praise;
Strength - en them, O Lord, and
Am7
D
G
keep them from the stran - ger's ways.
May God bless you
F
G
and grant you long lives.
(May the Lord ful - fill our Sab - bath prayer for you.)
F
E7♭9
May God make you good moth - ers and wives.
(May He send you hus - bands who will care for you.)

Am
D
Am7
D
Am
D
May the Lord pro - tect and de - fend you,
May the Lord pre - serve you from
Am7
D
Am
D
Am7
D
pain;
Fa - vor them, O Lord, with hap - pi - ness and peace, Oh,
Dm
E7
1
Am
D
Am7
D
hear our Sab - bath prayer, a - men.
a tempo
2
Am
D
Am7
D
Am
men.
a tempo
rit.

SEND IN THE CLOWNS

from the Musical A LITTLE NIGHT MUSIC

Music and Lyrics by
STEPHEN SONDHEIM

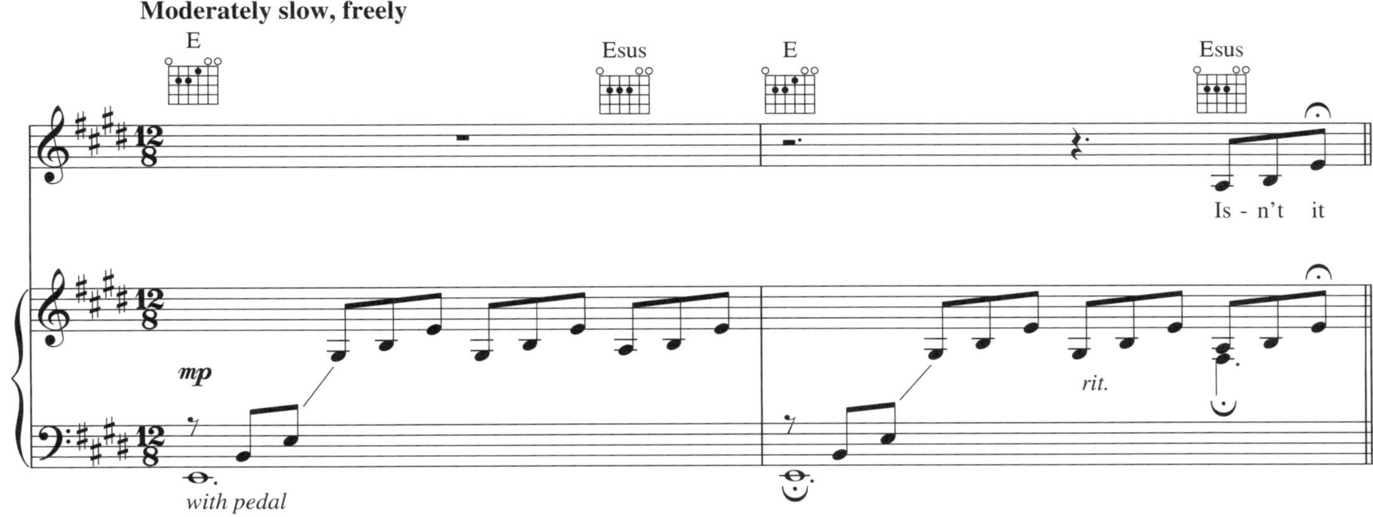

1.
B/E
A/E
Esus
2.
B/E
A/E
clowns.
Is-n't it
clowns?
Send in the
rit.
E
G♯m
D♯m7
G♯m
D♯m7
clowns.
Just when I'd
stopped
o-pen-ing doors,
fi-nal-ly
G♯m
C♯m(add2)
C♯m
C♯m(add2)
G♯/B♯
know-ing the one that I want-ed was
yours,
mak-ing my
C♯m/B
C♯m/A♯
C♯m/A
G♯7sus
F♯m7♭5
en-trance a-gain with my u-su-al
flair,
sure of my

B6/9
B6
A/B
B/E
A/E
B/E
Esus
lines, no one is there. Is-n't it
rit.
E
Esus
E
Emaj7
rich? Is-n't it queer, los-ing my tim-ing this late in my ca-
Amaj9
Amaj9♯11
4fr
Amaj9
B13/E
A/E
F♯m/E
G♯m/E
A/E
reer? And where are the clowns? Quick, send in the clowns. Don't both-er, they're
rit.
(♪= ♪)
E
Esus
E
E(add2)
here.
a tempo
rit.

SIXTEEN GOING ON SEVENTEEN

from THE SOUND OF MUSIC

Lyrics by OSCAR HAMMERSTEIN II
Music by RICHARD RODGERS

Refrain (assai moderato)
G9♭5 G9 C7♯9 C7 F Fdim F B♭/C
9fr 9fr 8fr
write on.
You are six - teen,
I am six - teen,
poco rit.
p with feeling and not fast
C7 F6 Dm7 G13
3fr
go - ing on sev - en - teen, Ba - by, it's time to think!
go - ing on sev - en - teen, I know that I'm na - ive.
C9 F Gm7 G13
3fr
Bet - ter be - ware, be can - ny and care - ful, Ba - by, you're on the
Fel - lows I meet may tell me I'm sweet and will - ing - ly I'll be -
C7 C+ F Fdim F B♭/C C7
8fr
brink! You are six - teen, go - ing on sev - en - teen,
lieve. I am six - teen, go - ing on sev - en - teen,
mf
p

F6 Dm7 G13 C9

Fel - lows will fall in line. Ea - ger young lads and
In - no - cent as a rose. Bach - e - lor dan - dies,

F Gm7 C9 F

rou - és and cads will of - fer you food and wine.
drink - ers of bran - dies, what do I know of those?

B♭ B♭(♭5) F7

To - tal - ly un - pre - pared are you To face a world of
To - tal - ly un - pre - pared am I To face a world of

mp

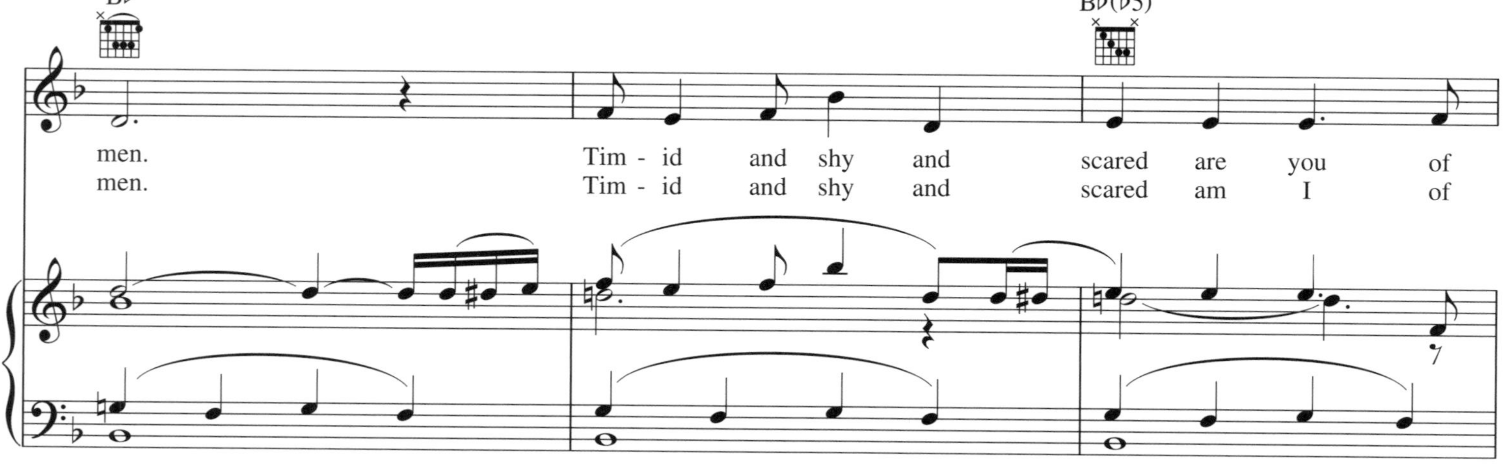

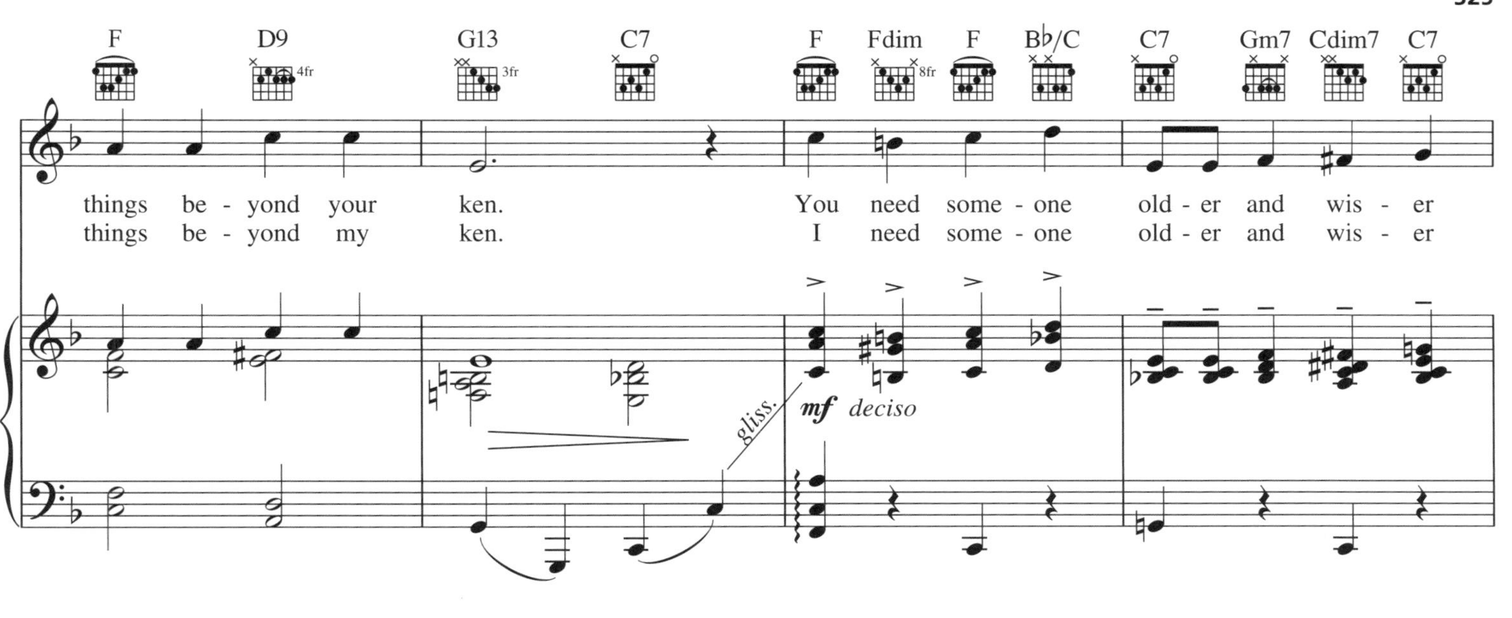
F D9 G13 C7 F Fdim F B♭/C C7 Gm7 Cdim7 C7
4fr
3fr
8fr
things be - yond your ken. You need some - one old - er and wis - er
things be - yond my ken. I need some - one old - er and wis - er
gliss.
mf deciso

F Fdim7/C F Gm7♭5 F Fdim F B♭/C D7 D9
8fr
4fr
Tell - ing you what to do.
Tell - ing me what to do.
I am sev - en - teen, go - ing on eigh - teen,
You are sev - en - teen, go - ing on eigh - teen,
mf

G9 C7♭9 1 F G9 C7
9fr
9fr
I'll take care of you.
I'll de - pend on

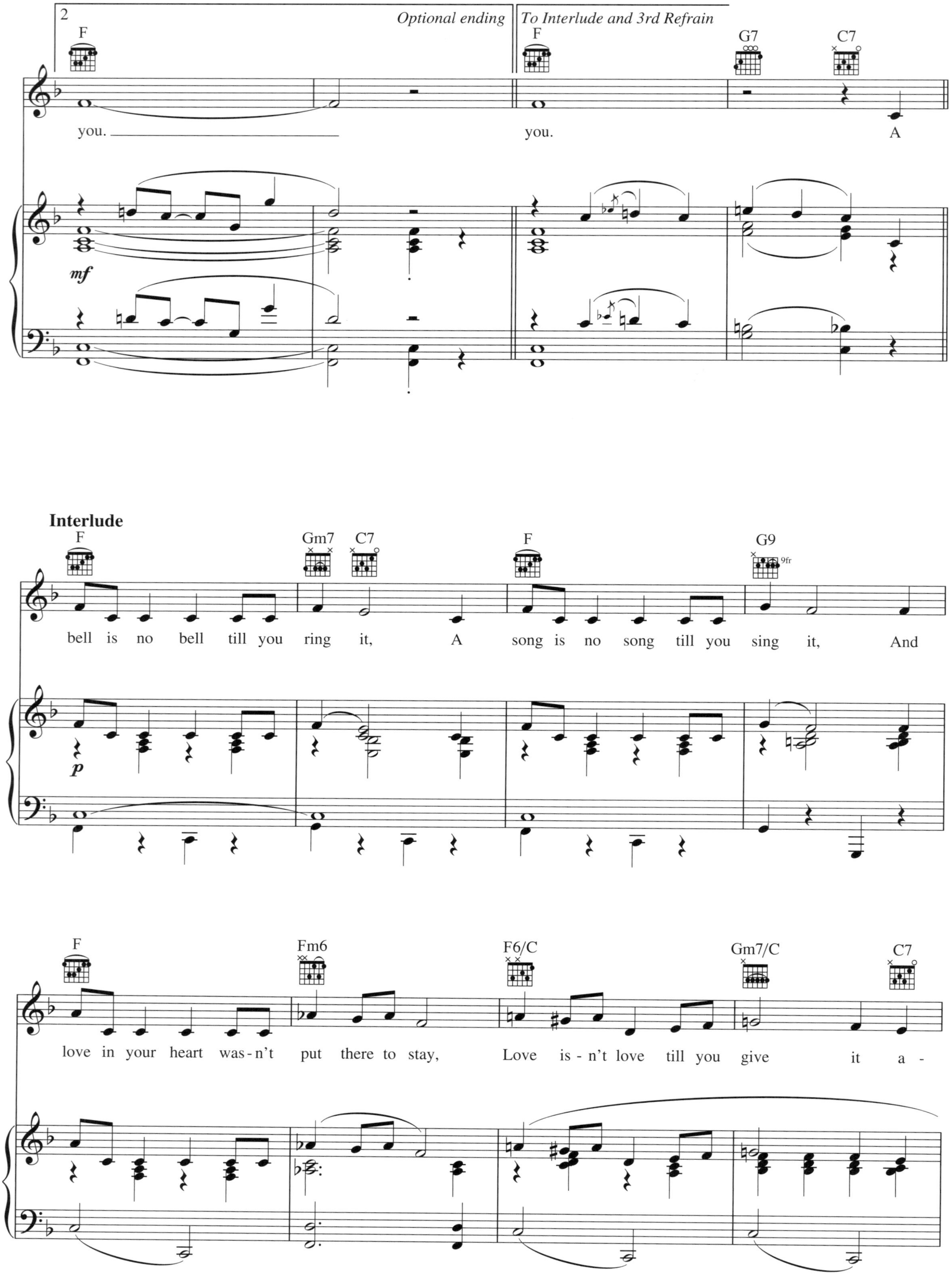

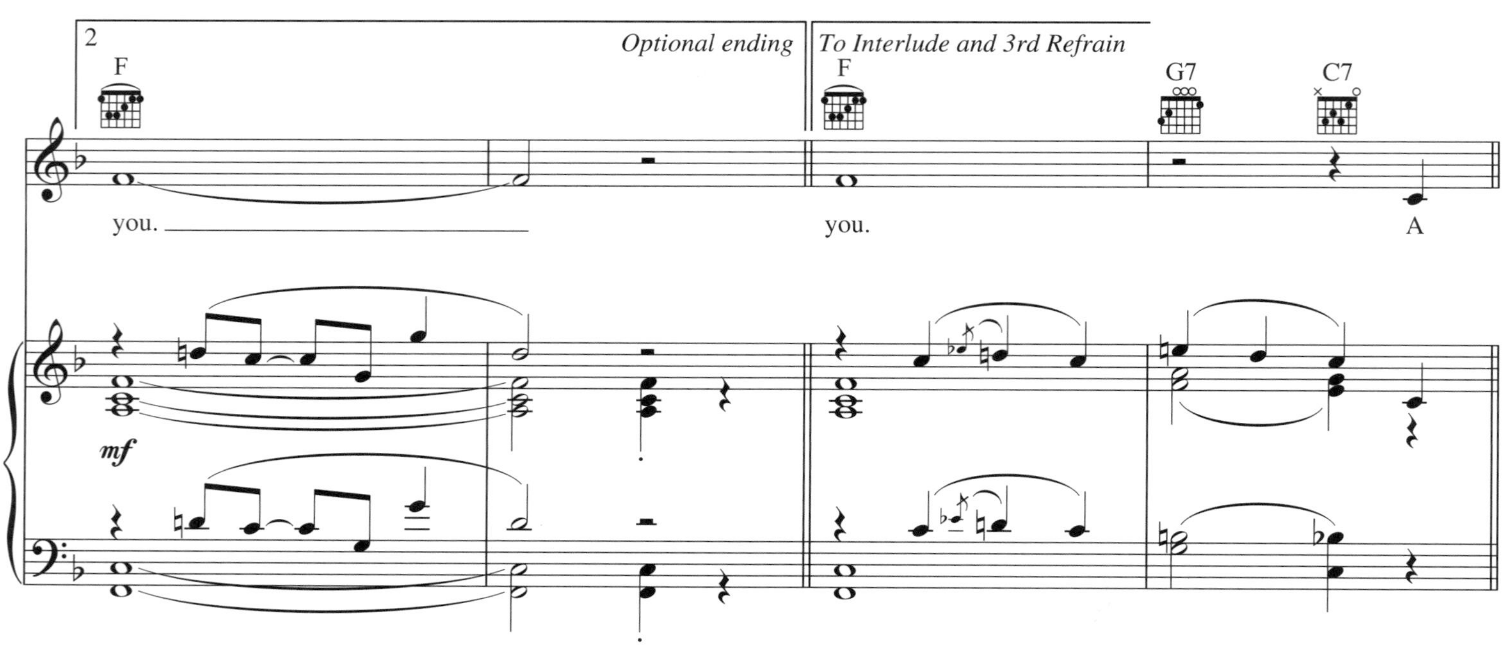

Interlude

F Gm7 C7 F G9 9fr

bell is no bell till you ring it, A song is no song till you sing it, And

p

F Fm6 F6/C Gm7/C C7

love in your heart was-n't put there to stay, Love is-n't love till you give it a-

3rd Refrain (assai moderato)
F7 F6 F+ F F Fdim F B♭/C
way.
When you're six - teen,
C7 F6 Dm7 G7
go - ing on sev - en - teen, Wait - ing for life to start,
C9 F Gm7 G7
Some - bod - y kind who touch - es your mind will sud - den - ly touch your
C7 C+ F Fdim F B♭/C C7
heart!
When that hap - pens, af - ter it hap - pens,
p
mf

F6
Dm7
G7
C9
noth - ing is quite the same.
Some - how you know you'll
F
Gm7
C9
F
jump up and go if ev - er he calls your name!
B♭
B♭(♭5)
F7
Gone are your old i - deas of life, the old i - deas grow
mp
B♭
B♭(♭5)
dim.
Lo and be - hold! You're some - one's wife and

F D9 4fr G7 C7 F Fdim 8fr F B♭/C
you be - long to him! You may think this
gliss.
mf deciso
C7 Gm7 Cdim7 C7 F Fdim/C F Gm7♭5
kind of ad - ven - ture nev - er may come to you
mf
F/C Fdim/C F/C B♭/C D7 D9 4fr G9 9fr
Dar - ling six - teen go - ing on sev - en - teen, Wait a
C7♭9 F
year or two.
mf

SOMEBODY LOVES ME

from GEORGE WHITE'S SCANDALS OF 1924

Words by B.G. DeSYLVA and BALLARD MacDONALD
Music by GEORGE GERSHWIN
French Version by EMELIA RENAUD

G
Am/D
D7
G6
Am7
D7sus
D7
G7
G7/C
Cmaj7
some - one has up - set
Heav - en's pret - ty
pro - gram, for we've
Cm6
3fr
D7
Em
Em6
Bm
Bm7
Bm6
E7
nev - er
met.
I'm
clutch - ing at straws,
just be - cause
Em7/A
A7
D7
D7♯5
G
Am7
Am/D
D
I may meet her
yet.
Some - bod - y
loves me,
G
C7
G
C7
Am7
D7
I won - der
who,
I won - der
who
she can be.
3

G
D7♭9
4fr
G
Some - bod - y
Am7
Am/D
D
G
A7
loves me, I wish I knew,
Bm
C♯7♭9
C♯m7/F♯
9fr
F♯7
Bm
Bm(maj7)
7fr
who can she be wor - ries me.
Bm7
E7
Am
Dm6/A
Am
Dm6/A
For ev - 'ry girl who pass - es me I shout, "Hey!

Am
Em7
A7
Em7
A7
may - be you were meant to be my lov - ing
D7
D+
G
Am7
Am/D
D
ba - by." Some - bod - y loves me,
G
C7
G
Em7
Am7
D7
I won - der who. May - be it's
3
1
G
D7
you.
2
G
Am/D
G
you.

SOMETHING GOOD

from THE SOUND OF MUSIC

Lyrics and Music by
RICHARD RODGERS

Note: In the film version, this song was written to replace "An Ordinary Couple."

F/C
C7
F6
F7
must have been a mo - ment of truth. For
Bb/D
Db7
4fr
F/C
F
here you are, Stand - ing there, Lov - ing me,
mf
Bb/D
Db7
4fr
C9
C7
Wheth - er or not you should. So,
mp
F
F7
Bb
Gm7b5
F/C
some-where in my youth or child - hood I must have done

E/C
C7
1
F
Gm7/C
C7
2
F
some - thing good. Per - good.
mf
Coda
C7/B♭
5fr
Am7
F/A
Gm7
Gm7♭5
Noth - ing comes from noth - ing, Noth - ing ev - er could. So,
mf
F/C
B♭/C
C7
some - where in my youth or child - hood I
F/C
E/C
C7
F
must have done some - thing good.
mf

S.O.S

from MAMA MIA!

Words and Music by BENNY ANDERSSON,
BJÖRN ULVAEUS and STIG ANDERSON

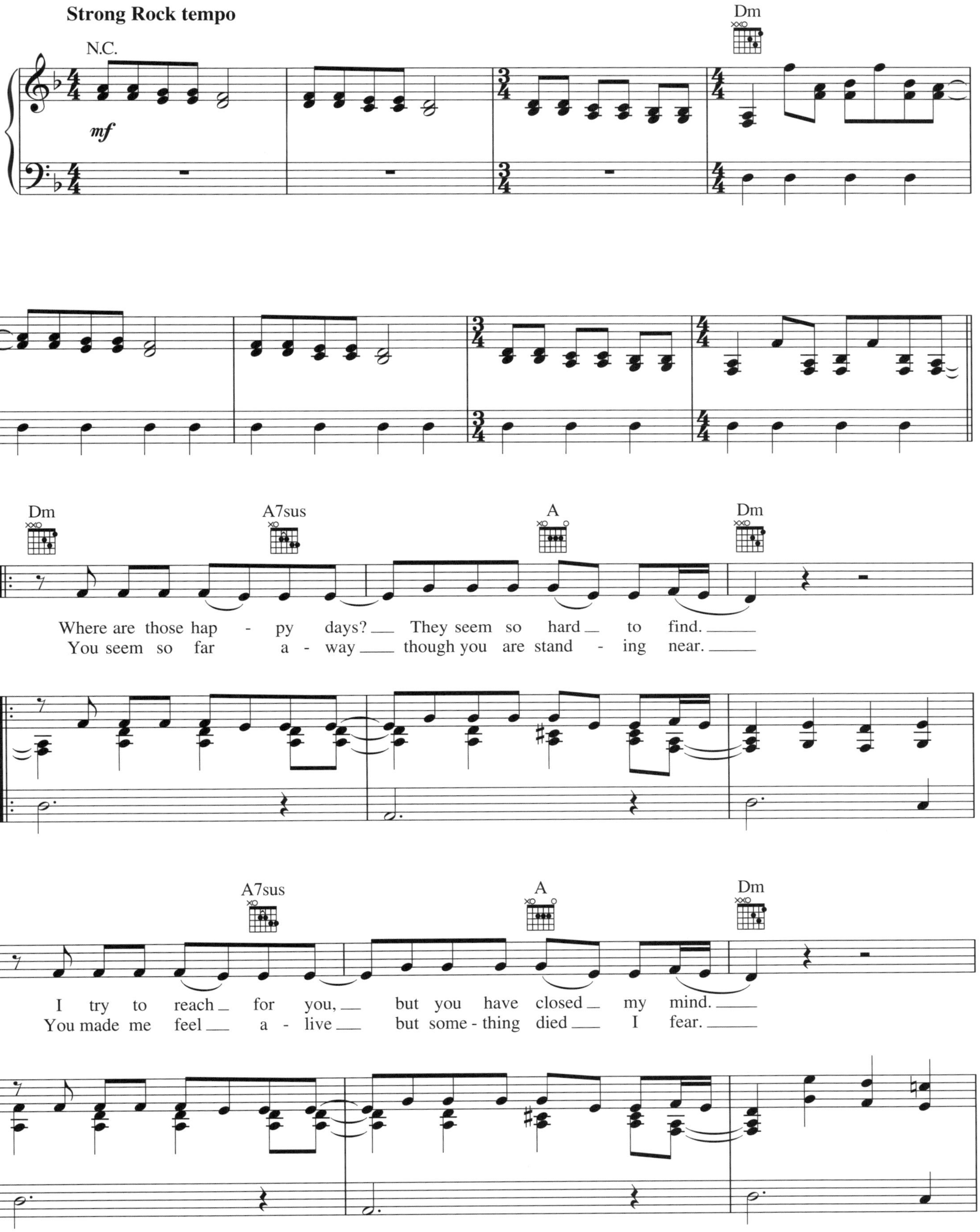

Strong Rock tempo
N.C.
mf
Dm
Dm
A7sus
A
Dm
Where are those hap - py days? They seem so hard to find.
You seem so far a - way though you are stand - ing near.
A7sus
A
Dm
I try to reach for you, but you have closed my mind.
You made me feel a - live but some - thing died I fear.

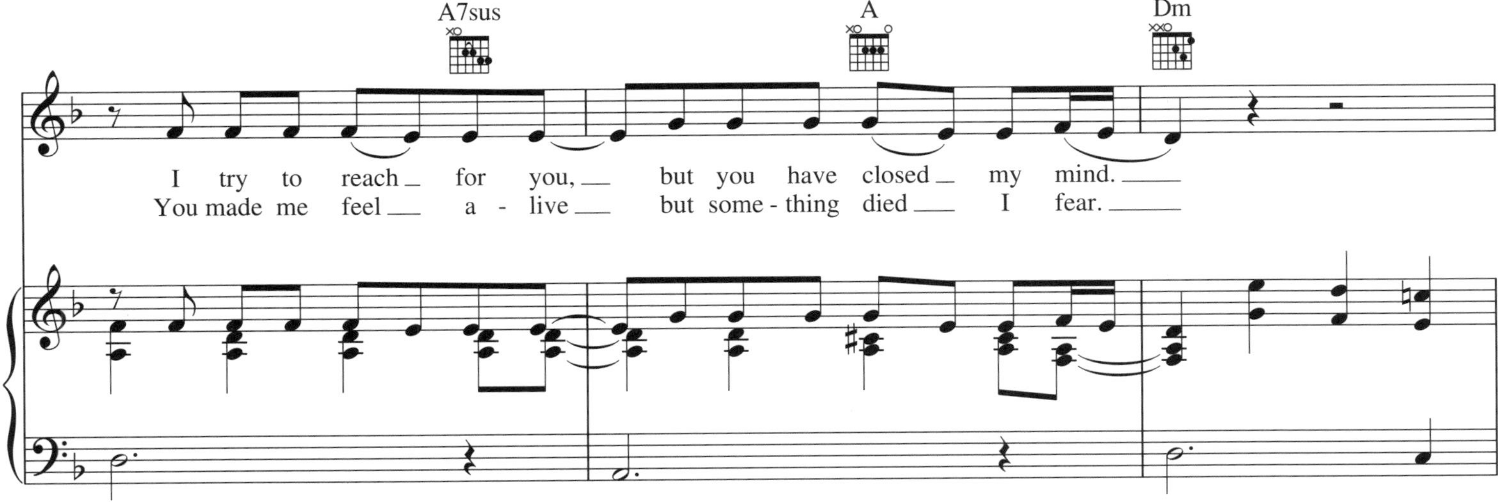

F
C
Gm
3fr
What-ev-er hap-pened to our love?
I real-ly tried to make it out.
I wish I un-der-stood.
I wish I un-der-stood.
Dm
A7sus
A
It used to be so nice.
What hap-pened to our love?
It used to be so good.
It used to be so good.
Dm
A/C♯
Dm
Edim
3fr
F
Gm7
F
C7/E
F
C
Gm
3fr
B♭
F
B♭/F
So when you're near me, dar - ling, can't you hear me S. O. S.?

F
B♭/F
F
C
Gm
3fr
B♭
The love you gave me, noth - ing else can save me, S.
O. S.
When you're gone, how can I
D♭
E♭
even try to go on?
When you're gone, though I try,

Db
Eb
3fr
To Coda
1
F
how can I car - ry on?
2
F
A7b9
5fr
F
A7b9
5fr
Dm
A7/E
F
C7
D.S. al Coda

CODA
F
When you're gone,
B♭
D♭
E♭
3fr
F
how can I even try to go on?
B♭
D♭
E♭
3fr
When you're gone, though I try, how can I car - ry on?
F
A/E
Dm
rit.

SONG ON THE SAND
(La Da Da Da)
from LA CAGE AUX FOLLES

Music and Lyric by
JERRY HERMAN

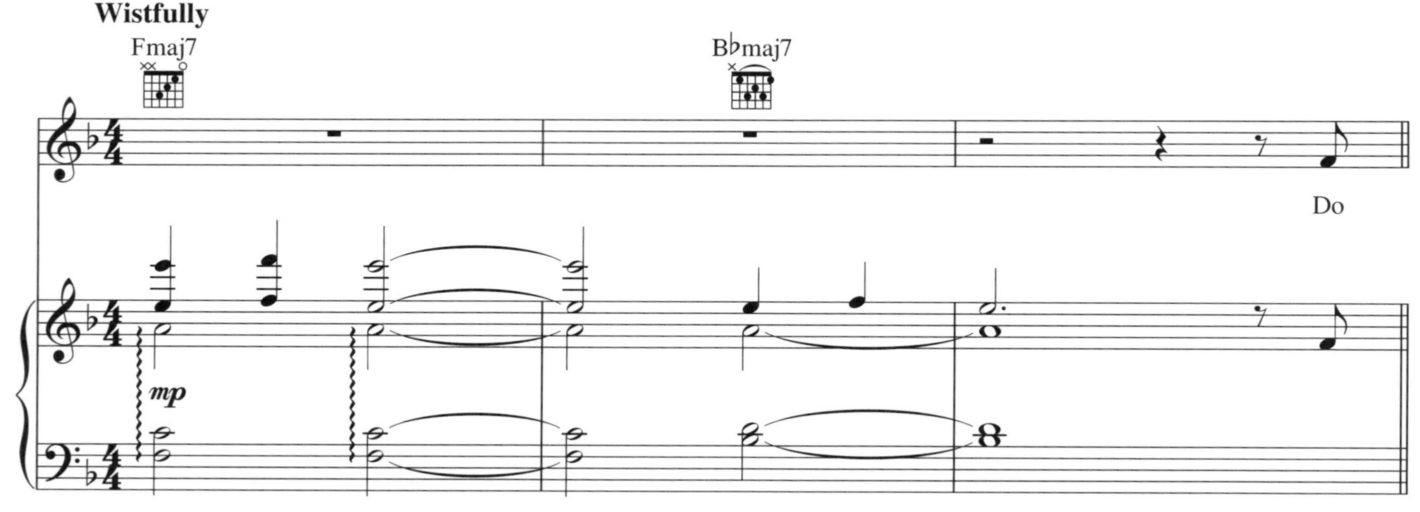

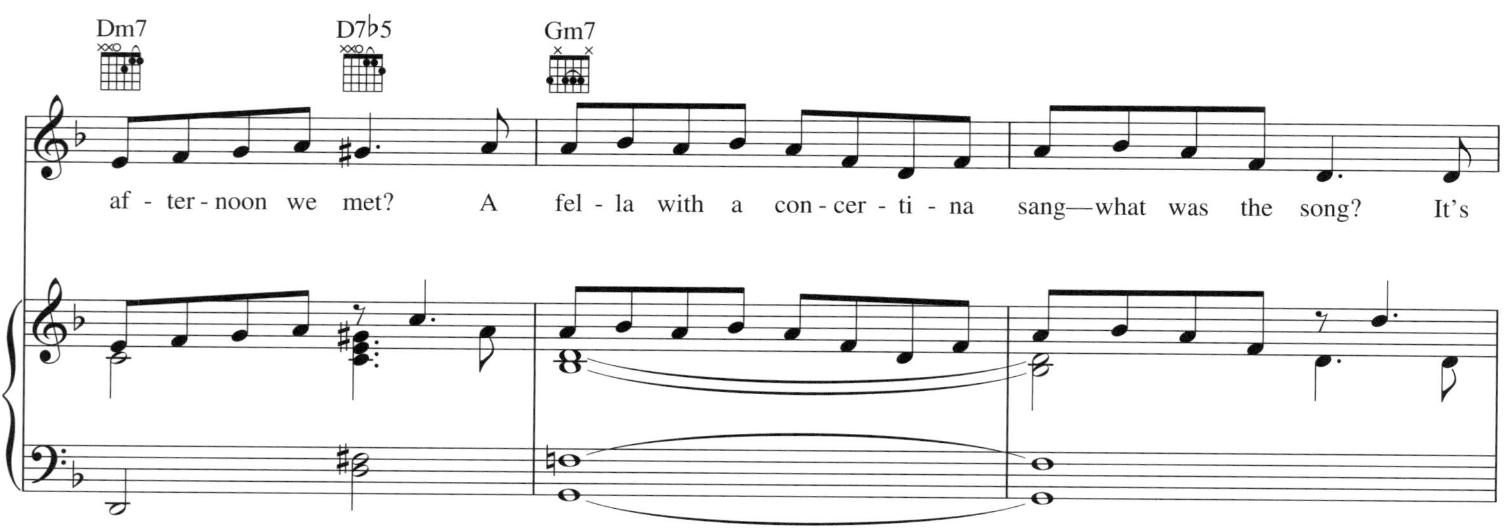

G7
Gm7
C7♭9
strange what we re - call, and odd what we for - get. I heard
F
Gm7
la da da da da da da da as we walked on the sand. I heard
C7sus
C7
Fmaj7
la da da da, I be - lieve it was ear - ly Sep - tem - ber. Through the
Am7♭5
D7
crash of the waves I could tell that the words were ro -

Gm
3fr
C7
man - tic— some-thing a - bout shar - ing, some-thing a - bout
F
C7
F
al - ways. Though the years race a - long, I still
Gm7
Gm7/C
Gm7
think of our song on the sand and I still try and search for the
C7
F
Am7♭5
words I can bare - ly re - mem - ber. Though the time tum - bles by, there is

D7
Gm
3fr
Gm7♭5
one thing that I am for - ev - er cer - tain of— I hear
F/C
Gm7
C7♯5
8fr
la da da da da da da da da da da da dum and I'm young and in
F
Gm7
D7♯5
love.
Gm7
C11
F
I be - lieve it was ear - ly Sep - tem - ber. Through the

Am7
D7
crash of the waves I could tell that the words were ro-
Gm
3fr
C
man - tic— some-thing a - bout shar - ing, some-thing a - bout
F
D7
G
al - ways. Though the years race a - long, I still
8va
B♭dim7
Am7
Am
F/A
think of our song on the sand and I still try and search for the

Am6 D7 Gmaj7 Bm7♭5
words I can bare - ly re - mem - ber. Though the time tum - bles by, there is
8va
E7/B Am Am7♭5
one thing that I am for - ev - er cer - tain of— I hear
G/D Am7 D7♭9
4fr
la da da da da da da da da da da da da, and I'm young and in
G G6 G
love.

THE SPARK OF CREATION

from CHILDREN OF EDEN

Music and Lyrics by
STEPHEN SCHWARTZ

C C6 C7 C6 C7
burn - ing in - side me can - not be de - nied.
let there be some - thing, some - thing made by me.
C C6 C7 C6 C7 C C6 C7
I've got a feel - ing that the Fa - ther who made us, when He was kin - dl - ing the
There's things wait - ing for me to in - vent them. There's worlds wait - ing for me
C6 C7 Dm
pulse in my veins, He left a ti - ny spark of that fi - re
to ex - plore. I am an ech - o of the e - ter - nal
C C6 C7 C6 C7 F(9 #11)
smol - der - ing in - side. The spark of cre - a - tion
cry of, "Let there be..." The spark of cre - a - tion
3

C C6 C7 C6 C7
is flick - er - ing with - in me. The
burn - ing bright with - in me . . . The
F(9 #11) C(9)
spark of cre - a - tion is blaz - ing in my
spark of cre - a - tion won't let me rest at
F(9 #11) Cmaj7/E F B♭/D
blood, A bit of the fire that lit up the stars and breathed
all, un - til I dis - cov - er or build or un - cov - er a
Em7 Am7 Dm7
life in - to the mud. The first in - spi - ra - tion,
thing that I can call my cel - e - bra - tion
3

G7sus
C
C6
C7
C6
C7
the spark of cre - a -
of the spark of cre - a -
C
C6
C7
1.
C6
C7
2.
C6
C7
tion . . .
tion . . .
The
F(9 #11)
Cmaj7/E
spark of cre - a - tion:
May it burn for - ev -
F(9 #11)
er.
The spark of cre - a - tion:
I am a

Cmaj7/E
keep - er of the flame.
F(9 ♯11)
Cmaj7/E
We think all we want is a
F
B♭/D
Em7
Am7
life - time of lei - sure, each per - fect day the same end - less va -
Dm7(11)
G7sus
ca - tion.
Well, that's all right, if you're a
kind of crus - ta - cean,
but when you're born with an i - mag - i - na - tion,

soon - er or la - ter, you're feel - ing the fire get hot - ter and high - er...
C C6 C7 C6 C7
The spark of
C C6 C7 C6 C7 F(9 #11) Cmaj7/E
cre - a - tion!
C# B G(4) C
8va

STANDING ON THE CORNER

from THE MOST HAPPY FELLA

A♭7
4fr
D7
Gmaj7
B7
Broth - er, you don't know a nic - er oc - cu -
Broth - er, if you've got a rich i - mag - i -
Broth - er, you can't go to jail for what you're
Em7
Am7♭5
D7
D7♭9
4fr
D7
D7♯5
pa - tion, mat - ter of fact, nei - ther do I than
na - tion, give it a whirl, give it a try. Try
think - ing, or for the "wooooo" look in your eye. You're on - ly
Gmaj7
Bm7
Am7
A♭7
4fr
Gmaj7
Am7♭5
stand - ing on the cor - ner watch - ing all the girls, watch - ing all the girls, watch - ing all the
To Coda
Adim
D7
Gmaj7
Am7
B♭7
B7
Em
Em/D♯
girls go by.
I'm the cat
Sat - ur - day,

Em/D
A7/C♯
Cmaj7
B♭
Am7
D7
that got the cream, have - n't got a girl, __ but I can dream.
and I'm so broke, could - n't buy a girl __ a nick - el coke.
Em
B/D♯
Em
E♭7
G
D7♯9
Have - n't got a girl, __ but I can wish, so I take me down to Main Street and
Still I'm liv - ing like __ a mil - lion - aire, when I take me down to Main Street and
Gmaj7
D7♯9
Gmaj7
D9
E♭7
D7
that's where I se - lect my i - mag - i - na - ry dish!
I re - view the ha - rem pa - rad - ing for me there.
E♭7
D7
D.S. al Coda
CODA
Gmaj7
E♭maj7
A♭maj7
Gmaj7(add13)
by. __

TRY TO REMEMBER

from THE FANTASTICKS

Words by TOM JONES
Music by HARVEY SCHMIDT

B♭
C7
F
F/A
kind of Sep - tem - ber when grass was green and
life was so ten - der that dreams were kept be -
nice to re - mem - ber with - out a hurt the

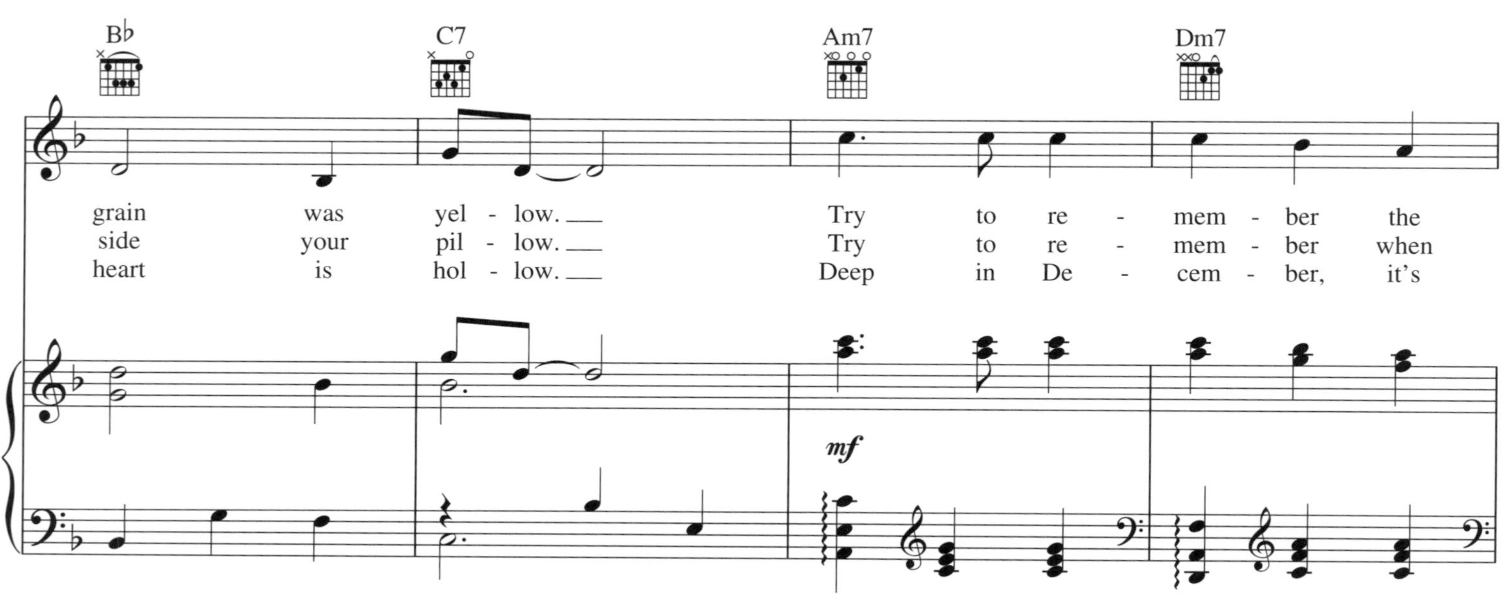
B♭
C7
Am7
Dm7
grain was yel - low. Try to re - mem - ber the
side your pil - low. Try to re - mem - ber when
heart is hol - low. Deep in De - cem - ber, it's
mf

Gm7
C7
Fmaj7
B♭maj7
kind of Sep - tem - ber when you were a ten - der and
life was so ten - der that love was an em - ber a -
nice to re - mem - ber the fire of Sep - tem - ber that

E♭
3fr
C7
F
F/A
cal - low fel - low. Try to re - mem - ber and
bout to bil - low. Try to re - mem - ber and
made us mel - low. Deep in De - cem - ber, our
decresc.
p
B♭
C7
1, 2
F
F/A
if you re - mem - ber, then fol - low.
if you re - mem - ber, then fol - low.
hearts should re - mem - ber and
B♭maj7
C7
3
F
F/A
fol - low.
B♭maj7
C7
F
Fol - low.
8va
rit. e decresc.
pp

STARS
from LES MISÉRABLES

Music by CLAUDE-MICHEL SCHÖNBERG
Lyrics by HERBERT KRETZMER and ALAIN BOUBLIL

A
F♯m7
B
yield till we come face to face, till we come face to
C♯m
F♯m
B
mp
face. He knows his way in the dark, but mine is the way of the
G♯m
F♯m
B7
Lord. And those who fol-low the path of the right-eous shall have their re-
E
E7
Am
D7
cresc.
mf
ward. And if they fall as Lu-ci-fer fell, the

G
B
flame, the sword!
dim.
E
G♯m/D♯
C♯m
E/B
B
Stars, in your mul - ti - tudes, scarce to be
p
A
F♯m7
B7
count - ed, fill - ing the dark - ness, with or - der and
E
G♯m/D♯
C♯m
E/B
B
light. You are the sen - ti - nels, si - lent and

A
F♯m7
B
sure, keep-ing watch in the night, keep-ing watch in the
mp
C♯m
F♯m
B
night. You know your place in the skies. You hold your course and your
mp
G♯m
F♯m
B7
aim. And each in your sea-son re-turns and re-turns and is al-ways the
E
E7
Am
D7
same. And if you fall as Lu-ci-fer fell, you
cresc.
mf

G
B
fall
in
flame!
And so it has
f
E
G♯m/D♯
Bm/D
A/C♯
4
been and so it is writ-ten on the door - ways to Par-a-dise, that those who
f
Am/C
E/B
F♯/A♯
fal - ter and those who fall must pay the
B
G
Bm/F♯
price.
cresc.
f

Em
G/D
D
C
Am
Lord let me find him, that I may
dim.
p
D
D7
G
Bm/F♯
D/F♯
see him safe be-hind bars. I will
mf
Em
G/D
D
C
Am7
nev-er rest 'til then, This I
cresc.
D
G
Bm/F♯
D/F♯
Em7
D
G
swear! This I swear by the stars!
f
rall.
a tempo
rall.

SUPERCALIFRAGILISTICEXPIALIDOCIOUS

from the Stageplay MARY POPPINS

Music and Lyrics by RICHARD M. SHERMAN
and ROBERT B. SHERMAN
Additional Music by GEORGE STILES
Additional Lyrics by ANTHONY DREWE

Freely
B♭7
E♭
3fr
C7sus
C7
con - ver - sa - tion keen. You need to find a way to say pre -
rit.
Bright 𝅗𝅥 = 110
C
B♭/D
E♭dim7
C7/E
F7
B♭
cise - ly what you mean. Su - per - cal - i - frag - il - is - tic -
G7/B
Cm7
3fr
F7sus
F7
ex - pi - al - i - do - cious! E - ven though the sound of it is
F7sus
F7/C♭
B♭
B♭maj7
some - thing quite a - tro - cious, if you say it loud e - nough, you'll

B♭7 E♭ Edim7 B♭/F Bdim7
al - ways sound pre - co - cious. Su - per - cal - i - frag - il - is - tic -
Cm7 F7 B♭
MRS. CORRY & CUSTOMERS:
ex - pi - al - i - do - cious. Um did - dle did - dle did - dle,
Cm7 F7 B♭ Cm7 F7
um did - dle ay. Um did - dle did - dle did - dle, um did - dle ay.
B♭ Cm7 F7 B♭
Um did - dle did - dle did - dle, um did - dle ay. Um did - dle did - dle did - dle,

Cm7
3fr
F7
B♭
G7/B
MARY:
um did - dle ay. When Stone Age men were chat - ting, sim - ply grunt - ing would suf -
Cm7
3fr
F7sus
F7
D♭(add2)/F
F7/C
3fr
COMPANY:
BERT:
fice. Ugh! Though if they'd heard this word, they might 'ave used it once or
B♭
B♭maj7
B♭7
MRS. CORRY:
twice. I'm sure E - gyp - tian Phar - aohs would have grasped it in a
E♭
3fr
Gm7/C
C7
jiff, then ev - 'ry sin - gle pyr - a - mid would bear this hie - ro -

A little faster
F7
B♭
G7/B
glyph... Oh, su - per - cal - i - frag - il - is - tic - ex - pi - al - i -
Cm7
3fr
F7sus
F7
Fm7
F7
do - cious! Say it and wild an - i - mals will not seem so fe -
B♭
MARY:
B♭maj7
ro - cious. Add some fur - ther flour - ish - es, it's
B♭7
E♭
3fr
MRS. CORRY:
so ro - co - co - co - co - cious. Ah.

MARY:
BERT:
BERT:
Edim7
Ah. Ah ah ah ah!
MARY POPPINS, JANE, MICHAEL & MRS. CORRY:
Su - per - cal - i -
B♭/F
G7♭9
Cm7
F7
B♭
ALL:
frag - il - is - tic - ex - pi - al - i - do - cious. Um did - dle did - dle did - dle,
Cm7
F7
B♭
Cm7
F7
um did - dle ay. Um did - dle did - dle did - dle, um did - dle ay.
B
C♯m7
F♯7
B
Um did - dle did - dle did - dle, um did - dle ay! Um did - dle did - dle did - dle,

C♯m7 F♯7 B B♯dim7
BERT:
um did - dle ay! The Dru - ids could 'ave carved it on their might - y mon - o -
C♯m7 F♯7 E/F♯ F♯7 E/F♯ F♯7/C♯
MRS. CORRY:
liths. The an - cient Greeks, I'm cer - tain, would have used it in their
B Bmaj7 B7
MARY:
myths. I'm sure the Ro - man Em - pire on - ly en - tered the a -
E C♯7
byss be - cause those Lat - in schol - ars nev - er had a word like

F♯
BERT, MARY & MRS. CORRY:
D
D♯dim7
this. Su - per - cal - i - frag - il - is - tic - ex - pi - al - i -
Em7
G/A
MARY:
Am7♭5
A7
do - cious! If you say it soft - ly, the ef - fect can be hyp -
p
D
Dmaj7
D7
BERT:
no - tious. Check your breath be - fore you speak in case it's hal - i -
mf
G
G♯dim7
D/A
B7
ALL:
to - tious. Su - per - cal - i - frag - il - is - tic -
f

Em7
A7
D
ex - pi - al - i - do - cious.
Um did - dle did - dle did - dle,
Em7
A7
D
Em7
A7
um did - dle ay.
Um did - dle did - dle did - dle,
um did - dle ay.
B/F♯
C/F♯
Um did - dle did - dle did - dle,
um did - dle ay.
Um did - dle did - dle did - dle,
sub. mp
F♯
um did - dle ay!
MARY: Of course, you can say it backwards, which is suoicodilaipxecitsiligarfilacrepus.
MICHAEL: She may be tricky, but she's bloody good.
ff
p
(vamp)

B
MARY:
B♯dim7
So when the cat has got your tongue, there's no need for dis -
f
C♯m7
F♯9sus
4fr
F♯9
3fr
may. Just sum - mon up this word and then you've got a lot to
B
BERT:
Bmaj7
B7
say. Pick out those eight - een con - so - nants, add six - teen vowels as
E
G♯m7/C♯
C♯7
F♯7
well, and put them in an or - der which is ver - y 'ard to spell.
rit.

Very slowly
B/F♯
E/F♯
F♯7
MARY:
S - u - p - e - r - c - a - l - i - f - r - a - g - i - l...
mp
Quickly
C♯m7
Bsus2/D♯
E
F♯7sus
Bsus
B
JANE & MICHAEL:
4fr
6fr
i - s - t - i - c - e - x - p - i - a - l - i - d - o - c - i - o - u - s.
Slower
C/G
F/G
G7
PRINCIPAL CHARACTERS:
S - u - p - e - r - c - a - l - i - f - r - a - g - i - l -
ENSEMBLE:
S - u - p - e - r - c - a - l - i - f - r - a - g - i - l -

Dm7(add4)
Csus2/E
F(add2)
G7sus
F/C
C
ALL:
i - s - t - i - c - e - x - p - i - a - l - i - d - o - c - i - o - u - s.
accel.
A little faster
Db/Ab
Gb/Ab
Ab7
S - u - p - e - r - c - a - l - i - f - r - a - g - i - l -
S - u - p - e - r - c - a - l - i - f - r - a - g - i - l -
mf
Ebm7(add4)
Bbm7/F
Gb6/9
Ab7sus
Db
Ab7/Db
Db
Ab7/Db
Db
A7
i - s - t - i - c - e - x - p - i - a - l - i - d - o - c - i - o - u - s.
accel.

Faster
D
D♯dim7
Em7
Su - per - cal - i - frag - il - is - tic - ex - pi - al - i - do - cious.
f
A7sus
A7
Am7
A7/E
D
E - ven though the sound of it is some - thing quite a - tro - cious,
Dmaj7
D7
G
if you say it loud en - ough, you'll al - ways sound pre - co - cious.
G♯dim7
D/A
B7♭9
JANE & MICHAEL:
G
G♯dim7
D/A
B7♭9
Su - per - cal - i - frag - il - is - tic! Su - per - cal - i - frag - il - is - tic!
mf

G
G♯dim7
D/A
B7♭9
ALL:
Su - per - cal - i - frag - il - is - tic -
ff
Em7(add4)
Gm
G♯m7♭5
A7
ex - pi - al - i -
D
D7
do - cious.
G
C♯/G♯
D/A
B7♭9
Em7(add4)
G/A
A7
D
Su - per - cal - i - frag - il - is - tic - ex - pi - al - i - do - cious!

TAKE THAT LOOK OFF YOUR FACE

from SONG & DANCE

Music by ANDREW LLOYD WEBBER
Lyrics by DON BLACK

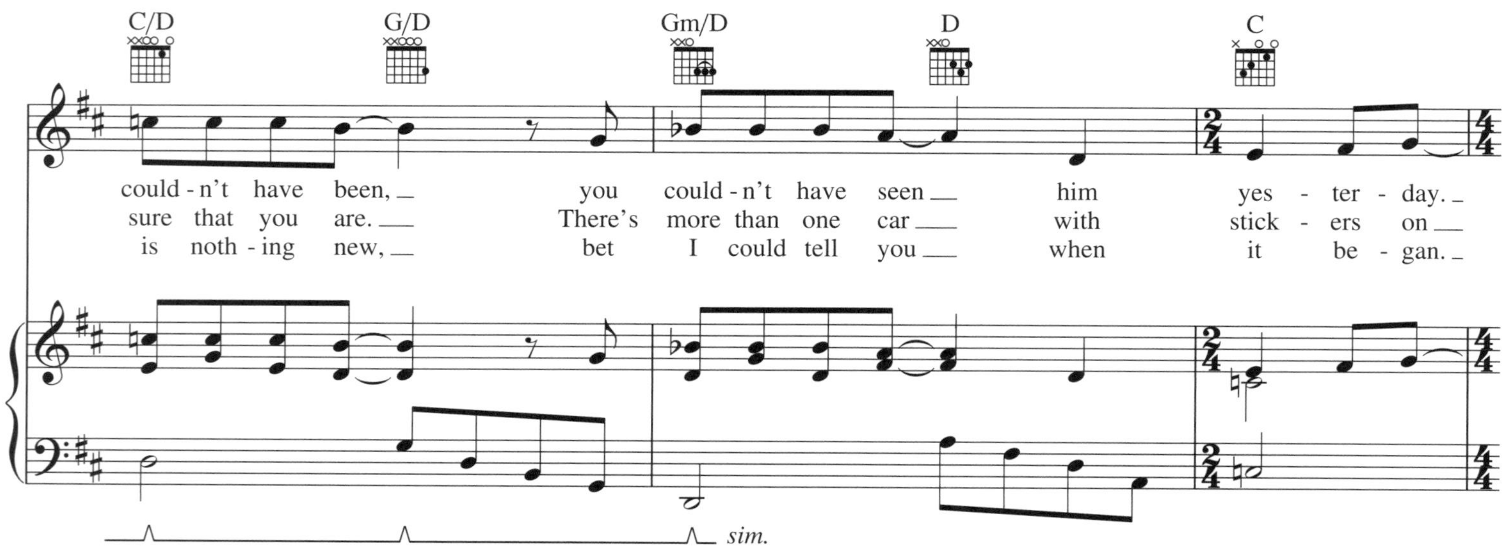

1
2, 3
G
G/A
3fr
D
A7
(Bkgd. vocals:)
hate it when he's a - way. You know if he had - n't gone.
on - ly a wom - an can.
Take that look off your face. (Take that look off your face.) I can
No, I did - n't dig deep. (No, I did - n't dig deep.) I did
see through your smile. (I can see through your smile.) You would
not want to know. (I did not want to know.) Well, you
love to be right, I bet you did - n't sleep good last night, could - n't wait to bring
don't in - ter - fere when you're scared of the things you might hear. When he's back, you think
f

G7 Bm

all of that bad news to my door. Well, I've
I will end it right there and then. Well, my

G7 D/F♯ Em7 D 1 G/D D

got news for you, I knew be - fore.
fair weath - er friend, you're wrong a - gain.

2 G(add2)/D

If (Take that

D

look off your face.) Take that look off your face. (I can

A7
see through your smile.) I can see through your smile. You would
D
A7
love to be right, I bet you did-n't sleep good last night, could-n't wait to bring
G7
Bm
G7
all of that bad news to my door. Well, I've got news for you,
G
D/F♯
Em7
D
G(add2)/D
Repeat and Fade
I knew be - fore. (Take that

THEY CALL THE WIND MARIA

from PAINT YOUR WAGON

Words by ALAN JAY LERNER
Music by FREDERICK LOEWE

Am
B♭maj7
Am7
Gm9
3fr
C9
F
fire is Joe, and they call the wind Ma - ri - a.
she had me, and the sun was al - ways shin - in'.
all a - lone, there ain't no word but "lone - ly."

Ma - ri - a blows the stars a - round, and
But then one day I lost my girl, I
And I'm a lost and lone - ly man, with -

Am
Dm
sends the clouds a - fly - in'. Ma - ri - a makes the
left her far be - hind me. And now I'm lost, so
out a star to guide me. Ma - ri - a blow my

Am
Gm7
C13
C7
F
moun - tain sound like folks up there are dy - in'.
gol - durn lost, not e - ven God can find me.
love to me; I need my girl be - side me.
Dm
Dm(maj7)
Dm7
Ma - ri - a!
Ma -
Am
Am(maj7)
Am7
Am6
B♭maj7
Am7
ri - a!
They call the
Gm9
C7
1, 2
F
wind Ma - ri - a!
Be -
Out

3
F
Dm
ri - a!
Ma - ri - a!
Dm(maj7)
Dm7
Am
Am(maj7)
Am7
Am6
Ma - ri - a!
F/C
C
B♭/C
C7
F
Blow my love to me!
8vb

THIS NEARLY WAS MINE

from SOUTH PACIFIC

Lyrics by OSCAR HAMMERSTEIN II
Music by RICHARD RODGERS

E♭
Fm/B♭
E♭
This nearly was mine.
One
Fm7
F♯dim
E♭/G
B♭/D
D♭dim
girl for my dream,
One partner in
A♭/C
A♭m/C♭
E♭/B♭
Cm/A
paradise,
This promise of
A♭
A♭m
E♭
Fm/B♭
paradise
This nearly was

E♭
A♭
E♭7
A♭
mine.
Close to my heart she came
B♭
On - ly to fly a - way,
On - ly to fly as day
cresc.
F7
Fm7/B♭
B♭7
flies from moon - light.
f
dim. e poco rit.

E♭
Fm7
E♭/G
E♭/B♭
B♭/D
3fr
6fr
Now, now I'm a - lone, Still
mp a tempo
D♭dim
A♭/C
A♭m/C♭
E♭/B♭
4fr
dream - ing of par - a - dise, Still
Cm/A
A♭maj7
Cm/A
E♭
say - ing that par - a - dise Once
f allargando
Fm/B♭
To Coda
1
E♭
Em6
B♭7
2
E♭
near - ly was mine. mine.
a tempo

Verse
D7
Gm
3fr
D7♯5
So clear and deep are my fan - cies
mf
D7
Gm
3fr
D7sus
D7
Of things I wish were true. I'll
Gm
3fr
Cm/A
4fr
D7
G
keep re - mem - b'ring eve - nings I wish I'd
D+
G
Gm
3fr
spent with you. I'll keep re -
mp

D♭13
3fr
G♭
mem - b'ring kiss - es
From lips I'll
F13
B♭
nev - er own,
And all the
E♭m
6fr
B♭/F
E♭dim/F
love - ly ad - ven - tures
That we have nev - er
f espressivo
mf
B♭
D.S. al Coda
known.
rit.
CODA
E♭
3fr
mine.
f

THOROUGHLY MODERN MILLIE

from THOROUGHLY MODERN MILLIE

Words by SAMMY CAHN
Music by JAMES VAN HEUSEN

F/C
G7
C7
heav - en knows, the world has gone to rack and to
F6
Fdim7
F6
Fdim7
ruin.
F6
Fdim7
F6
A7
What we
f
mf
Dm
Dm(maj7)
Dm7
think is chic, u - nique, and quite a - dor - a - ble,

G9
F6/C
D♭7♭5
they think is odd and Sod - om and Go -
cresc.
C
D♭/C
B♭7♭5
mor - rah - ble!
f
A7
N.C.
D
But the fact is ev - 'ry - thing to - day is thor - ough - ly
mf
E9
E13
N.C.
A7
A7/B
mod - ern. (Check your per - son - al - i - ty.) Ev - 'ry - thing to -

Cdim7
A7/C♯
D7
D9
4fr
N.C.
day makes yes - ter - day slow.
(Bet - ter face re - al - i - ty.)
G
Gm6
3fr
D
F♯7/C♯
It's not in - san - i - ty, says Van - i - ty
Bm
E13
F♯m
Gdim
E7/G♯
Fair. In fact, it's styl - ish to
N.C.
A7
Adim7
A7
Adim7
raise your skirts and bob your hair,
Raise your skirts and bob your hair,
Raise your skirts and

F9
E9
A7
D6
bob your hair!
bob your hair!
Have you seen the way they kiss in the
E9
E13
N.C.
A7
movies? (Isn't it delectable?) Painting lips and
N.C.
F♯13
N.C.
pencilining your brow now is quite respectable.
G
Gm6
3fr
D
Goodbye, good goody girl, I'm changing, and
3
3

B9
Em7
A
Em7
A7
Em7
A7
Em7
how. So beat the drums 'cause here comes Thor - ough - ly Mod - ern
G/A
A7
D6
B♭7
D
Bdim7
Mil - lie now!
F♯7
Bm
Bm(maj7)
What we think is chic, u - nique, and quite a -
Bm7
E9
Bm
dor - a - ble, they think is odd and

E7
A
Sod - om and Go - mor - rah - ble! But the fact is,
F
N.C.
G9
9fr
ev - 'ry - thing to - day is thor - ough - ly mod - ern.
mp
N.C.
C7
(Bands are get - tin' jazz - i - er.) Ev - 'ry - thing to - day is start - ing to
F13
N.C.
N.C.
B6
go. (Cars are get - tin' snaz - zi - er.) Men say
mf

B♭m
F/C
A7
Dm
it's crim - i - nal what wom - en - 'll do.
G9
9fr
N.C.
C7
What they're for - get - ting is this is nine - teen
F
twen - ty - two!
f
G7
Am7
B♭m6
6fr
G7/B
C9

F9
Bb6
Good - bye,
Bbm
good good -
- y girl,
F/C
I'm chang - ing, and
D9
4fr
how!
mf cresc.
N.C.
I'm chang - ing, and
A7
D9
4fr
how!
So
f
mp

N.C.
beat the drums 'cause here comes thor - ough - ly Hot off the press! One step
grad. cresc.
a - head! Jazz Age! Whoop - ee, ba - by! We're so Thor - ough - ly
Gm7
Mod - ern
N.C.
Mil - lie
f
R.H.
gliss.
F
Db7
4fr
F6
now!
ff
gliss.
gliss.

TO LIFE

from the Musical FIDDLER ON THE ROOF

Words by SHELDON HARNICK
Music by JERRY BOCK

B♭m7
G7
D7♭9
D7
G7sus
G7
Drink l' - chai - im to life, to life, l' -
Cm
C7
chai - im! L' - chai - im, l' - chai - im, to
Fm
B♭7
E♭maj7
life!
One day it's hon - ey and rai - sin cake,
A gift we sel - dom are wise e - nough
A♭maj7
D♭
D♭maj7
B♭maj7
G7
next day a stom - ach ache,
ev - er to prize e - nough,
drink l' - chai - im to

C C7 Fm Cm
life!
Our great men have writ - ten words of
God would like us to be joy - ful,
D7 G7 Cm C7
wis - dom to be used when hard - ship must be faced;
E - ven though our hearts lie pant - ing on the floor;
Fm Cm D7
Life o - blig - es us with hard - ship, so the words of wis - dom
How much more can we be joy - ful, when there's real - ly some - thing
G D7♭9 D7 G7sus G7
should - n't go to waste. To us and our good
to be joy - ful for. To life! To life! L' -
3fr
4fr

Cm
3fr
C7
Fm
for - tune, Be hap - py, be health - y, long life!
chai - im. L'- chai - im, l' - chai - im, to life!
B♭7
E♭maj7
3fr
A♭maj7
D♭
D♭maj7
And if our good for - tune nev - er comes, here's to what - ev - er comes,
It gives you some-thing to think a - bout, some-thing to drink a - bout,
B♭m7
G7
1
Cm
3fr
drink l' - chai - im to life!
2
Cm
3fr
G7
Cm
3fr
To life!
8vb

TOO CLOSE FOR COMFORT

from the Musical MR. WONDERFUL

Words and Music by JERRY BOCK,
LARRY HOLOFCENER and GEORGE WEISS

Moderately
E/B
A/B
B7
E
Am7
D7
a wom-an and man in love. Since I can - not con - sult a book of
G
Am7
D7
G
knowl - edge that may be ly - ing on a shelf, I
Not too slowly, with a beat
B♭7
E♭
3fr
Dm7
guess I'll have a con - fi - den - tial dis - cus - sion with my - self.
Passionately
G7
C6
Be wise, be

Cm6
3fr
Gm6
3fr
A7
smart, be - have, my heart. Don't up -
Fm6
G7
C6
Cmaj7
set your cart when {she's / he's} so close. __
C7
C6
Cm6
3fr
Be soft, be sweet, but
Gm6
3fr
A7
Fm6
G7
be dis - creet. Don't go off your beat. {She's / He's} too

C
C6
C+
F6
F7
close for com - fort, too close, too
Fm6
C
C7
close for com - fort. Please, not a - gain.
F6
F7
Fm6
A♭7
4fr
Too close, too close to know just when to say when.
G7
C6
Cm6
3fr
Gm6
3fr
Be firm, be fair, be sure, be -

A7
Fm6
G7
C
ware. On your guard, take care while there's such temp -
C6
C+
F6
F7
Fm6
ta - tion. One thing leads to an - oth - er,
Cm6
D7
A♭9
G9
too late to run for cov - er. She's / He's much too
To Coda
G7♭9
Cm7
D7
G7
D.S. al Coda
close for com - fort now! Be

CODA
Cm7
3fr
now!
Too close,
too close.
Cm6
Ab9
G9
G7b9
Cm
Cm/Bb
She's
He's
much too close for com - fort now!
F7/A
Ab7
Cm/G
Ab/Gb
F7
Db7b5
Cm
sfz

WHAT DID I HAVE THAT I DON'T HAVE?

from ON A CLEAR DAY YOU CAN SEE FOREVER

Words by ALAN JAY LERNER
Music by BURTON LANE

Ab
Ab+
Ab6
Ab+
4fr
4fr
3fr
4fr
What did I have that I don't have?
rall.
pp
Ab
Ab6
Adim7
Bbm7
Eb7
Ab7
What did he like that I lost track of?
What did I do that
Dbmaj7
C7
Fm7
Bb7sus
Bb7
Eb7
I don't do the way I did be - fore?
Ab
Ab+
Ab6
Ab+
Ab
Ab6
What is - n't there that once was there?
What have I got a

G7 Cm7 Fm7 B♭7 E♭maj7 A♭maj7
great big lack of? Some-thing in me then he could see then
D♭maj7 B♭7 E♭7 N.C. D♭6 D♭+
beck-ons to him no more. I'm
D♭6 E♭7 A♭6 Cm7 Bdim7
just a vic-tim of time, ob-so-lete in my
B♭m7 E♭7 G7 C7 F7
prime, out of date and out-classed

B♭m7
E♭7
A♭
A♭+
A♭6
A♭+
by my past.
What did he love that there's none of?
pp
A♭
A♭6
Adim7
B♭m7
E♭7
A♭7
What did I lose the sweet warm knack of?
Would-n't I be the
D♭maj7
C7
Fm
Fm/E♭
B♭7/D
B♭7
E7
late, great me If I knew how?
Oh!
rall.
A♭maj7/E♭
B♭m7
E♭7
A♭6
What did I have I don't have now?
fp

E♭7
N.C.
D♭6
D♭+
D♭6
E♭7
Where can I go to re -
mf
A♭6
3fr
G7
Bdim7
pair all the wear and the
B♭m7
E♭7
G7
tear, till I'm once a - gain
C7
F7
B♭m7
E♭7
A♭
4fr
A♭+
4fr
the pre - vious me?
What did he like that
pp

A♭6
A♭+
A♭
A♭6
Adim7
B♭m7
E♭7
I'm not like?
What was the charm that I've run dry of?
A♭7
D♭maj7
C7
Fm
Fm/E♭
What would I give if my old know - how still knew
B♭7/D
B♭7
E7
A♭maj7/E♭
how!
Oh!
What did I have I
rall.
fp
B♭m7
E♭7
A♭6
don't have now?
ff

WHAT KIND OF FOOL AM I?

from the Musical Production STOP THE WORLD—I WANT TO GET OFF

Words and Music by LESLIE BRICUSSE
and ANTHONY NEWLEY

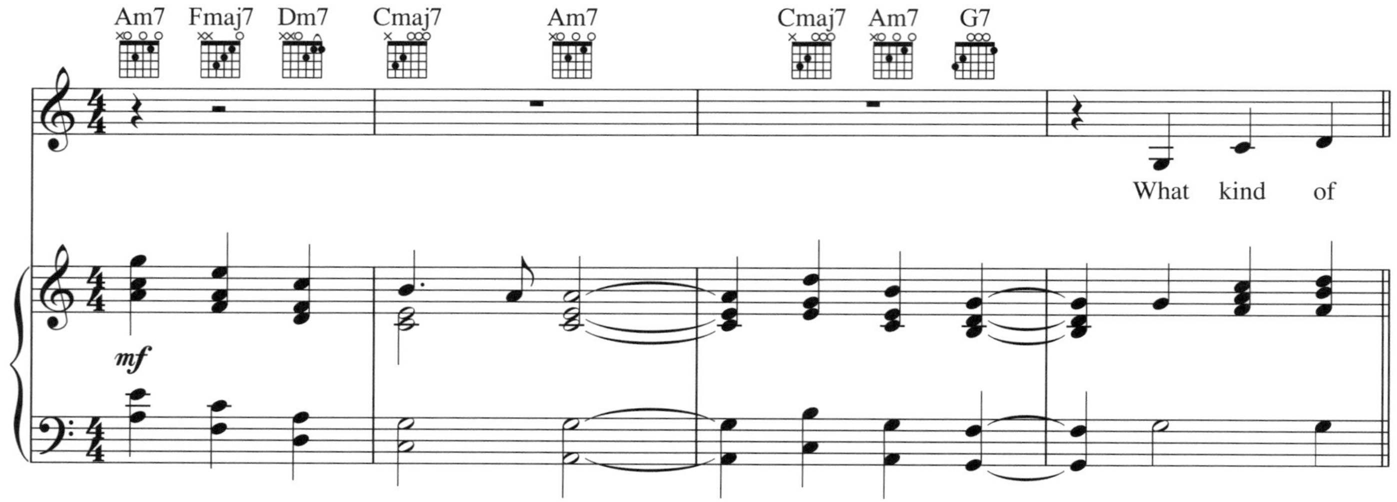

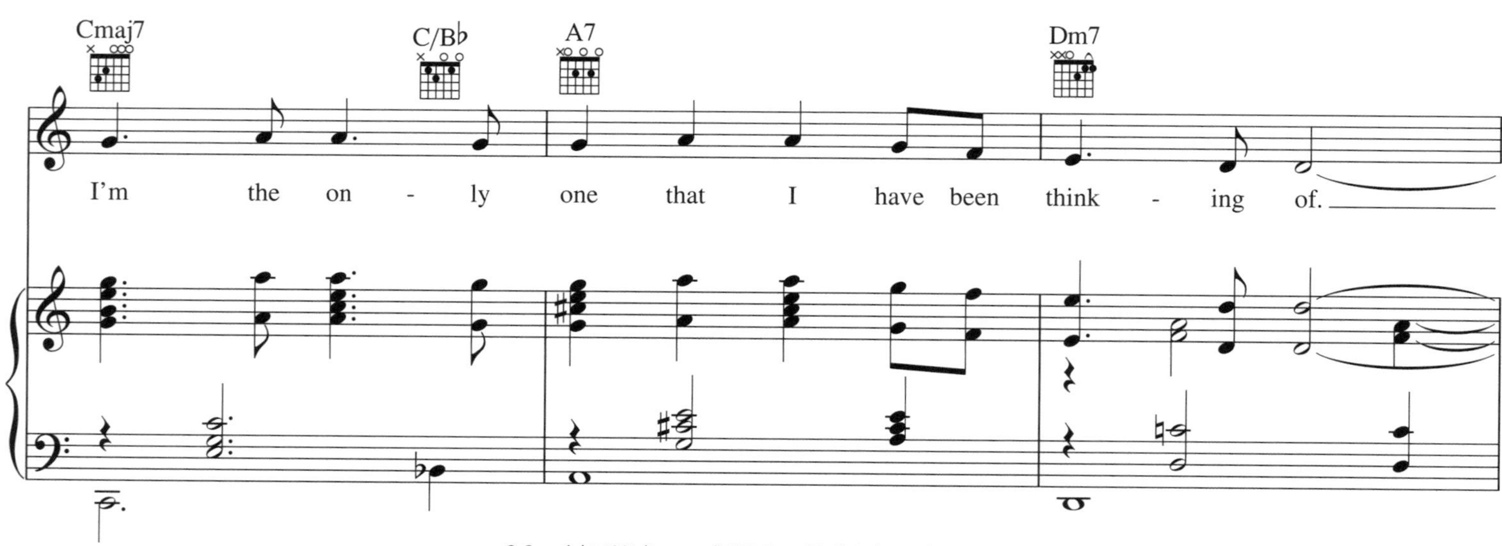

Dm7/G
G7
C
Am7
What kind of
man
life
is this?
An emp - ty
D7
G/B
Em7
Am7
D7
shell,
a lone - ly
cell
in which
an
emp - ty
heart
must
Gsus
3fr
G7
Cmaj7
dwell.
What kind of
lips
are
these
that
lied
with
clown
am
I?
What
do
I
Dm7(add4)
3fr
G7
Cmaj7
ev - 'ry
kiss?
That
whis - pered
emp - ty
words
of
know
of
life?
Why
can't
I
cast
a - way
the

Gm/B♭
A7
Gm7
C7
love that left me a - lone like this? Why can't I
mask of play and live my life? Why can't I
F6
Dm7♭5
C/E
fall in love like an - y oth - er man
fall in love 'til I don't give a damn
D7
Dm7
Fm
G7♭9
and may - be then I'll know what kind of fool I
1
C
Cmaj7
Am7
Fmaj7
Fmaj7/G
F/G
G7
am. What kind of
2
C
Cmaj7
Am7
Fmaj7
Dm7
Cmaj7
am.

THE WINNER TAKES IT ALL

from MAMA MIA!

Words and Music by BENNY ANDERSSON
and BJÖRN ULVAEUS

A♭m/E♭
D♭
me, now it's his - to - ry.
sense, build - ing me a fence,
same when she calls your name?
stand you've come to shake my hand.

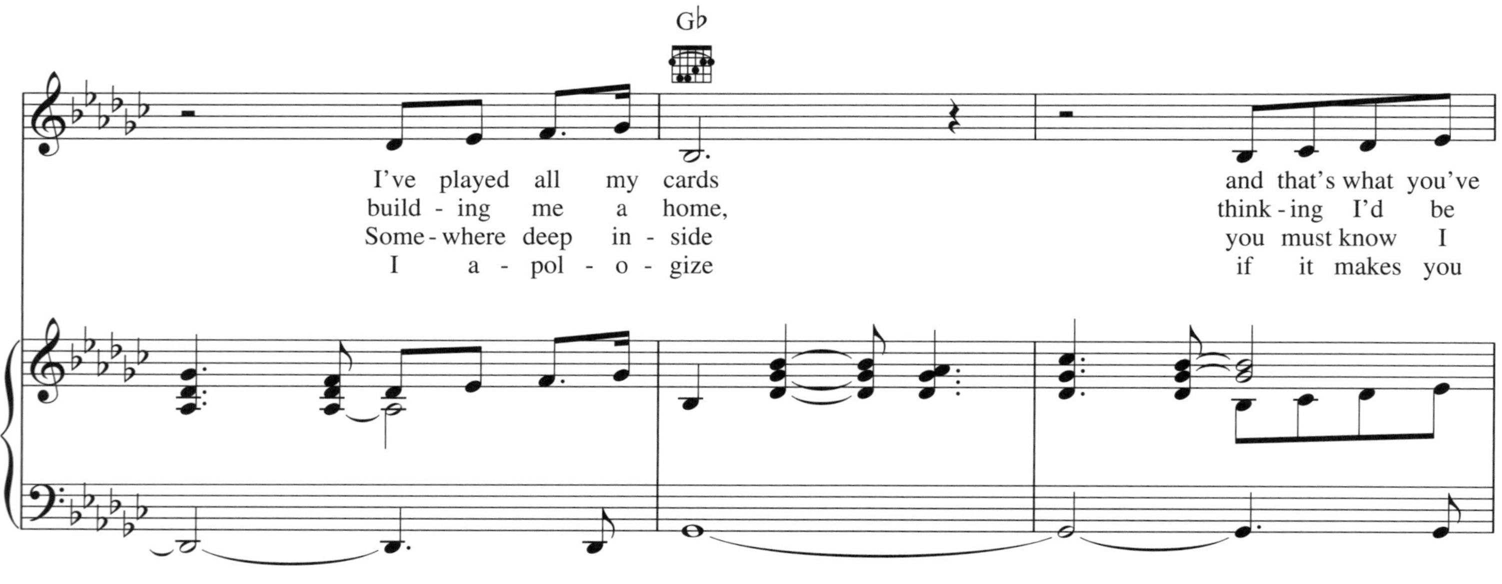
G♭
I've played all my cards and that's what you've
build - ing me a home, think - ing I'd be
Some - where deep in - side you must know I
I a - pol - o - gize if it makes you

D♭/F
A♭m/E♭
done, too, noth - ing more to say,
strong there, but I was a fool,
miss you, but what can I say,
feel bad see - ing me so tense,

To Coda
D♭
no more ace to play.
play - ing by the rules.
rules must be o - beyed.
no self con - fi - dence.
The win - ner takes it
The gods may throw a
The judg - es will de -
The win - ner takes it

G♭
B♭7/D
E♭m
6fr
all, the los - er stand - ing small
dice, their minds as cold as ice,
cide, the likes of me a - bide,

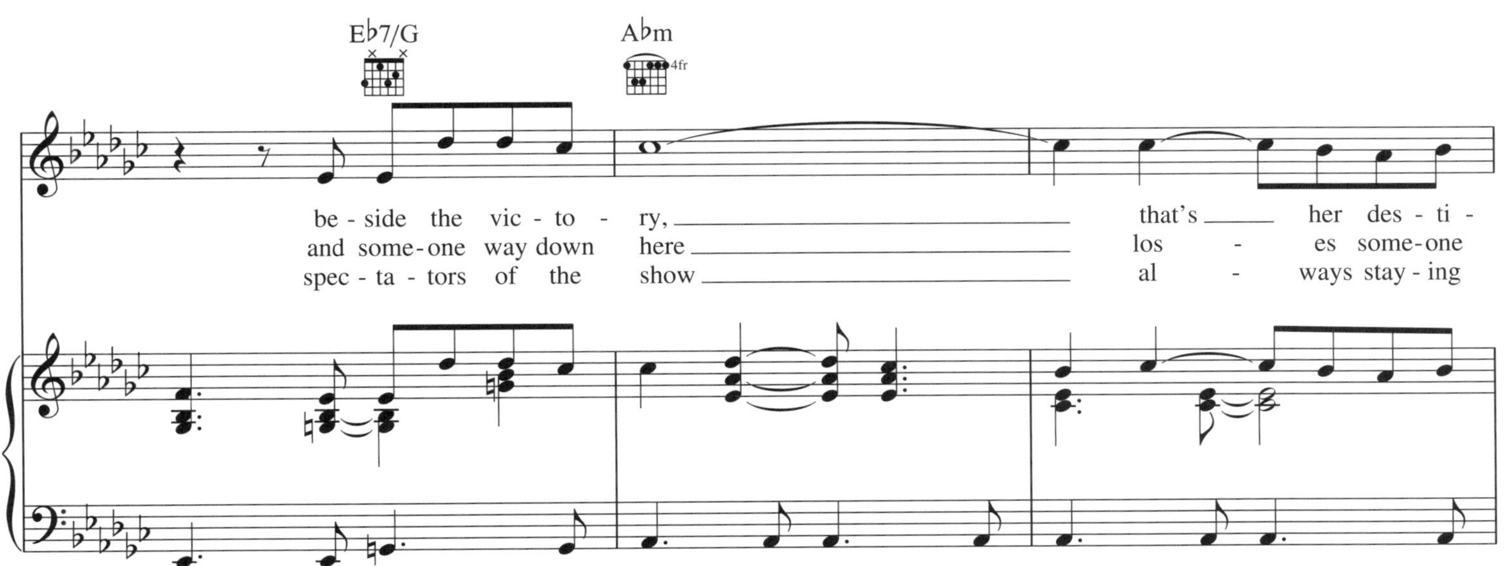
E♭7/G
A♭m
4fr
be - side the vic - to - ry, that's her des - ti -
and some - one way down here los - es some - one
spec - ta - tors of the show al - ways stay - ing

D♭
1
2, 3
ny. I was in your
dear. The win - ner takes it
low. The game is on a -
G♭
B♭7/D
E♭m
E♭7/G
all, the los - er has to fall, it's sim - ple and it's
gain, a lov - er or a friend, a big thing or a
A♭m
D♭
plain, why should I com - plain.
small, the win - ner takes it all.
1
2
D.S. al Coda
But tell me, does she
I don't wan - na

CODA
G♭
B♭7/D
E♭m
6fr
all.
E♭7/G
A♭m
4fr
D♭
The win-ner takes it all.
G♭
B♭7/D
E♭m
6fr
E♭7/G
A♭m
4fr
D♭
Repeat and Fade

WHY WAS I BORN?

from SWEET ADELINE

Lyrics By OSCAR HAMMERSTEIN II
Music by JEROME KERN

side me, I picture the pret - ti - est sto - ries on - ly to
F7
wake up, All by my - self.
B♭
D
What is the good of me, by my - self?
F7
L.H.
poco rit.
B♭
B♭/D
C♯dim7
Edim7
F7/C
F
Why was I born? Why am I
p
a tempo
con pedale

E♭/G F7/A Gm/A Gm B♭/F Em7♭5 E♭6 E♭6/G
liv - ing? What do I get? What am I
F7/A F7 B♭ B♭/D E♭maj7
giv - ing? Why do I want a thing I dare - n't hope for?
sostenuto
Ped.
F7 B♭7 E♭ E♭m(maj7) E♭m6 B♭/D
What can I hope for? I wish I knew.
Cm7 F7 B♭ B♭/D C♯dim7 Edim7 F7/C F7
Why do I try To draw you
con pedale

Eb/G F7/A Gm/A Gm Bb6/F E7b5 Eb6 Eb6/G
near me? Why do I cry? You nev - er
F7/A F7 Bb Bb6/D
hear me. I'm a poor fool, but what can I
sostenuto
Ped.
C9 Bb/F C#dim7/F Cm7/F F7
do? Why was I born to love
L.H.
3
rall. e dim.
1
Bb C9/E F7/Eb Bb/D Cm7 F7/C
you?
a tempo
f
2
Bb Eb9 Bb
you?
morendo
Ped.

WITH A SONG IN MY HEART

from SPRING IS HERE

Words by LORENZ HART
Music by RICHARD RODGERS

B♭m7
E♭7
A♭
4fr
B
time ev - 'ry meet - ing's a mar - vel - ous past - time you're in -
light not a note of our mu - sic is played out, it will
E♭/B♭
6fr
Cm
3fr
Fm7
B♭7
E♭
3fr
A♭
4fr
creas - ing - ly sweet, so when - ev - er we hap - pen to meet
be just as sweet, and an air that I'll live to re - peat:
E♭
3fr
E7/B
B♭7
B♭7♯5(♭9)
E♭
3fr
B♭7
I greet you with a song in my heart.
rall.
a tempo
E♭
3fr
B♭7
E♭
3fr
G7
I be-hold your a - dor - a - ble face, just a song at the start,
R.H.

Cm
G7
Cm
Cm/B♭
But it soon is a hymn to your grace. When the mu - sic
Am7♭5
A♭
Fm7
E♭6
D7
swells I'm touch-ing your hand; it tells that you're
Fm7
D7
G7
C7
Fm7
B♭7
E♭
stand - ing near, and at the sound of your
B♭7
E♭
B♭7
voice heav - en o - pens its por - tals to me.

E♭
G7
Cm
Can I help but re - joice
that a song such as
G7
Cm
Cm/B♭
Am7♭5
F7
E♭/B♭
ours came to be?
But I al - ways knew
I would live life
F7
E♭/B♭
A♭6
B♭7
through
with a song in my heart for
rall.
1
E♭
E7/B
B♭7
B♭7♯5(♭9)
2
E♭
you.
you.
a tempo

THE WIZARD AND I

from the Broadway Musical WICKED

Music and Lyrics by
STEPHEN SCHWARTZ

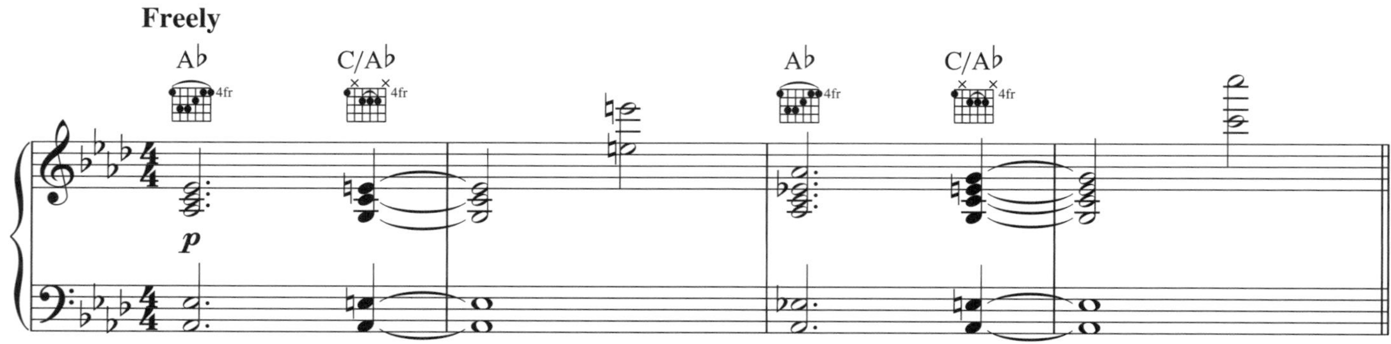

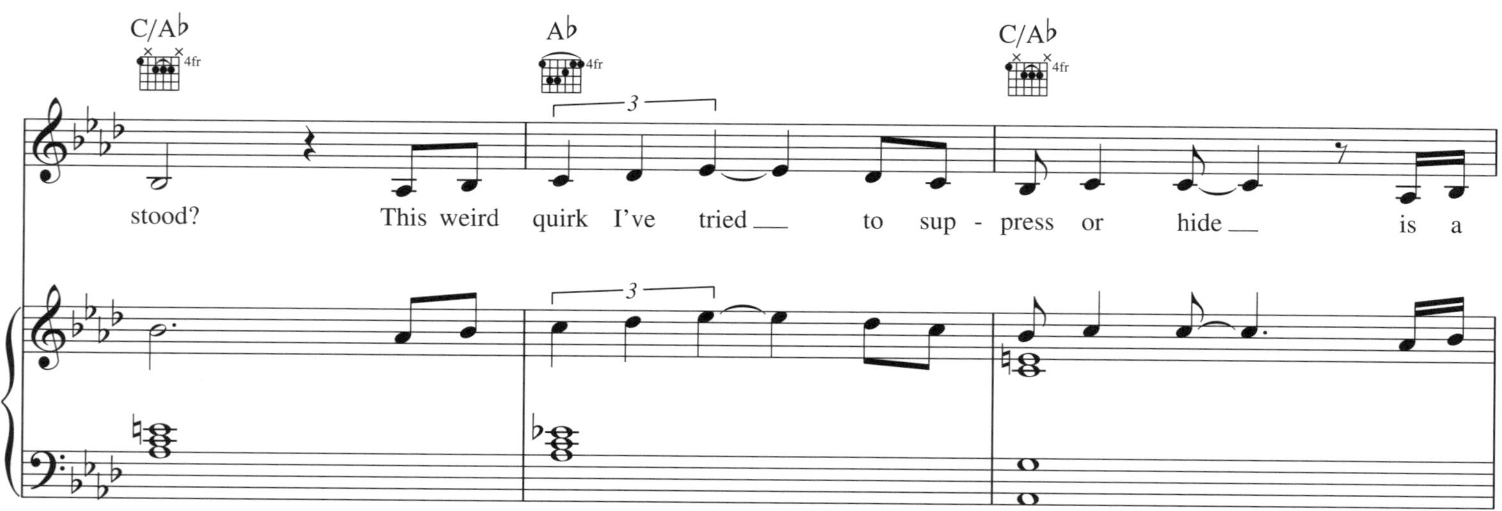

Fm/A♭
A♭7(add4)
A♭7♯5
D♭maj9
tal - ent that could help me meet the Wiz - ard
mf
B♭m7
E♭7/G
Cm7
G♭(add9)
if I make good! So I'll make
rit.
dim.
Pulsing with excitement
C
Dm/C
G7sus/C
G/C
good...
p
When I meet the Wiz - ard
Once I prove my worth,

C
C/B
Am7
Dm7
C/F
Gsus
3fr
and then I meet the Wiz - ard
What I've wait-ed for since—
G/C
C
Dm/C
G7sus/C
G/C
since birth!
And with all his Wiz-ard wis - dom, by my
C
Em
B♭maj7/F
looks, he won't be blind - ed...
Do you think the Wiz - ard is
C/G
B♭maj7/F
Gsus
G
dumb?
Or like Munch-kins, so small-mind - ed?
No!
He'll

Am7 Dm7(add4) G/B C/E Am7 Dm7(add4)
3fr
say to me: "I see who you tru-ly are: A girl on whom I can re-
Gsus G C Dm7 C/E Fsus F
ly!" And that's how we'll be-gin, the Wiz-ard and I...
C Dm7 Gsus C Dm7 Gsus
C Dm7 Gsus G C Dm7 Gsus
Once I'm with the Wiz-ard, my whole life will change

C C/B Am7
'Cause once you're with the Wiz - ard,
Dm7 C/F Gsus C Dm7 Gm7(add4)
no one thinks you're strange. No fa - ther is not proud of
C C/B Em7
you; no sis - ter acts a - shamed. And
F/B♭ Csus2 F/C C F/B♭ B♭maj7 Gsus
all of Oz has to love you, when by the Wiz - ard you're ac - claimed.

G
Am7
Dm7
G/B
C/E
And this gift or this curse I have in - side,
Am7
Dm7
Gsus
G
C
Dm7
C/E
May - be at last I'll know why, as we work hand in hand,
Più mosso
Fsus
F
Amaj7
the Wiz - ard and I! And
ad lib.
Dmaj9
C♯m11
Dmaj9
one day, he'll say to me: "El - pha - ba, A girl who is so su -
mf

C♯m11
Fmaj9
Em7(add4)
pe - ri - or—
Should-n't a girl who's so good in - side
Dm7(add4)
Em7(add4)
Cm9
B♭/E♭
F(add4)
have a match - ing ex - te - ri - or? And since folks here to an ab -
rhythmically
B♭(add9)/D
Cm9
B♭/E♭
F(add4)
B♭(add9)/D
surd de - gree seem fix - at - ed on your ver - di - gris, Would
D♭
Csus
C
Freely
B♭m7
it be all right by you If I de - green - i - fy
dim. e rit.
mp

A tempo
Csus
3fr
C
Am7
Dm7
G/B
C/E
you?" And though of course that's not im - por - tant to me,
Am7
Dm7
Gsus
3fr
G
C
Csus/D
C/E
"All right, why not?" I'll re - ply. Oh, what a pair we'll be
mf
Fsus
F
Am7
Dm7
Gsus
3fr
G
The Wiz - ard and I!
C
Dm7
C/E
Fsus
F
What a pair we'll be, The Wiz - ard and..
3
3

Dreamily
C♭maj9♯11
f p sub.
With pedal
Un - lim - it - ed
My fu-ture is
E♭m9
C♭maj9♯11 G♭maj9/D♭
G♭maj7
un - lim - it - ed...
And I've just had a
C♭maj9♯11
B♭m11
E♭m11
A♭dim/E♭♭
Freely
G♭/D♭
D♭9sus
vi-sion al-most like a proph-e - cy—
I know, it sounds tru-ly cra-zy, and

G♭/D♭
D♭9sus
A(add9)
Amaj7
A6
true, the vi - sion's ha - zy,
But I swear, some - day there'll
warmly
Dmaj9
G♭/D♭
F/D♭
be a cel - e - bra - tion through-out Oz that's
A tempo
C♭/D♭
B♭7sus
B♭7
B♭7sus
B♭7
all to do with me!
rall.
f
Broadly
Gm7
Gm9
B♭maj7/C
C7
B
Bsus/C♯
And I'll stand there with the Wiz -
cresc.
rall.
ff

Bsus/F♯
B
Bsus/C♯
Bsus/F♯
4fr
- ard, feel - ing things I've nev - er felt,
accel.
B
Bsus2/A♯
G♯m7
Bsus/G♯
G♯m7
C♯m7
B/E
F♯sus
And though I'd nev - er show it, I'll be so hap - py, I could melt!
poco a poco accel.
Bright, triumphant
F♯
G♯m7
Bsus/C♯
F♯/A♯
B/D♯
And so it will be for the rest of my life, and I'll
G♯m7
Bsus/C♯
F♯5
F♯sus
F♯
B
C♯m7
B/D♯
Esus
want noth - ing else till I die! Held in such high es - teem,

E
C
Dm7
C/E
Fsus
F
when peo-ple see me, they will scream for half of
cresc.
C
Csus/D
C/E
Fm(maj7)/A♭
G7sus
Oz-'s fav-'rite team:
The Wiz-ard and
f
molto rall.
A tempo
C
Dm7
G
Am(add9)
5fr
Am
Fmaj9
D♭(add♯4)
4fr
B(add♭6)
C
I!
ff
3
rall.

WONDERFUL

from the Broadway Musical WICKED

Music and Lyrics by
STEPHEN SCHWARTZ

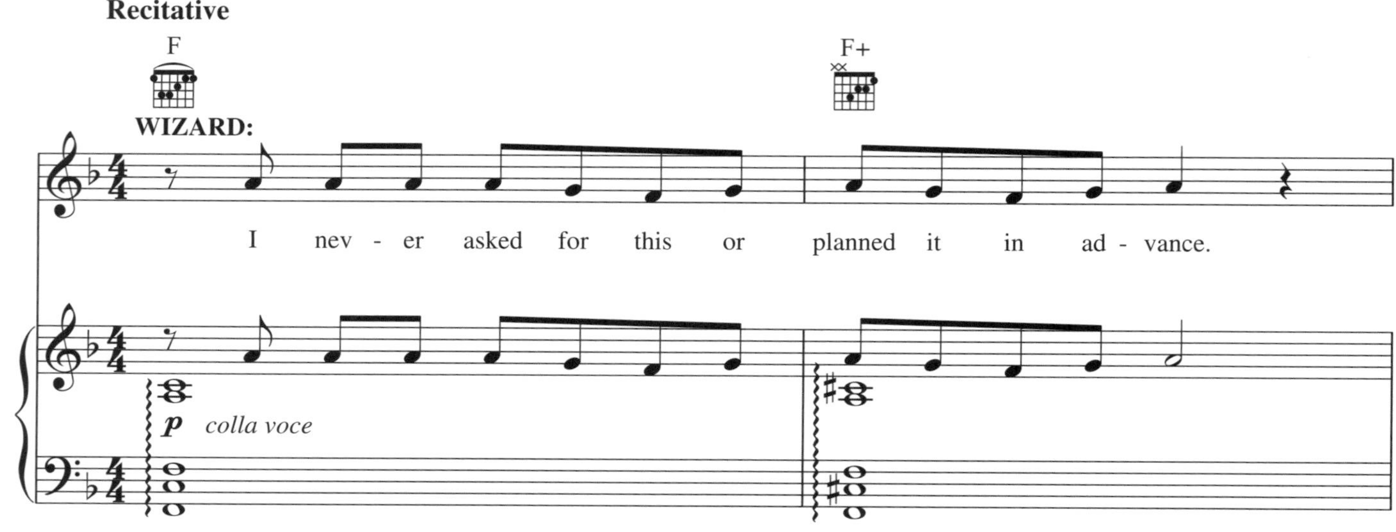

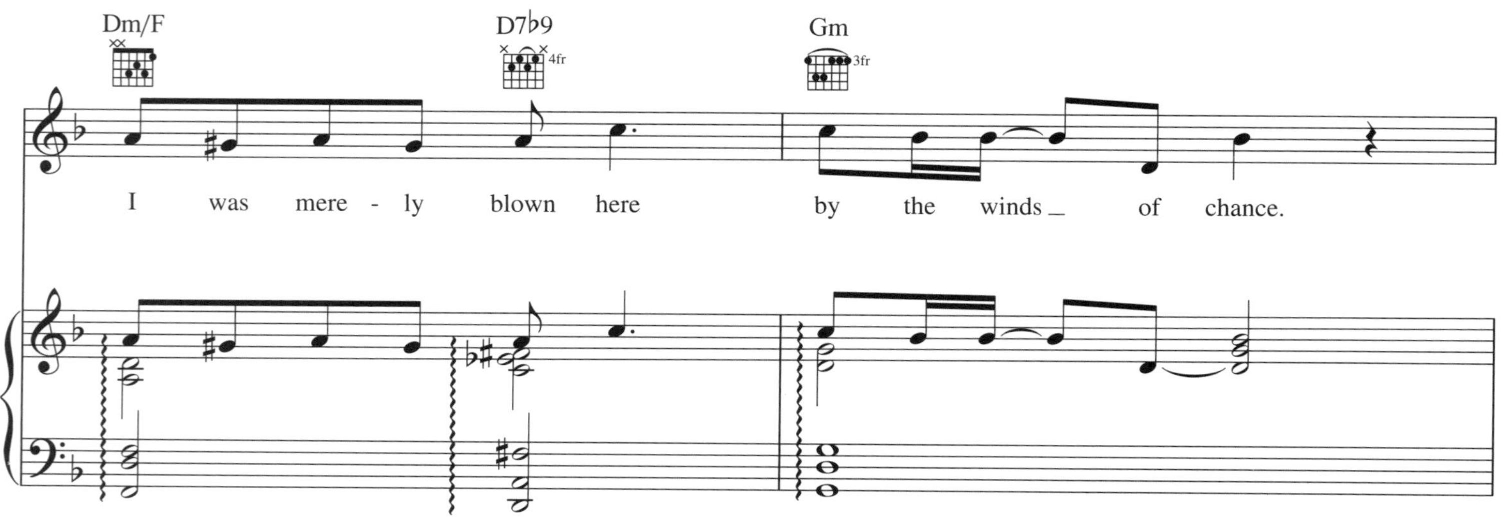

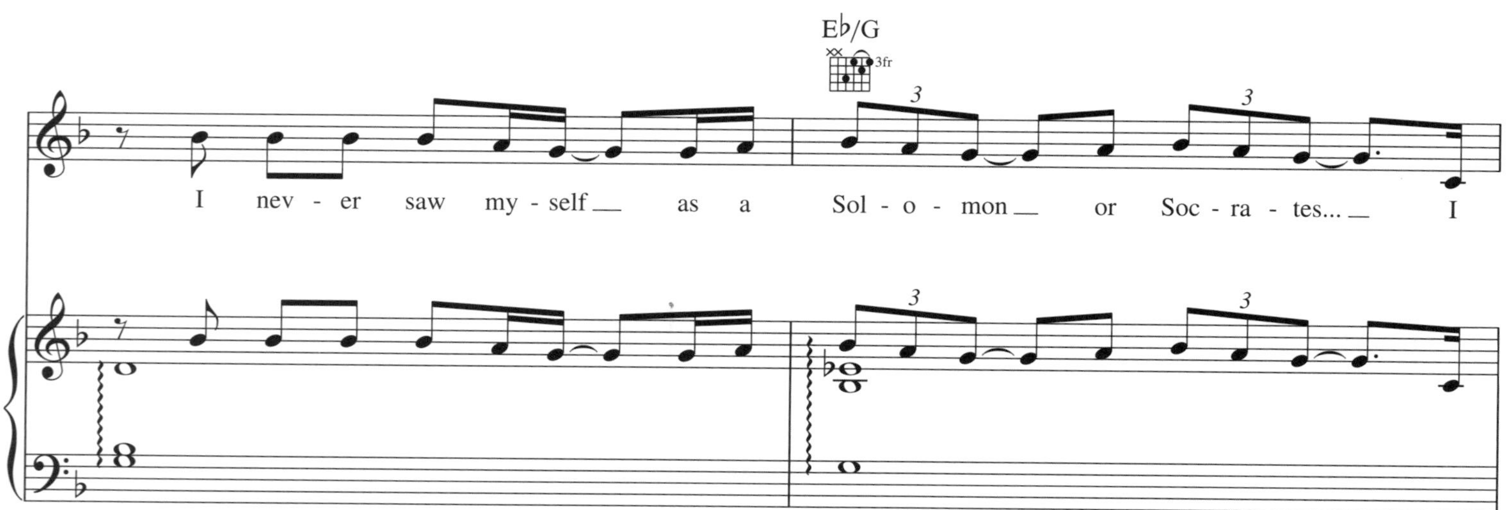

C7sus
C7
D♭7
4fr
F
knew who I was: _ One of your dime - a - doz - en me - di - oc - ri - ties.
3
A7
Dm
Then sud - den - ly I'm here, re - spect - ed, wor - shipped e - ven,
B♭m/D♭
F/A
Bm7♭5
C9
just be - cause the folks in Oz need - ed some - one to be - lieve in
F
F+
Dm/F
F9
B♭(add9)
6fr
Does it sur - prise you I got hooked, and all too soon?
8va

Gdim/B♭
F
D7
G9
What can I say...? I got car - ried a - way, and not just by bal -
C7
loon...
8va
Freely
F6
Dm6/F
"Won - der - ful." They called me "Won - der - ful."
Gm9♭5/F
C7♯5
So I said, "Won - der - ful... if you in -

Slow Ragtime
F
Gm7
C7
F
F6
sist... I will be won - der - ful," And they said,
D7♭9
4fr
D7
G
Am
"Won - der - ful..." Be - lieve me, it's hard
G/B
G7
C7
C9
B♭maj7/C
C7♭9(♭13)
to re - sist, 'cause it feels
Faster, light 2
F
F6
G7
won - der - ful! They think I'm won - der - ful!

Gm7♭5
C9
Hey, look who's won - der - ful: this corn - fed
Am7♭5
D7
G9
9fr
hick, who said, "It might be keen
3
3
3
C9
C9/B♭
Am7
D7
Dm7/F
D7/F♯
to build a town of green... and a
G9
9fr
C9
F
F6/A
won - der - ful road of yel - low brick!"

Gm9
C7sus
C9
Where I come from, we believe all sorts of things that aren't true—we call it..."history."
A
rall.
Soft-shoe
F
A/C
Dm/F
F+/C
man's called a trai - tor or lib - er - a - tor; A
F
D7
Gm
rich man's a thief or phi - lan - thro - pist. Is
Gm
B♭maj7♯5/D
Gm
D+
one a cru - sad - er or ruth - less in - vad - er? It's

G7
C13
2fr
F
all in which la - bel is a - ble to per - sist.
A7
Dm
These are pre - cious few at ease with mor - al am - bi - gu - i - ties,
G
G/B
C7
C9
B♭maj7/D
3fr
C7♯5/E
7fr
straight 8ths
so we act as though they don't ex - ist! They called me
Moderate Ragtime
F6
G7
won - der - ful So I am won - der - ful...

F♯dim
Gm7♭5
C7♭9
C9/B♭
In fact: it's so much who I am, it's part of my
Am7♭5
D7
G9
C13
name! And with my help, you can be the
A little slower
F
F7
Fmaj7/B♭
Em7/A
same... At long, long last re-ceive your due, long o-ver-
rit.
Freely
Am7/D
B♭m7
F/A
B♭(add2)
due El - pha - ba... The most cel - e - brat - ed are the
Alt. lyric: Don't you know...

F/A
B♭6
A♭(add9)
4fr
re - ha - bil - i - tat - ed There'll be such a whoop - de -
D♭maj7
F/C
E/C
D♭/A♭
4fr
doo A cel - e - bra - tion through - out Oz that's all to do with
A7sus
A7
A♭9
4fr
A tempo
G
G6
you! Won - der - ful,
molto rit.
7
7
poco a poco accel.
A9
5fr
They'll call you "Won - der - ful" Does it sound

In tempo, fast
Am7♭5
D7♭9
Bm7♭5
E7
won - der - ful? Trust me, it's fun! When you are
Am9
D9
Bm7
won - der - ful Won't it be won - der - ful?
E7
F♯m7
Edim/G
E/G♯
A9
D13
When you're the won - der - ful
G
G7/B
C
C♯dim
A9♯11(♭13)
D+/C♯
G
one!
8va

A WONDERFUL DAY LIKE TODAY

from THE ROAR OF THE GREASEPAINT—THE SMELL OF THE CROWD

Words and Music by LESLIE BRICUSSE
and ANTHONY NEWLEY

Fm7
Gm7
Cm7
Fm7
B♭7
mo - ment I woke with the lark, we were both of us sing - ing a -
Gm7
Cm7
A♭maj7
D♭9
Gm7
Cm9
way. And the sky was so blue, I in - stinc - tive - ly knew we were
Cm7
F7
F7♭5
E♭
Cm7
in for a won - der - ful day. As I came through the door, as I
A♭maj7
A♭6
C9
Fm7
B♭13
N.C.
told you be - fore, I was ter - ri - bly tempt - ed to say: On a

Brightly
E♭ 3fr
E♭6
E♭maj7 3fr
won - der - ful day like to - day
won - der - ful morn - ing like this,
E♭6
E♭ 3fr
E♭6
I de - fy an - y cloud to ap -
when the sun is as big as a
Fm7
B♭7
Fm7
B♭7
pear in the sky. Dare an - y rain -
yel - low bal - loon, e - ven the spar -
Gm7
C9
C7♯5 8fr
- drop to plop in my eye on a
- rows are sing - ing in tune on a

1
A♭maj7 F9 F7 Fm7
won - der - ful day like to - day.
won - der - ful morn -
2
B♭7 B♭7♭9 E♭ Fm7
On a - ing like this.
3fr
F♯dim G7 A♭ A♭+ A♭6
9fr 4fr 4fr 3fr
On a morn - ing like this I could kiss ev - 'ry -
A♭7 Adim E♭ Fm7 B♭9 E♭maj9
4fr 3fr
bod - y, I'm so full of love and good - will.

E♭6 E♭7 A♭ A♭maj7 A♭6
Let me say fur - ther - more I'd a - dore ev - 'ry -
A♭7 Adim Gm C7 F9
bod - y to come and dine. The pleas - ure's mine, and I will pay the
B♭13 E♭ E♭6 E♭maj7
bill. May I take this oc - ca - sion to say
E♭6 E♭ E♭6 Fm7 B♭7
that the whole hu - man race should go down on its knees,

Fm7
Bb7
Show that we're grate - ful for
Gm7
C9
C7#5
8fr
Abmaj7
D7
morn - ings like these, for the world's in a won -
G7b9
Cm
3fr
Cm(maj7)
8fr
Cm7
3fr
- der - ful way, on a
F9
Fm7
Bb13
6fr
Eb6
won - der - ful day like to - day.

WOULDN'T IT BE LOVERLY

from MY FAIR LADY

Words by ALAN JAY LERNER
Music by FREDERICK LOEWE

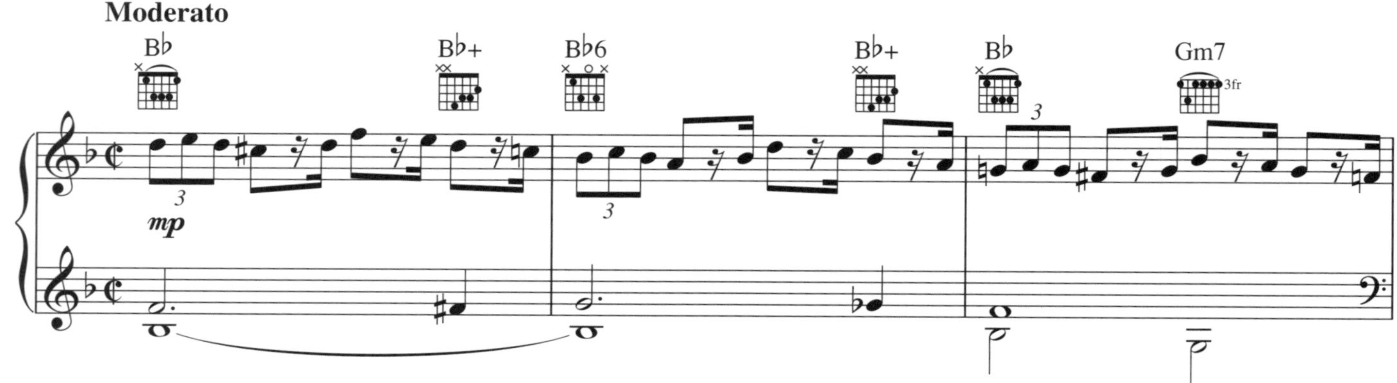

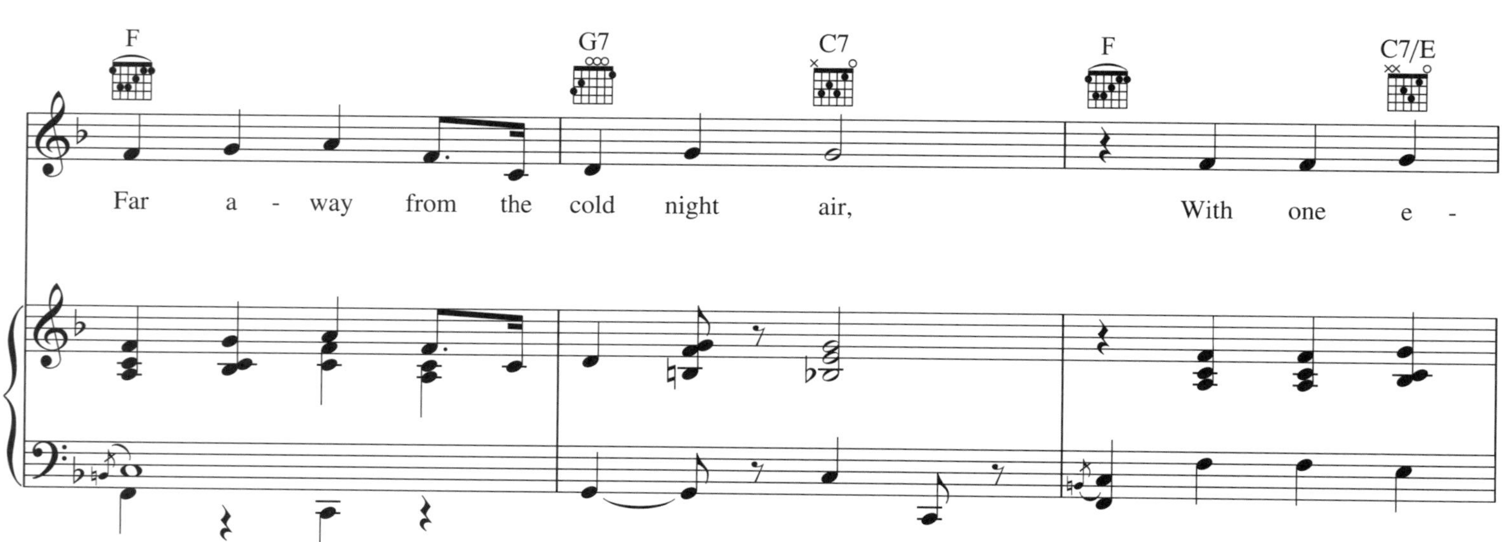

Cm6/E♭ D7 B♭m/D♭ F/C Cdim Gm7/C B♭m6/C C7
3fr
nor - mous chair; Oh, would - n't it be lov - er - ly?
F B♭ Gm7 C7 F
3fr
Lots of choc' - late for me to eat; Lots of coal mak - in'
G7 C7 F C7/E Cm6/E♭ D7 B♭m/D♭
lots of heat; Warm face, warm hands, warm feet, Oh,
F/C C9 F C C♯dim7
would - n't it be lov - er - ly? Oh, so
mf

G/D
G
C
E7/B
Am
E/G♯
C7/G
lov - er - ly sit - tin' ab - so - bloom - in' - lute - ly still!
F6
E7
Am
E7/B
Am/C
D7
G
C♯dim7
I would nev - er budge 'til spring crept
Gm/C
3fr
C7
F
B♭
Gm7
3fr
C7
o - ver the win - dow - sill. Some - one's head rest - in' on my knee,
p
F
G7
C7
F
C7/E
Warm and ten - der as he can be; Who takes good

Cm6/E♭
D7
B♭m/D♭
F/C
Dm
Gm7
3fr
C7
care of me. Oh, would - n't it be
F
lov - er - ly?
1
C9
Ddim7/C
F/C
Dm/C
B♭/C
Gm9
3fr
C13
2fr
2
C13
2fr
F
Lov - er - ly! Lov - er - ly!
B♭
F
Lov - er - ly! Lov - er - ly!
rall.
p

WRITTEN IN THE STARS

from Elton John and Tim Rice's AIDA

Music by ELTON JOHN
Lyrics by TIM RICE

C/G G C G/C F/C
go, so well. Female: Nev - er won - der what I'll feel as
Male: Noth - ing can be al - tered. Oh, there is
C E7sus E7/G♯ Am Am/G
liv - ing shuf - fles by. You don't have to ask me and
noth - ing to de - cide. No es - cape, no change of heart, nor
F Gsus G/B C G/D F/C
I need not re - ply. Ev - 'ry mo - ment of my life, from
an - y place to hide. Female: You are all I'll ev - er want but
C E7sus E7/G♯ Am Am/G
now un - til I die, I will think or dream of you and
this I am de - nied. Some - times in my dark - est thoughts I

F
C/E
Dm7
To Coda
fail to un-der-stand how a per-fect love can be con-found-ed
wish I nev-er learned what it is to be in love and have that
C/G
G
C
G/B
out of hand. Both: Is it writ-ten in the stars? Are we
Am
C/G
F
pay-ing for some crime? Is that all that we are good for, just a
Dm7
C/G
G
C
G/B
stretch of mor-tal time? Is this God's ex-per-i-ment in

Am
Am/G
F
which we have no say?
In which we're giv - en par - a - dise,
but
Dm7
C/G
G
C
G/C
F/C
C
G/C
F/C
D.S. al Coda
on - ly for a day.
CODA
C/G
G
C
G/B
love re - turned.
Both: Is it writ - ten in the stars?
Are we
Oh
Am
Am/G
F
C/E
pay - ing for some crime?
Is that all that we are good for,
just a

Dm7
C/G
G
C
G/B
stretch _ of mor - tal time? ___ Is this God's ex - per - i - ment, _ oh, in
Am
Am/G
F
which we have _ no say? _ In which we're giv - en par - a - dise, ___ but
Dm7
F/G
C/G
C
G/B
on - ly for a day. ___
Male: Is it writ - ten in the stars? ___ Are we
Am7
Em/G
F
F/E
pay - ing for some crime? _ Is that all that we _ are good for, just a

Dm7
F/G
C
G/B
stretch of mor - tal time? Both: Is this God's ex - per - i - ment Male: in
Am
Am/G
F
F/E
which we have no say? In which we're giv - en par - a - dise
Female: In which we have no say, giv - en par - a -
Dm7
F/G
C
G/C
F/C
on - ly Both: for a day.
dise
C
G/C
F/C
G♭(add2)
A♭(add2)
B♭(add2)
C
6fr
4fr
3fr
rall.

YA GOT TROUBLE

from Meredith Willson's THE MUSIC MAN

By MEREDITH WILLSON

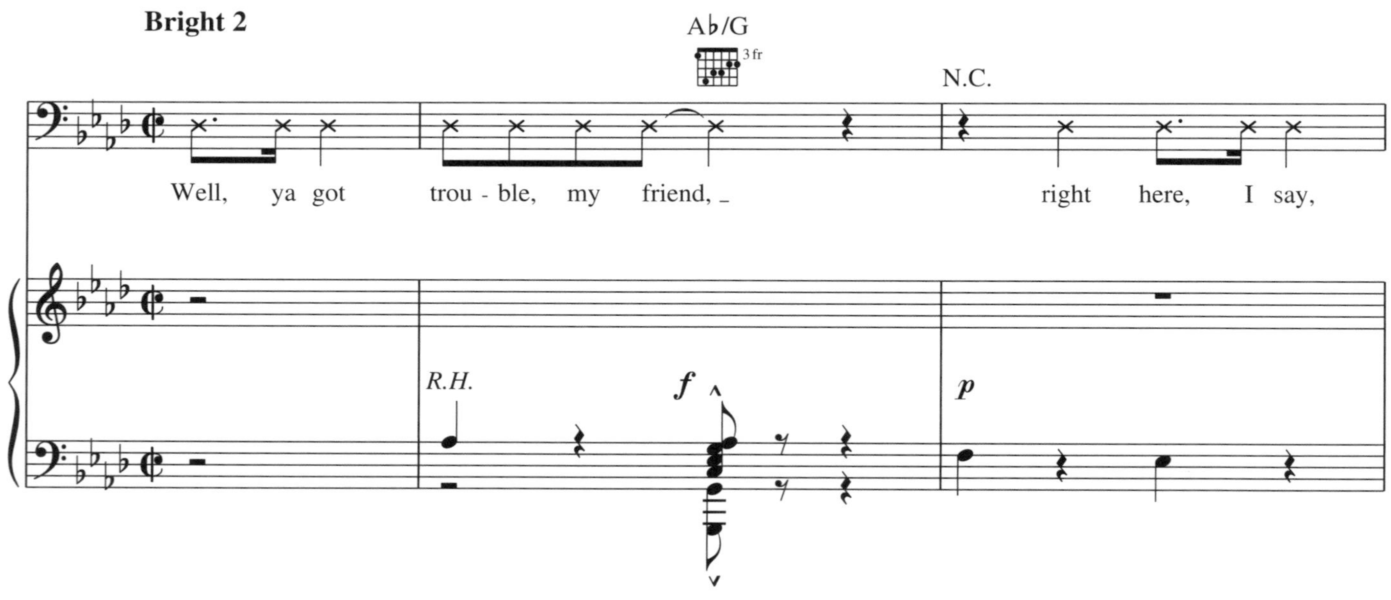

Eb7
Db(add9)/F
Ebm7b5/F#
hours I spend with a cue in my hand are gold - en.
pp
sfz
Eb7/G
Bbm7
Eb7
Bbm7/F
F#dim7
Help you cul - ti - vate horse sense and a cool head and a
pp
Eb7#5/G
Fm7/Ab
N.C.
keen eye. 'Jev - er take 'n' try to give an i - ron - clad leave to your -
sfz
ppp
E9
Eb7(add13)
self from a three - rail bil - liard shot? But just as I
sfz

A♭
say it takes judg - ment, brains and ma-tur - i - ty to score in a balk - line
pp
A♭7
game, I say that an - y boob kin take 'n' shove a
3
D♭6
3
ball in a pock - et, And I call that sloth! The first big
pp
Ddim7
A♭/E♭
E♭m6/G♭
F7♯5
F7
step on the road to the depths of de - gra - da... I say, first it's a

B♭7
E♭7
A♭6
3 fr
lit - tle, ah, me-dic - i - nal wine from a tea - spoon, then beer from a
E♭6/9
A♭
4 fr
bot - tle. And the next thing you know, your son is play - in' fer
mon - ey in a pinch - back suit and list' - nin' to some big out -
Adim7
B♭m7
Adim7
B♭m7
- ta - town jas - per, hear - in' him tell a - bout horse race gam - blin'.

Eb7
Db6/9/F
Ebm7b5/F#
Not a whole - some trot - tin' race, no, but a race where they se' down
sfz
Eb7/G
Gdim7/Bb
5 fr
right on a horse! Like to see some stuck - up jock - ey boy
f
3
p
Ab6
3 fr
Ab
4 fr
set - tin' on Dan Patch? Make your blood boil? Well, I should
3
8
say. Now friends, lem - me tell you what I mean. Ya got
8
mf

A♭7
4 fr
D♭6
3 fr
one, two, three, four, five, six
Ddim7
pock-ets in a ta-ble! Pock-ets that mark the dif-f'rence be-tween a
A♭6/E♭
F
B♭m7
gen-tle-man and a bum, with a cap-i-tal "B" and that rhymes with
E♭7
A♭
4 fr
"P" and that stands for pool. And all week long your

River City-y youth-'ll be fritern away, I say, your young men-'ll be
fritern.
Fritern away their noontime, supper time,
chore time too!
Get the ball in the pocket! Never mind gettin'
dande-li-ons pulled or the screen door patched or the beef-steak pound-ed.
Bbm7
Eb7
Bbm7(add4)
Eb7
Db(add9)/F
Ebm7b5/F#
Eb7

N.C.
Nev - er mind pump - in' an - y wa - ter 'til your par - ents are caught with a
sfz
pp
Ab
4fr
cis - tern emp - ty on a Sat - ur - day night, and that's trou - ble, oh yes, ya got
lots 'n' lots - a trou - ble. I'm think - in' of the kids in the knick - er - bock - ers,
Ab7
4fr
Db6
3fr
shirt - tails, young ones, peek - in' in the pool hall win - dow af - ter school. Ya got

D♭maj7
Ddim7
A♭/E♭
C7
trou - ble, folks, right here in Riv - er Cit - y.
sfz
pp
F7
B♭7
E♭7
Trou - ble with a cap - i - tal "T" and that rhymes with "P" and that stands for
sfz
p
A♭
4 fr
pool! Now I know all you folks are the right kind of par - ents.
I'm gon - na be per - fect - ly frank. Would ya like to know

Eb7/Bb
F#m7/A
what kind - a con - ver - sa - tion goes on while they're loaf - in' a - round the
Eb7/Bb
Eb7
Db6/F
hall? They'll be try - in' out Be - vo; try - in' out Cu - bebs; try - in' out Tail
sfz
F#dim7
Eb7/G
Eb7#5(b9)
5fr
or Mades like cig - a - rette fiends, and brag - gin'
Ab
4fr
all a - bout how they're gon - na cov - er up a tell - tale breath with Sen - Sen.

One fine night, they leave the pool hall head - in' for the
dance at the Arm - 'ry. Lib - er - tine men and scar - let wom - en and
rag - time, shame - less mu - sic that - 'll drag your son and
your daugh - ter to the arms of a jun - gle an - i - mal in - stinct
p
Ab7
4fr
Db6
3fr
Ddim7
Ab/Eb
Cm7b5
F+
F7
3

B♭7♭9
E♭7
N.C.
mass - ter - i - a! Friends, the i - dle brain is the
sfz
pp
A♭
4 fr
dev - il's play - ground, trou - ble! Right here in Riv - er
Cit - y With a cap - i - tal "T" and that rhymes with
E♭7
"P" and that stands for pool. We've sure - ly got

E♭7♯9
E♭7
D♭(add9)/F
F♯dim7
E♭7/G
trou - ble! Right here in Riv - er Cit - y!
E♭7
Got - ta fig - ger out a way to keep the young ones mor - al af - ter
p
A♭
4fr
school. Our chil - dren's chil - dren gon - na have trou - ble. Oh ___ we got
cresc.
trou - ble. We're in ter - ri - ble, ter - ri - ble trou - ble. That game with the

Ab7
4fr
Db6
3fr
fif - teen num-bered balls __ is the dev-il's tool!
Oh, yes, we've got
mf
Ddim7
Ab/Eb
C7b5/Gb
F7
trou - ble, trou - ble, trou - ble. Yes, we got trou-ble here, _ we got big big trou-ble with a
Bb7
Eb7
Fm6
Eb/G
3fr
"T." Got - ta rhyme it with "P" and that stands for
Ab6
3fr
Bbm7/Ab
6fr
Ab
4fr
Bbm7/Ab
6fr
Abm7b5
6fr
Ab
4fr
pool!
f
ff

YOU'LL BE IN MY HEART

from Disney Presents TARZAN THE BROADWAY MUSICAL

Words and Music by
PHIL COLLINS

B
F♯/B
B
Bsus2
For one so small, you seem so strong.
My arms will hold you, keep you
F♯/B
B
E(add2)/B
safe and warm.
This bond be-tween us
can't be bro - ken.
C♯m7
4fr
E6
E♭
3fr
A♭(add2)
4fr
I will be here, don't you cry.
'Cause you'll be in my
mp
D♭(add2)
E♭
3fr
E♭/D♭
Cm7
3fr
heart.
Yes, you'll be in my heart
from

Fm7
D♭(add2)
G♭
G♭maj7
this day on, now and for - ev - er more.
E♭(add2)
6fr
A♭(add2)
4fr
D♭(add2)
You'll be in my heart no
E♭
3fr
E♭/D♭
Cm7
3fr
Fm7
mat - ter what they say. You'll be here in my
D♭(add2)
G♭
G♭/F
E♭(add2)
6fr
heart al - ways. Don't

D♭sus
D♭
D♭sus2
D♭
lis - ten to him, 'cause what does he know? We
des - ti - ny calls you, you must be strong. I
ENSEMBLE:
Love is all that we know.
We watch our love grow.
mf
D♭sus/B♭
D♭/B♭
D♭sus2/B♭
D♭/B♭
need each oth - er to have, to hold. He'll
may not be with you, but you've got to hold on. They'll
Oo.
Fm
1
G♭(add2)
see in time, I know.
see in time, I
In this par - a - dise we are
In this par - a - dise.

2
G♭(add2)
A♭(add2)
E♭(add2)
When know. We'll show them to-geth-er 'cause
fam-i-ly.
B♭(add2)
E♭
F
F/E♭
you'll be in my heart. Yes, you'll be in my
You'll be in my heart
Dm
Gm7
E♭
heart from this day on, now and for-ev-er
now and for al-ways. For-ev-er

A♭(add2)
F(add2)
B♭(add2)
E♭
more.
Oh, you'll be in my heart no
more.
You'll be in my
F
F/E♭
Dm
Gm7
E♭
mat-ter what they say.
You'll be here in my heart al-
heart now and for al-ways, al-
A♭
A♭/G
F(add2)
B♭(add2)
-ways.
Al-ways.
Al-ways.
-ways.
molto rit.

YOUNGER THAN SPRINGTIME

from SOUTH PACIFIC

Lyrics by OSCAR HAMMERSTEIN II
Music by RICHARD RODGERS

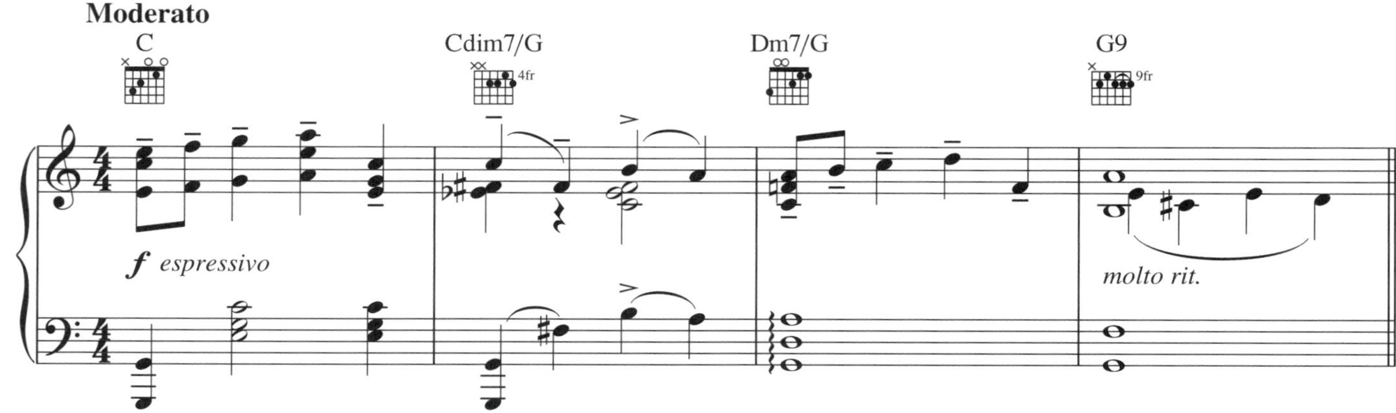

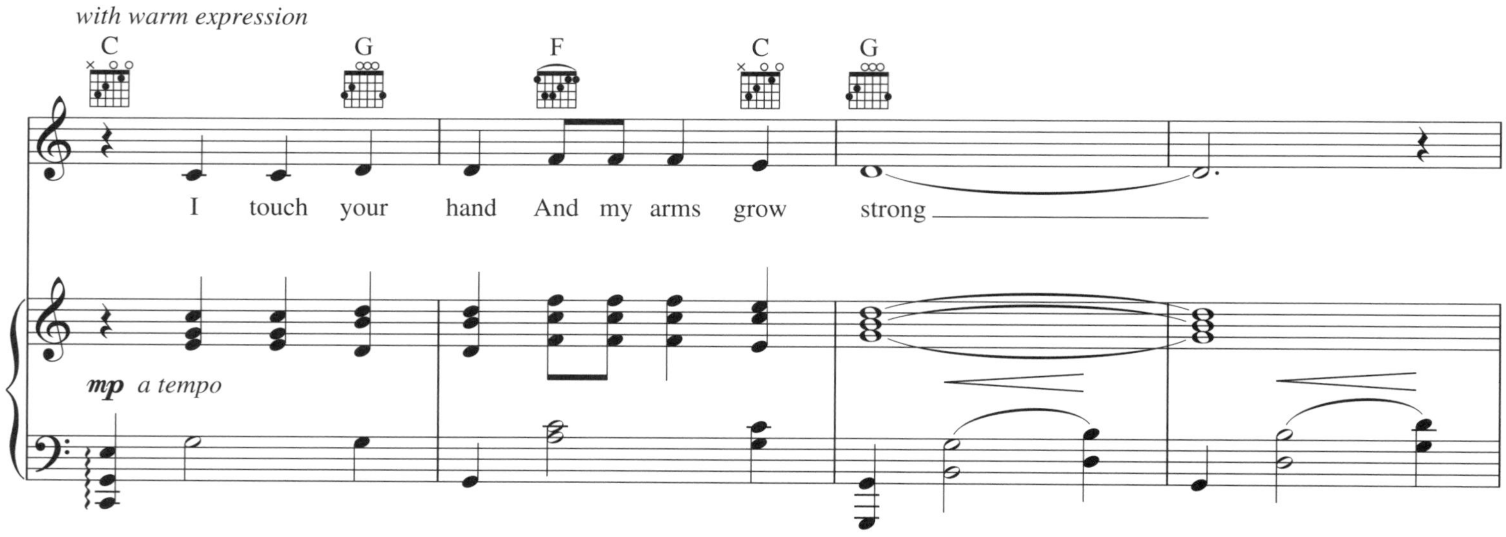

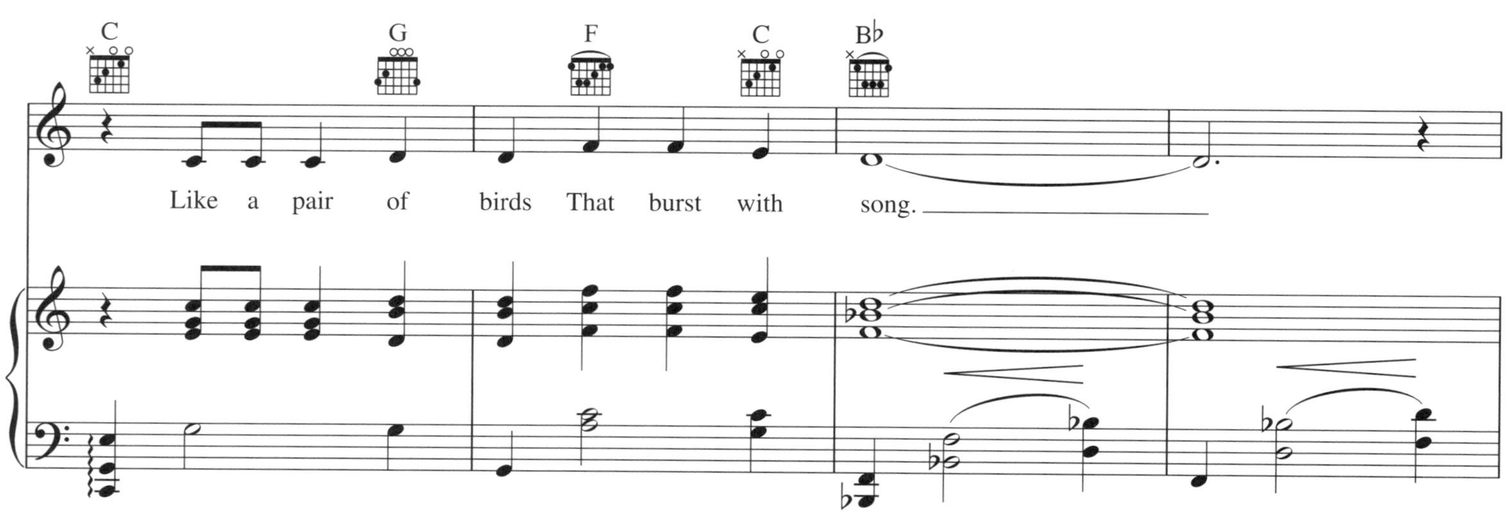

Dm
Gdim
A7♭9
5fr
Dm
Fm6
My eyes look down At your love - ly face
And I hold the
f
C
C♯dim7
Dm7
G7
world
In my em - brace.
mf
molto rit.
Refrain (slowly, with great warmth)
C
G/B
Young - er than Spring - time are you,
Soft - er than star - light
p-mf
C
Am
D
are you,
Warm - er than winds of June are the gen - tle lips you

Gmaj7 G7 C G/B
gave me. Gay - er than laugh - ter are you, Sweet - er than mu - sic
p
C Am D
are you, An - gel and lov - er, heav - en and earth are you to
G D7 G D7
me. And when your youth and joy in - vade my
mf
cresc.
G D7 G Dm7
arms And fill my heart as now they do...

G7
C
G/B
C
G/B
then...
Young-er than Spring-time
am I,
Gay-er than laugh-ter
mp
C
G7/B
C
with passion
Am
am I,
An-gel and lov-er,
heav-en and earth am
cresc.
Am7/D
G7
1
C
G7/B
I
with
you!
f
allarg.
a tempo
2
C
you!
f dim.
morendo
p
Ped.
*

WITHOUT YOU

from RENT

Words and Music by
JONATHAN LARSON

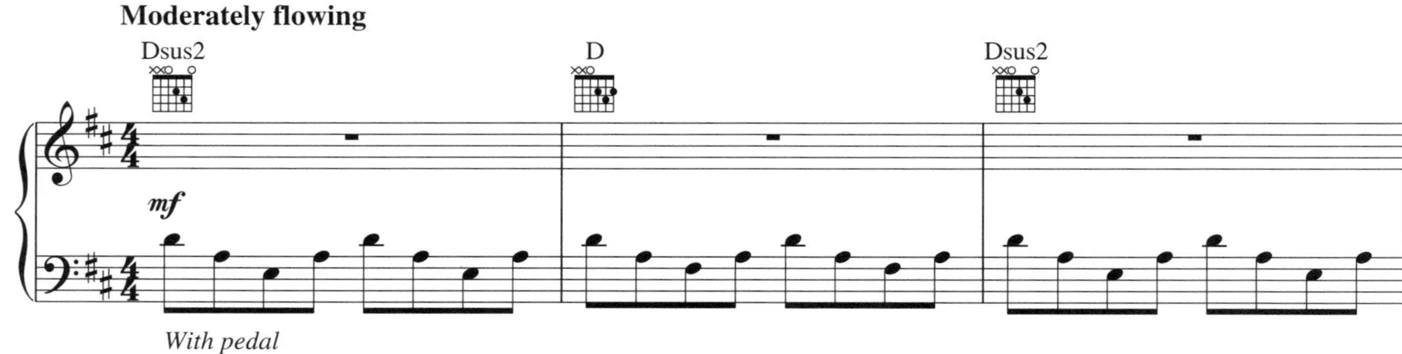

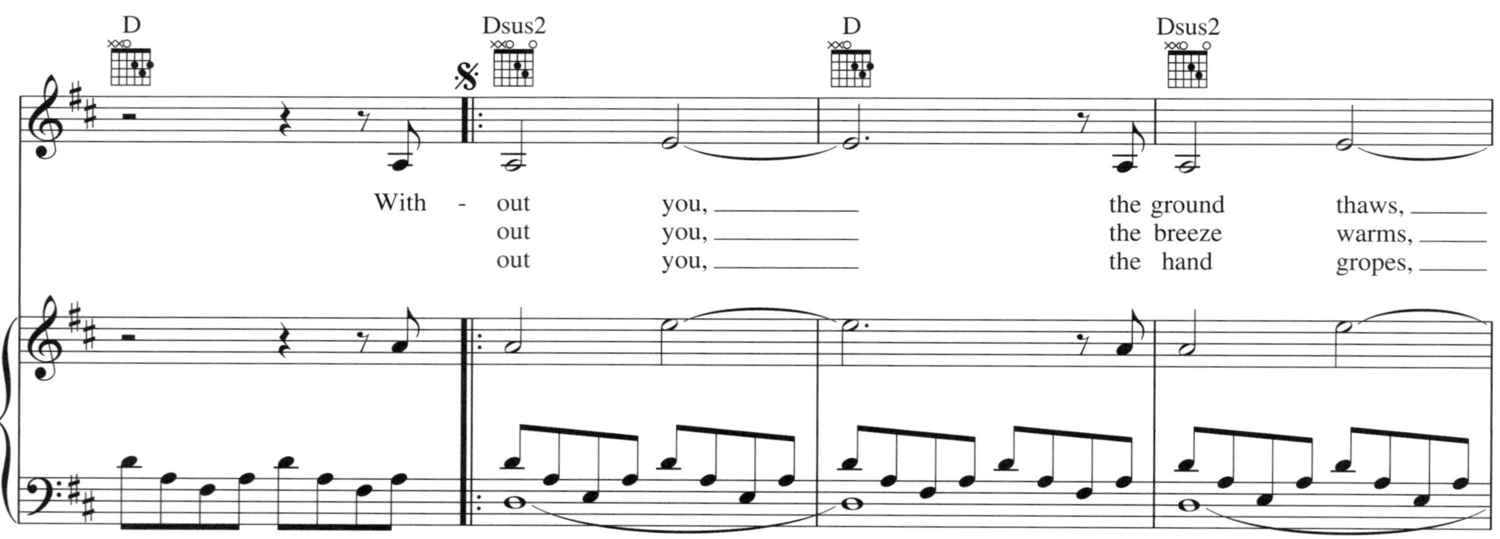

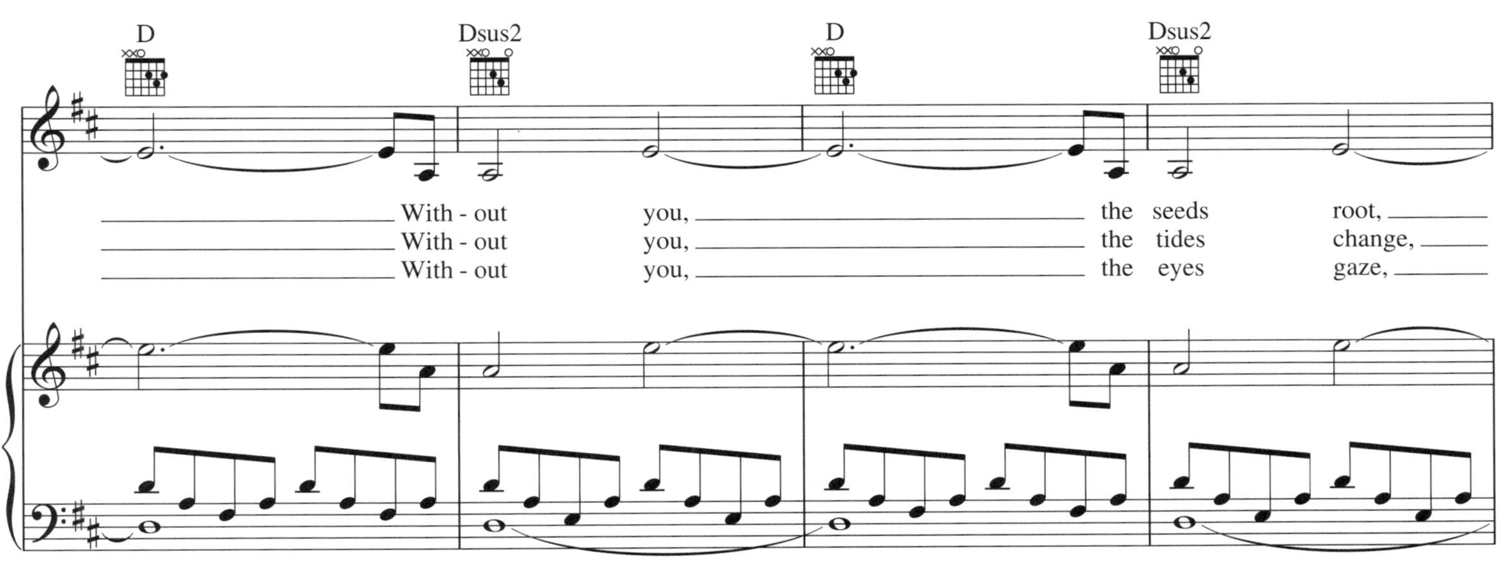
D
Dsus2
D
Dsus2
With - out you, the seeds root,
With - out you, the tides change,
With - out you, the eyes gaze,

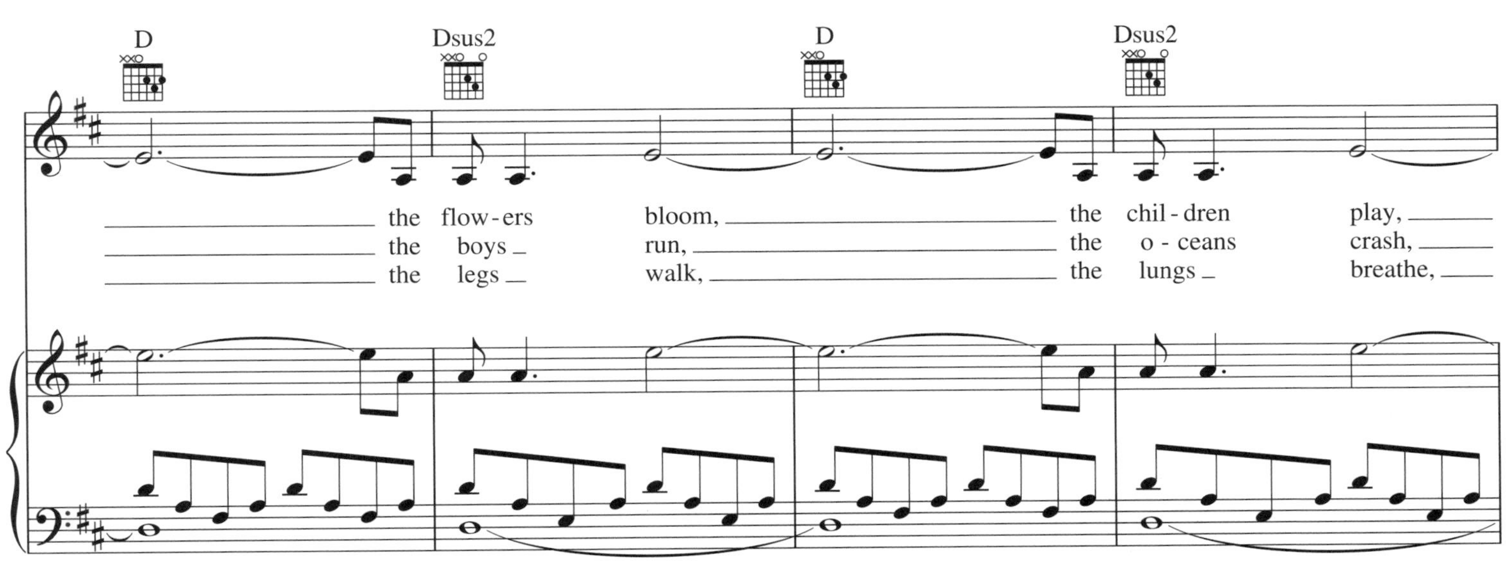
D
Dsus2
D
Dsus2
the flow - ers bloom, the chil - dren play,
the boys run, the o - ceans crash,
the legs walk, the lungs breathe,

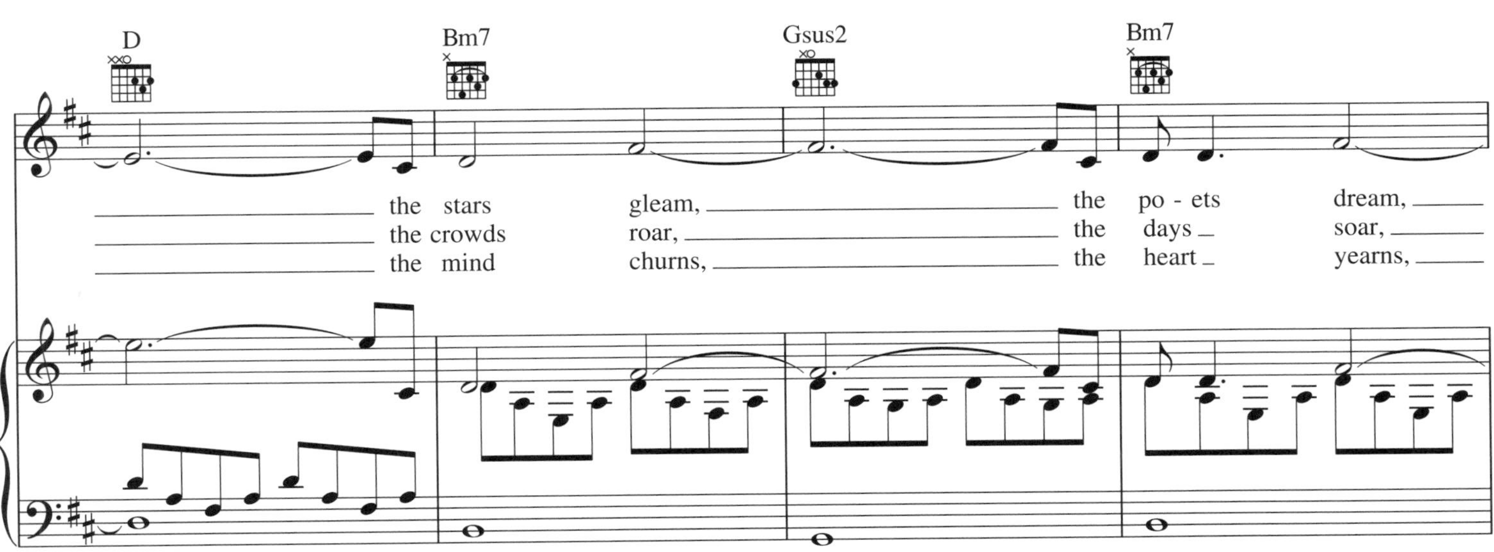
D
Bm7
Gsus2
Bm7
the stars gleam, the po - ets dream,
the crowds roar, the days soar,
the mind churns, the heart yearns,

Gsus2
F♯m
Gsus2
Dsus2
the ea - gles fly with - out you.
the ba - bies cry with - out you.
the tears dry with - out you.
D
Bm7
Gsus2
To Coda
The earth turns, the
The moon glows, the
Life goes on, but
Bm7
Gsus2
F♯m
Gsus2
sun burns,
riv - er flows,
but I die
Dsus2
1
D
with - out you.

2
Dsus2
D
D
B♭sus2/D
With -
The world re-
Dsus2
B♭sus2/D
Dsus2
B♭sus2/D
vives,
col - ors re - new,
but I know
A/C♯
Am/C
G/B
Gm/B♭
blue,
on - ly blue,
lone - ly
D/A
Gm/B♭
Asus
A
blue,
with - in me
blue
rit.

Dsus2
D
Dsus2
D
D.S. al Coda
with - out
you.
With -
a tempo
CODA
Bm7
Gsus2
F♯m
Gsus2
I'm
gone
'cause
I
die
with - out
Dsus2
D
Dsus2
D
you,
with - out
you,
with - out
Dsus2
D
Dsus2
D(add2)
you,
with-out
you.
rall.

HAL LEONARD:
Your Source for the Best of Broadway

THE BEST BROADWAY SONGS EVER

Over 70 songs from Broadway's latest and greatest hit shows: As Long as He Needs Me • Bess, You Is My Woman • Bewitched • Comedy Tonight • Don't Cry for Me Argentina • Getting to Know You • I Could Have Danced All Night • I Dreamed a Dream • If I Were a Rich Man • The Last Night of the World • Love Changes Everything • Oklahoma • Ol' Man River • People • Try to Remember • and more.
00309155 Piano/Vocal/Guitar $24.95

THE BIG BOOK OF BROADWAY

This edition includes 70 songs from classic musicals and recent blockbusters like *The Producers, Aida* and *Hairspray*. Includes: Bring Him Home • Camelot • Everything's Coming Up Roses • The Impossible Dream • A Lot of Livin' to Do • One • Some Enchanted Evening • Thoroughly Modern Millie • Till There Was You • and more.
00311658 Piano/Vocal/Guitar $19.95

BROADWAY CLASSICS

Piano Play-Along Series, Volume 4

This book/CD pack provides keyboardists with a full performance track and a separate backing track for each tune. Songs include: Ain't Misbehavin' • Cabaret • If I Were a Bell • Memory • Oklahoma • Some Enchanted Evening • The Sound of Music • You'll Never Walk Alone.
00311075 Book/CD Pack $14.95

BROADWAY DELUXE

125 of Broadway's biggest show tunes! Includes such showstoppers as: Bewitched • Cabaret • Camelot • Day by Day • Hello Young Lovers • I Could Have Danced All Night • I Talk to the Trees • I've Grown Accustomed to Her Face • If Ever I Would Leave You • The Lady Is a Tramp • My Heart Belongs to Daddy • Oklahoma • September Song • Seventy Six Trombones • Try to Remember • and more!
00309245 Piano/Vocal/Guitar $24.95

BROADWAY SONGS

Get more bang for your buck with this jam-packed collection of 73 songs from 56 shows, including *Annie Get Your Gun, Cabaret, The Full Monty, Jekyll & Hyde, Les Misérables, Oklahoma* and more. Songs: Any Dream Will Do • Consider Yourself • Footloose • Getting to Know You • I Dreamed a Dream • One • People • Summer Nights • The Surrey with the Fringe on Top • With One Look • and more.
00310832 Piano/Vocal/Guitar................................$12.95

CONTEMPORARY BROADWAY

44 songs from 25 contemporary musicals and Broadway revivals. Includes: And All That Jazz (*Chicago*) • Dancing Queen (*Mamma Mia!*) • Good Morning Baltimore (*Hairspray*) • Mein Herr (*Cabaret*) • Popular (*Wicked*) • Purpose (*Avenue Q*) • Seasons of Love (*Rent*) • When You Got It, Flaunt It (*The Producers*) • You Rule My World (*The Full Monty*) • and more.
00310796 Piano/Vocal/Guitar................................$18.95

DEFINITIVE BROADWAY

142 of the greatest show tunes ever, including: Don't Cry for Me Argentina • Hello, Dolly! • I Dreamed a Dream • Lullaby of Broadway • Mack the Knife • Memory • Send in the Clowns • Somewhere • The Sound of Music • Strike Up the Band • Summertime • Sunrise, Sunset • Tea for Two • Tomorrow • What I Did for Love • and more.
00359570 Piano/Vocal/Guitar................................$24.95

ESSENTIAL SONGS: BROADWAY

Over 100 songs are included in this top-notch collection: Any Dream Will Do • Blue Skies • Cabaret • Don't Cry for Me, Argentina • Edelweiss • Hello, Dolly! • I'll Be Seeing You • Memory • The Music of the Night • Oklahoma • Seasons of Love • Summer Nights • There's No Business like Show Business • Tomorrow • and more.
00311222 Piano/Vocal/Guitar..........................$24.95

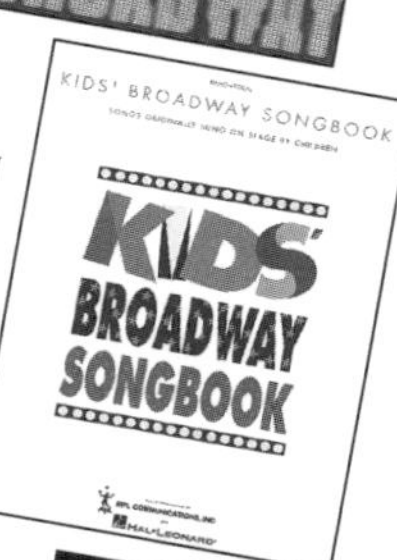

KIDS' BROADWAY SONGBOOK

An unprecedented collection of songs originally performed by children on the Broadway stage. Includes 16 songs for boys and girls, including: Gary, Indiana (*The Music Man*) • Castle on a Cloud (*Les Misérables*) • Where Is Love? (*Oliver!*) • Tomorrow (*Annie*) • and more.
00311609 Book Only......................................$14.95
00740149 Book/CD Pack................................$24.99

THE OFF-BROADWAY SONGBOOK

42 gems from off-Broadway hits, including *Godspell, Tick Tick...Boom!, The Fantasticks, Once upon a Mattress, The Wild Party* and more. Songs include: Always a Bridesmaid • Come to Your Senses • Day by Day • Happiness • How Glory Goes • I Hate Musicals • The Picture in the Hall • Soon It's Gonna Rain • Stars and the Moon • Still Hurting • Twilight • and more.
00311168 Piano/Vocal/Guitar..........................$16.95

THE TONY AWARDS SONGBOOK

This collection assembles songs from each of Tony-winning Best Musicals through "Mama Who Bore Me" from 2007 winner *Spring Awakening*. Songs include: Til There Was You • The Sound of Music • Hello, Dolly! • Sunrise, Sunset • Send in the Clowns • Tomorrow • Memory • I Dreamed a Dream • Seasons of Love • Circle of Life • Mama, I'm a Big Girl Now • and more. Includes photos and a table of contents listed both chronologically and alphabetically.
00311092 Piano/Vocal/Guitar..........................$19.95

THE ULTIMATE BROADWAY FAKE BOOK

Over 700 songs from more than 200 Broadway shows! Songs include: All I Ask of You • Bewitched • Cabaret • Don't Cry for Me Argentina • Edelweiss • Getting to Know You • Hello, Dolly! • If I Were a Rich Man • Last Night of the World • The Music of the Night • Oklahoma • People • Seasons of Love • Tell Me on a Sunday • Unexpected Song • and more!
00240046 Melody/Lyrics/Chords......................$47.50

ULTIMATE BROADWAY PLATINUM

100 popular Broadway songs: As If We Never Said Goodbye • Bye Bye Birdie • Camelot • Everything's Coming Up Roses • Gigi • Hello, Young Lovers • I Enjoy Being a Girl • Just in Time • My Favorite Things • On a Clear Day • People • Sun and Moon • Try to Remember • Who Can I Turn To • Younger Than Springtime • and many more.
00311496 Piano/Vocal/Guitar..........................$22.95

Prices, contents, and availability subject to change without notice.
Some products may not be available outside the U.S.A.

For More Information, See Your Local Music Dealer,
Or Write To:

7777 W. Bluemound Rd. P.O. Box 13819 Milwaukee, WI 53213

Get complete songlists and more at **www.halleonard.com**

0209